Anthony Summers, formerly a deputy editor of the BBC's *Panorama*, is the author of eight investigative books and the only two-time winner of the Crime Writers' Association's top award for non-fiction. Robbyn Swan, his co-author and wife, has partnered Summers on three previous biographies and investigations. Their book *The Eleventh Day*, on the 9/11 attacks, was a finalist for the 2012 Pulitzer Prize.

LOOKING FOR MADELEINE

ANTHONY SUMMERS
& ROBBYN SWAN

headline

First published in 2014 by
HEADLINE PUBLISHING GROUP

First published in paperback in 2015 by
HEADLINE PUBLISHING GROUP

2

Cataloguing in Publication Data is available from the British Library

Paperback ISBN 978 1 4722 1159 0

Typeset in Berkeley Book by Palimpsest Book Production Limited, Falkirk, Stirlingshire

www.headline.co.uk
www.hachette.co.uk

For Ava, who will be two on her next birthday

Authors' Note

The authors wish to make clear at the outset that, after more than two years studying this controversial case, they have seen not a shred of evidence to indicate that Gerry and Kate McCann, any member of their holiday group, or Robert Murat, were at any stage – in May 2007 or subsequently – guilty of malfeasance of any kind in connection with Madeleine McCann's disappearance or the repercussions that followed.

Allegations or innuendos about their role made or published by others, when referenced in the text of this book, are published only in the interests of reporting the history of the case – and to demonstrate the very point that such allegations are based on no factual evidence or are simply egregious.

This book has been researched and written independently of Gerry and Kate McCann.

A night in 2007. A seaside resort in Europe, just north of where the Atlantic meets the Mediterranean. Spring, but early spring, and the breeze from the north – two hours after sunset – is chilly. On the beach, named after Our Lady of Light, the tide has sucked the water to its lowest point.

Four hundred yards inland, a swimming pool. Palm trees, sun loungers tidied away for the night. Dinner tables and waiters. The clink of glasses. The sound of laughter, English voices.

Across the water, a sixty-second walk away, a five-storey apartment block.

There is movement in the darkness, undetected movement.

Is it a child, wandering alone into the night? Is it a person, male or female, furtively making away with a child?

Moments later, a man is seen walking purposefully nearby, carrying something in his arms. The something appears to be a small child, warm from its slumber, still in nightclothes.

A child will go missing this night, May 3rd 2007, a child who has since become enduringly famous for an absence that has lasted years. As circulated by Interpol at the request of Portugal's Polícia Judiciária, the disappearance is that of a little girl:

File No: 2007123403
Present Family Name: McCann
Forenames: Madeleine Beth.

1

'There she was, perfect,' Kate McCann would recall of Madeleine's birth in May 2003 at Leicester's Royal Infirmary. 'We were just so happy . . . She was lovely.' For her and her husband, Gerry, this was no cliché. Kate had wanted to have a large family, as many as 'six or seven' children.

It had seemed possible, though, that she would not be able to have even one baby. The couple had resorted to in vitro fertilisation, and the process had been difficult. Not least for that reason, Kate would say, they both had 'the most incredible bond' with Madeleine.

Gerry and Kate McCann were both doctors in their mid-thirties. He, a Scot, had moved south to take up a post in cardiology in the Midlands. Though Kate's speciality had been anaesthetics, she had switched to work as a GP – hoping that the schedule would prove less disruptive to family life than a hospital post.

Books on the origin of names say that 'Madeleine' means 'tower of strength' – probably from the Aramaic word signifying 'tower', 'elevated' or 'magnificent'. It is a variant of Magdalene, the Mary Magdalene who – the Gospels say – bravely stood by Jesus to the last. It is perhaps no coincidence that Madeleine McCann's mother is a devout Catholic.

By Kate's account, the new baby demanded patience worthy of a saint. She suffered badly from colic, cried incessantly, and had to be carried around almost all the time. She slept astonishingly little. Kate would recall her big blue-green eyes as seemingly ever open – one of them, the right eye, bearing a rare blemish in the iris. The mark, known as a coloboma, would one day receive worldwide publicity.

Always with Madeleine at bedtime was a soft toy named Cuddle Cat. Another favourite was a toy lamb that, if squeezed, played the words of 'You Are My Sunshine'.

The McCanns waited hardly at all before trying for another baby – again by IVF – and promptly succeeded. Their reward this time was the birth of twins in early 2005, a boy they named Sean and a girl, Amelie. Madeleine for her part seemed to enjoy her role as elder sister. On the other hand – she had been walking for some time by now – she would run up and down screaming for more attention. With walking came nocturnal expeditions. If she woke in the night, she would find her way to her parents' bed and spend the rest of the night there.

As the months passed, and after a move to a larger house in the Leicestershire village of Rothley, Madeleine's parents got their firstborn under better control. She would be awarded stars for sleeping all night long. The stars mounted up, stuck on the refrigerator door in the kitchen for all to see, and earned her presents. In the bedroom she had to herself now, Madeleine would lie back, blonde hair spread on the pillow, and say 'Lie with me, Mummy. Lie with me.' Kate was beguiled.

The McCann family were popular. Karen McCalman, a family friend and a mother herself, thought Gerry and Kate exemplary parents, and Madeleine, whom she cared for on occasion, 'fun-loving, smart . . . [She] expressed herself with ease . . . like she was an adult.' Hayley Plummer, who taught at Madeleine's nursery school, remembered her as polite and affectionate, sometimes shy, but good at making friends. She liked dancing and dressing up.

At three, and talking, Madeleine would come out with, 'Oh, I love your earrings, Mummy,' or – out shopping with her mother – 'Oh Mummy, I like that top.' Her parents were both keen on sport – Gerry the cardiologist had long been a runner – and she would ask if she could go jogging. She liked swimming and had a go at tennis.

'You forget,' Kate was to reflect, 'how precious life is – until something awful happens . . .'

On Christmas Day 2006, camera phone in hand, Gerry McCann filmed Madeleine as she ripped the paper from one of her presents. 'Oh wow!' Gerry is heard to exclaim as the package turns out to contain a small pink roll-along bag. Just a week later, on New Year's Day, the McCanns began planning a spring holiday.

It was their friends David and Fiona Payne who had come up with the idea. A week's break with the children at a resort in Portugal, they thought, would be just the thing. They themselves had spent time the previous year in Greece, at one of a chain of resorts run by a British tour operator named Mark Warner Ltd. This year, they suggested, they could try another of the company's resorts – the Ocean Club, in the Algarve region of Portugal.

It sounded like the sort of holiday the McCanns favoured. The Ocean Club offered good amenities, sporting activities for the grown-ups and crèche facilities for young children. There would be other couples they knew – Matt and Rachael Oldfield, Russell O'Brien and Jane Tanner – and Fiona Payne's mother, Dianne Webster. Six of the adults were doctors by profession. The couples had eight small children between them.

Though she was won over by the enthusiasm of everyone else, Kate McCann was initially hesitant about the trip. She has explained this by saying she had concerns about what it would cost, and all the trouble and organisation involved in getting three small children to Portugal and back for just a few days. Fiona Payne would remember her friend's hesitation a little differently. 'I don't know why,' she recalled Kate saying on the phone, 'I've just got an uneasy feeling about it.'

Come April, with the trip only a week away, the three-year-old daughter of Jane Tanner and her partner Russ O'Brien came down with a foot infection. Their decision to travel was made only at the last minute. 'It was all a bit weird,' Rachael Oldfield was to reflect, 'almost like the holiday should never have happened in the first place.'

Madeleine was very excited about the trip. She chattered on about it at her nursery school, to teachers and children alike. Early on April 28th, the day of departure, the McCanns and the Paynes piled into a people carrier and headed for East Midlands Airport. As she clambered up the steps to board their flight, Madeleine had a mishap. With the Paynes' two-year-old clutching her by one hand and with a bag in the other – the one she had been given for Christmas – she slipped and grazed her shin. 'She started crying but stopped almost immediately,' her father would recall. 'She was really brave.'

Camera-phone footage taken on the airport bus – after the families' arrival in Faro – shows the children seated in a row, Madeleine in shocking-pink pants. Her father has a frazzled look on his face, prompting Payne to exclaim, 'Cheer up, Gerry! We're on holiday!'

They reached the Ocean Club, an hour's drive away, by mid-afternoon. The remainder of the party had flown in earlier from Gatwick, and everyone got together by the swimming pool. The weather was chilly, the water cold, but Madeleine insisted on going for a dip. She was, by general agreement, irrepressible.

Essential baggage for the trip had included the children's picture books. Madeleine loved books. While her parents were packing, she had proudly regaled an aunt with the words of one of them, a story about a bear hunt with the chorus:

> What a beautiful day!
> We're not scared.

The Ocean Club sprawls across what is left of a centuries-old fishing village named Praia da Luz – *praia* is Portuguese for 'beach' and *luz* means 'light' – though it has only had the name since tourism overwhelmed the fishing industry. Foreigners pounced on the place, bought up the fields where once wheat and barley grew and – as elsewhere along the coast – built the villas and apartment blocks that lure visitors to this part of Portugal. Half of the approximately three-thousand-strong population is now said to be made up of British, Dutch or German expatriates. Many thousands more live in or own properties in the region.

The centre of Praia da Luz today makes little pretence at being Portuguese. It looks and feels like what it is, a holiday development simulating a developer's idea of what a quaint but up-to-date seaside village should look like. It has everything such a place requires: windsurfing and diving schools, discos, restaurants, shops and, inevitably, 'British' pubs with names like The Bull and The Duke Bar.

The Ocean Club is advertised as comprising 'purpose-built, self-catering cottages and low-rise apartments . . . attractively designed reflecting traditional Portuguese and Moorish styles and set among beautifully landscaped gardens.' It boasts four pools, five tennis courts, a restaurant and two snack bars. Because the Club consists of four separate areas in the village, anyone can wander freely from one to another.

Many of the apartments were not owned by the Club but rented out under an arrangement with the owners. The apartment allocated to the McCanns was owned by a British woman – no relation – named Ruth McCann. It was a ground-floor apartment, number 5A, positioned on the corner of a five-storey block overlooking one of the Club's swimming pools. The block had been built on a hill at the point where one street, Rua Dr Francisco Gentil Martins, rises to form a T-junction with another, the Rua Dr Agostinho da Silva (see street plan in photo section).

There was access to Apartment 5A at two points: from Rua Dr Gentil Martins via a small wrought-iron gate and steps up to a veranda and sliding patio doors; and – on the opposite side of the building – via the main entrance door, which opened on to a walled parking area on the Rua Dr Agostinho da Silva.

Inside, the apartment was roomier than the McCanns had expected. The patio doors on the pool side gave access to a sizeable lounge and a dining area adjoining the kitchen. Off the lounge, and to the left, was a door to a bedroom with a window on to the veranda. This was the bedroom Gerry and Kate chose to use – they pushed together the two single beds it contained.

Opposite this first bedroom, and beyond a bathroom, was a

second bedroom for the children. The McCanns decided that Sean and Amelie would sleep in travel cots in the middle of the room, while Madeleine was assigned a bed just inside the door. A second bed, allocated to no one, was positioned beneath the window that looked on to the parking area. Inside, that window had curtains. On the outside there were shutters, which could be opened or closed by pulling a cord inside the bedroom. According to the McCanns, they closed both the curtains and the shutters soon after their arrival – and left them closed.

Given what was going to happen to Madeleine, and given the heated aspersions that would later be cast on her parents, an observation is needed here. It is that the authors will in this chapter relate events very neutrally and – wherever possible – as corroborated by others.

The McCann family would enjoy five days of ordinary holiday, uncomplicated days. From the first of those days, life took on what was to be the basic routine. All the parents planned to take advantage of the Ocean Club's facilities to have time to themselves. They would deliver their children each morning to the Club's crèche, pick them up at lunchtime, then usually return them to the care of the nannies until late afternoon.

The arrangement seemed to suit the whole McCann family. A cleaning woman who saw them on the first day of the holiday was charmed by the sight of Kate heading out of the apartment with her brood. The three children were wearing trainers that flashed with every step, each was carrying a slice of bread on a plate, and Madeleine led the way. Having a break from the children meant rare down time for Kate and Gerry – a chance, above all, for open-air activity. They signed up for tennis lessons and on occasion went running.

At the crèche, Madeleine joined the Mini Club for tots aged three to five, while the twins were cared for at the Toddler Club, for infants aged one to two. The Mini Club was divided in turn into two groups, the Lobsters and the Sharks. Madeleine was a Lobster.

Madeleine thrived at the crèche. Catriona Baker, the experienced English nanny who spent most time with Madeleine, would remember her as having been a little shy at first, but then 'active, sociable'. Another nanny, Amy Tierney, thought her 'very intelligent for her age'. Some nannies would remember her as 'Maddy', a shortening of her name that the media would adopt with relish in the months to come. 'She hated it when we called her "Maddy",' her mother would remember. 'She'd say, "My name is Madeleine," with an indignant look on her face.' At the Mini Club, she seems not to have objected.

The consensus among the parents, too, was that this was a bright, pretty little girl who was enjoying herself. David Payne thought her 'almost unique-looking . . . doll-like . . . good fun'. Russ O'Brien, who had not seen much of Madeleine before the holiday, thought her 'full of beans' and – importantly for him – that she was getting on especially well with his daughter Ella. The two girls, his partner Jane Tanner thought, were having 'a whale of a time'.

The time the adults and children saw most of each other as a group was generally in the early evening. Madeleine was bubbly, cheery, Rachael Oldfield said, 'sort of caring, very good with smaller children. I remember Grace falling over and Madeleine going to pick her up and help.' 'It was all, you know, fun,' Rachael's husband Matt was to say later, 'the children running around. They'd all jump on Dave or jump on Gerry. And the awful thing was that Madeleine always used to say, "Oh come on, be a monster! Chase me!" It was all pretend at that point, but of course not – as it turned out. The fact she said that was . . .' His voice trailed off.

How to spend the evenings had posed a problem even before the families left England, and the solution they found would bring down lasting opprobrium on Kate and Gerry McCann. It concerned how to combine appropriate care for their children with getting together to dine and socialise.

The resort offered what it described as 'an evening service for the younger children, enabling you to have a relaxing dinner . . . from 7.30 p.m. until 11.30 p.m. and allows you to drop off your children at our crèche where they will be entertained with films or games or – if they can – go to sleep in a designated quiet area.'

The crèche did not appeal to the McCanns and their friends. For Kate, using the facility would have disrupted the children's usual 7 p.m. bedtime. 'We did what we thought was best in the kids' routines . . . the whole bath, bed, story, type thing.' Their friends had similar concerns. Matt Oldfield worried that his eighteen-month-old daughter Grace 'wouldn't go to sleep particularly well with, sort of, strangers – in a room where people would be coming in and out to collect their children.'

David Payne, who had the principal role in organising the holiday, had initially thought there would be an alternative to the crèche. He had expected the resort to offer 'a listening service. What that involves is that . . . the parents can go and have their evening meal . . . and they [the Club staff] will go and listen outside the room, of each of the rooms, just to check whether the baby's crying or there seem to be any problems.'

The Ocean Club, however, had no baby-listening service. It seemed to the McCanns and the other couples, though, that they could do the job themselves. There was a restaurant at which they could eat, they discovered, without even leaving the Ocean Club. This was the Club's own Tapas restaurant, a small, cano-pied addition to a bar of the same name that was pleasantly located beside a large swimming pool. The apartment block in which the group were staying was some sixty yards away, on the other side of the pool from the restaurant. On foot, going around the pool and a short distance uphill on the public road to the patio doors, it was ninety yards – less than a minute's walk away.

Going across to the Tapas for dinner seemed to the group to offer a satisfactory solution. 'We ate there and enjoyed it,' Russ O'Brien was to say, 'thought it was going to be convenient for us and the children. In relation to the childcare issues, it was a collective decision.' Rachael Oldfield recalled: 'We just thought we'd do our own sort of baby-listening. Basically we just thought we'd go and have dinner and run back, you know, every fifteen, twenty minutes and have a listen at the door and make sure nobody's screaming their head off . . . It was so quiet, you know, the beginning of the season . . . just like dead . . . which is why we kind of [felt] comfortable in leaving the children and going back and checking them . . . If it had been really busy we wouldn't have done that.'

It was Rachael who, on Monday, April 30th, arranged with the Tapas that the party would eat there for the remainder of their stay. The booking was for 8.30 p.m., and they gathered there that evening and the three evenings that followed.

For Kate and Gerry McCann, and for the other parents who had left their offspring with the nannies, the end of the day was marked by what the nannies called the children's high tea. Madeleine and her fellow Mini Club members would be ushered into the swimming-pool area in single file, holding on to coloured rings on a long rope known as 'Sammy Snake'. After playing a while longer, the McCann children would then be taken back to the apartment to get into their pyjamas, drink a glass of milk and listen to stories. Kate and Gerry would then get cleaned up and have a first glass of wine before heading over to the Tapas restaurant.

Interviewed later, the staff at the Tapas restaurant would have only good things to say about the British party. Jeronimo Salcedas, who worked in the bar and waited tables, thought them a polite group, always courteous to the staff. In the weeks that followed, some would suggest that the party drank excessively. Salcedas – and other staff – described them as moderate drinkers.

Svetlana Vitorino would remember them as a 'very happy' crowd, and the diners themselves do not disagree. Given the number of doctors in the party, there was a good deal of medical shop talk – and ribaldry. 'A bit rude, this,' Jane Tanner would recall of the night she innocently told the friends she was heading back to the apartment to relieve her partner Russ, who was minding their sick daughter. Her use of the word 'relieve' led to chuckles and – when she came out with the phrase on another occasion – knowing cries of, 'Oh, Jane's off to *relieve* Russ again . . .'

Gerry McCann's addiction to tennis and running could be off-putting. Matt Oldfield would remember the night he avoided sitting next to Gerry because 'he'd bored the pants off me yesterday when we were talking about his sports.' However, he could also be entertaining. He was noticeable, waiter Salcedas thought, because he 'told many jokes'.

On Wednesday night, May 2nd, the jollity went on later than on any previous night. Instead of leaving before midnight –

Salcedas and a colleague named Ricardo Oliveira would recall – some members of the party stayed on until 12.20 a.m. or later. Some of them drank almond bitters – the nearest thing the bar stocked to Amaretto – then moved into the bar. 'I think it was midnight that night,' Jane Tanner was to say. 'We went into the bar area for, you know, a nightcap . . . definitely much later than any of the other nights we'd been there.'

Though they were apparently not amongst the last to leave, the night did not end well for Kate and Gerry McCann. Shortly before midnight, according to Kate, Gerry abruptly declared that he was off to bed. Kate followed soon afterward, feeling slighted, and got back to find her husband already asleep and snoring. She decided not to join him, and spent the night on the unused bed in the children's room.

On the Thursday morning when the family got up, no more was said about the incident. It was something Madeleine said at breakfast, according to Kate, that got her attention. Why had her mother not come the previous night, the little girl wanted to know, 'when me and Sean were crying'? Perplexed, her mother asked when she and her brother had cried – early the previous evening or later? Madeleine did not answer. Her attention had turned to something else.

That day, Thursday, May 3rd, the prospects for the rest of the holiday seemed to be looking up. The weather had so far been disappointingly chilly, with rain. Now it turned dry and warm, which was what British people hope for in spring in Portugal. More than usual, the day called for activity outdoors.

As Ocean Club coach Georgina Jackson was to recall, Kate and Gerry were on the tennis courts in both the morning and the afternoon. At one point, while Kate and others in the party watched from the sidelines, there was an odd little episode – one that would later come to haunt them. A fellow guest with a video camera, who was filming his three-year-old daughter as she tried wielding a tennis racket, made a remark none of them would forget.

'He said something like,' Russ O'Brien remembered, '"the way things are these days, you feel like a criminal or a dirty old man taking a photo of your own kid." I don't know if he used the word "perv", but the conversation went . . . you know, that society can make normal parents feel uncomfortable about what ten, twenty, thirty years ago would have been considered a completely innocent thing like taking a photograph . . . We kind of said, "It's ridiculous, isn't it?"'

During the morning that day, over at the Mini Club, nanny Cat Baker decided to take her charges out on the water. With Baker heading their 'snake', the line of children trooped down to the beach for an outing on a boat. As it was launched, Baker recalled, Madeleine 'was fearful, and cried on my lap, "I'm scared."' She soon got over it, though. When some of the other children returned to shore, she stayed on board. After that, there was swimming.

When handed over to Kate that evening, her mother was to recall, Madeleine seemed 'really tired, very very tired'. She asked her mother to carry her back to the apartment.

'Mummy,' Madeleine confided, 'I've had the best day ever. I'm having lots of fun.' The next day, when the children were due to perform a dance they had been rehearsing, was also going to be exciting.

After the children's bathtime that evening, the weary Madeleine sat on Kate's lap. She was allowed to try on her mother's engage-ment ring, something she often asked to do. In the bedroom, everyone settled down on Madeleine's bed for one last story. It featured a veritable menagerie of animals, with the children joining in the chorus:

> If you're happy and you know it,
> And you really want to show it,
> If you're happy and you know it,
> SHOUT!

At the end, the song called for everyone to holler really loudly, 'WE ARE!' By that time, however, Madeleine was already almost asleep.

By about 7.15 p.m., according to Kate, she was putting on make-up and her husband – who had got back from a last game of tennis in time to join in the bedtime kisses – was taking a shower. Then they sat and talked over a drink for a while. Forgotten, long since, was a notion that they might keep the children up and take them along to dinner for once. Now, around 8.30 p.m., they headed out, down the hill and around the pool to the Tapas restaurant. Gradually, their friends joined them.

David and Fiona Payne were last to arrive – they always were. David, who had stopped by the McCanns' apartment earlier, said as he sat down that Madeleine and the twins had 'looked like perfect children . . . all clean in their pyjamas, having a story.' Over dinner, however, in conversation with Fiona and Jane Tanner, Kate McCann told them how Madeleine had asked that morning where her parents had been the previous night, when she and her little brother 'woke up'.

'You could see,' Fiona would recall, 'she was just a bit sort of concerned . . . It was just sort of like, "I wonder if she did wake up." I think she thought Madeleine was just saying it . . . So I think Kate was more worried that night, you know, whether leaving them was the right thing – so to speak.'

Members of the group would say later that, while all the parents checked on their children at regular intervals that week, the McCanns – as Russ O'Brien put it – did their checks 'by the clock'. 'Out of everybody,' Tanner thought, 'Kate and Gerry were the most strict on that . . . We almost took them as the lead for when we checked, because they were definitely every half an hour.'

Just before 9.00 that Thursday evening, on his way back to the restaurant after a check on his own child, Matt Oldfield paused for a moment outside the window of the McCann apartment, 'had a listen' and told Gerry minutes later that all was quiet.

At 9.05 p.m., nevertheless, Gerry returned to Apartment 5A to check for himself for the first time. Madeleine, he would recall, was lying in her bed as she had been when he left. 'I had one of those really proud father moments,' he said, 'I just thought, "You're absolutely beautiful and I love you . . . "'

At about 9.25, the friends would later agree, Kate, Matt Oldfield and Russ O'Brien were about to leave the table – all at the same time – to go and make sure their children were all right. When Oldfield offered to stop at 5A and check for her, Kate accepted the favour. He entered the McCann apartment, peered into the children's room without going in, then returned to say all was quiet.

Half an hour later, at 10 p.m., Kate rose from the table to go and check yet again. Then she came running, shouting from the entrance to the pool complex, panic in her voice. What she shouted, repeated, was: 'Madeleine's gone.'

Gerry's first reaction was, 'She can't be gone.' He raced towards

Kate, their friends at his heels. Long minutes later, still in the restaurant, waiter Jeronimo Salcedas heard what he would come to assume had been Kate screaming.

'Never in my life,' he would tell the police later, 'had I heard a cry like that . . .'

2

Even before the friends got back to Apartment 5A, David Payne was to say, Kate McCann's 'Madeleine's gone' had changed to 'They've taken her!' According to a woman in an apartment on a higher floor, Susan Moyes, that would shortly become, 'The fucking bastard's taken her!' or 'The fucking bastards have taken her!'

Kate jumped to that conclusion for good reason, the statement she would soon give to the Portuguese police suggests. When she entered the apartment to check on her children, she said, she had found the door to their bedroom 'completely open' – not ajar, as it had been left. Its window, which earlier had been closed, was also 'open, the shutters raised and the curtains open'. Madeleine's bed, where her husband had seen their daughter sleeping peacefully less than an hour earlier, was now empty, the coverlet 'pulled back'.

Kate looked in her own room, thinking Madeleine might be there. Then it dawned on her. 'I kind of looked and double-looked. There was twenty seconds of, you know: "She must be here . . . " Then there was panic, and fear . . . I was screaming her name. I ran to the group.'

By the time she came rushing back to the Tapas restaurant to raise the alarm, Payne recalled, the look on her face was one of 'disbelief . . . grief . . . horror'. He reached the apartment with Kate, entered briefly, and stayed long enough to see that 'with all the pandemonium and the shouting' Madeleine's baby brother and sister were still sound asleep. Wanting not to 'run around like a headless chicken', to be doing something useful, Payne then headed outside to join the first, frenzied, impromptu search.

Members of the group hoped against hope that Kate was wrong in thinking Madeleine had been snatched. 'Surely,' Matt Oldfield recalled thinking, 'she must have just wandered off. And we're just going to find her and she's just going to be there.' Even as everyone first rushed to respond to Kate's call, Fiona Payne had told her mother Dianne to stay in the restaurant. 'I said to Mum, "You stay put here just in case Madeleine comes down to the pool area." Then, 'Pretty much immediately, Dave, Matt, Russell and myself split up in four different directions just to do a search, you know, again assuming that she must have just wandered off.'

Fiona hunted around behind the apartments and the tennis courts, then cut down in front of the nearby Baptista supermarket. Her husband David checked on their own children, then 'did a sweep of the pool and the area immediately around the Ocean Club, then met up with Matt and Russell. I remember saying, "Right. What're we going to do?" And Matt was saying, "We've got to try and be systematic here . . . " I started venturing up towards the Millennium [another restaurant] . . . and it was just so quiet . . . Again I was just building up hope that she'd run off . . . I went down towards the seafront, you know, along the whole length of the beach, looking under beach huts . . . shouting, "Madeleine!"'

In the jumble of testimony made long afterwards, it is not

quite clear who searched in which areas and at what stage. 'I searched mainly on my own,' Russ O'Brien said, 'although we were all close by to each other . . . There may have been places we missed. It was haphazard and panicked. I met Dave, and he was running down the hill with sort of panic in his eyes . . . and it was him who said to me, "This is bad. This is really bad. They haven't found her. She's missing."'

At Apartment 5A, the McCanns' emotions were spiralling out of control. Kate and Gerry were both, Rachael Oldfield recalled, 'pretty much most of the rest of the night . . . hysterical and screaming and shouting . . . it was just awful.' Fiona Payne, who is a hospital anaesthetist, said of Kate, 'I've never seen such horrible raw emotion in my life, and I've seen a lot of it in my job. She was just bereft . . . extremely frightened for Madeleine.

'The helplessness of not being able to do anything . . . She was angry, really angry, punching walls, kicking walls. She was covered in bruises the next day . . . She was angry at herself. She kept saying, "I've let her down. We've let her down, Gerry. We should have been here." . . . She was just howling.'

The cry of 'We've let her down' was loud enough to be heard by Pamela Fenn, an elderly resident in the apartment immediately above the McCanns' place. She leaned over the balcony, caught sight of Kate and Gerry, and asked what was happening. A little girl, Gerry told her, had been 'abducted'.

By the time the men making the initial search got back to Apartment 5A, Russ O'Brien said, panic had really set in. Normally 'a very determined, very strong guy [who] doesn't get flustered easily,' Gerry was 'lying on the floor in hysterics. He had a high voice, crying like a baby. I didn't know what to say.' Madeleine's father would get a grip on himself, talk about what was best to do, then break down again.

'Is it normal to react the way they did?' Fiona Payne would reflect long afterwards. 'How can anyone ever put themselves in their situation – the transition from utter, relaxed happiness to the worst thing that could ever happen? I couldn't tell you what's normal. But they were just distraught.'

In the midst of panic, there was common sense – now muddled in memory. Far in the future some Portuguese officials, as senior as the then Attorney General and the president of the police union, would talk as though Madeleine's disappearance had not been reported until many hours later. All the facts indicate otherwise.

The Ocean Club receptionist, Helder Sampaio, said that, having learned from a staff member at the Tapas restaurant that a little girl was missing, he phoned the police at once. As Kate recalled it, Gerry asked Matt Oldfield to go to the Ocean Club reception and have a call put through to the police. Oldfield thought it had been his initiative, and that the reaction he got at the reception desk was 'surreal'.

'I said, "You've got to phone the police . . . a child's been taken." And they went, "Oh no, she's probably just woken up . . . probably sort of wandered off." . . . It was sort of a weird kind of lack of urgency. You know, he'd ring, but you sort of had to stand there and say, "Ring now. Ring now." So I don't know if they rang at that point.'

So far as one can see from phone company records, the first call from the Ocean Club to the local headquarters of the GNR – Portugal's Guarda Nacional Republicana, or Republican National Guard – went out at 10.41 p.m. A message was then passed to two officers in a patrol car some eight miles away, tasking them to head for the Ocean Club, where a girl had 'gone missing'.

At the Club, staff had begun to react. Alerted by one of the nannies on night duty, crèche manager Lyndsay Johnson initiated the procedure to be followed in the event of a child going missing. She called Ocean Club manager John Hill at home, and he hurried to reception. Services manager Silvia Batista also responded. Staff on night duty, with others summoned from home, were assigned to fan out across the property and beyond in search of Madeleine.

One of the recruits was Jeronimo Salcedas, the Tapas waiter who knew and liked the McCann party and had quickly become aware of the emergency. 'We were sent to the beach area,' he remembered, 'and looked in all the lanes and called out the name of the child but did not find her.' Joined as time passed by locals, tourists and residents – perhaps forty or fifty people in the end – the search would continue into the night.

Club nannies Amy Tierney and Emma Knight, meanwhile, had hurried to Apartment 5A to offer help. Tierney, who went into the children's bedroom 'to see if the girl was hiding', looked in the wardrobes. As she recalled it, the bedclothes of Madeleine's empty bed had been 'pushed back'. A 'small child's blanket and a cuddly toy' were on the bed.

A bed near the window was 'rumpled as if someone had been sitting there . . . The shutter was raised . . . [and] the window partially open.' On learning that Madeleine's shoes were still in the apartment, she thought the little girl might indeed have been abducted.

Nanny Emma Knight, who introduced herself to Kate, remembered her as having been 'hysterical and desperate . . . crying and calling Madeleine's name, shouting "Where is she?"' and banging on the headboard of a bed. Gerry, though 'visibly upset' and crying, tried to be helpful.

To the frantic parents and their friends, the police seemed to be taking an age to come. 'It was, you know, "Where are the police? Where are the police?"' Matt Oldfield recalled. 'And so [it was] back to the reception . . . Gerry had come down as well.'

In fact, phone records show that only eleven minutes had passed between the initial call to local police, at 10.41 p.m., and a second call, made at 10.52. A later statement by Officer Nelson Costa, one of the two members of the police car unit detailed to head for the Ocean Club following the first call, suggests that the second call really got them moving. Told that the missing person was a 'very young child', he said, he and his partner José Roque drove the final mile and a half to the Club at speed.

The officers arrived at reception at 11 p.m. or thereabouts – not much more than twenty minutes after the first call – to be met by the waiting Gerry, Matt Oldfield and two Ocean Club employees. Gerry, Oldfield recalled, was 'intermittently calm and then completely hysterically upset'.

Officer Costa and Silvia Batista, the senior Ocean Club employee who translated for Gerry, painted a more vivid picture. 'Gerry knelt down,' Batista recalled, 'and slamming his two hands on the floor, like an Arab praying, screamed twice in indescribable anguish.'

Shortly afterwards, when the policemen arrived at Apartment 5A, things did not go smoothly. 'They were Portuguese obviously,' Fiona Payne recalled, 'didn't really speak any English. And that was awful . . . because we were obviously desperate and frantic . . . conscious of every second that was passing . . . We were just trying to get over the urgency, and it just didn't feel that they were recognising the urgency . . . Kate was getting hysterical . . . because she just wanted somebody who she felt was doing something that was going to make a difference.'

Officers Roque and Costa, the plodding language of their reports indicate, did the routine things that one would expect beat policemen to do to establish that Madeleine really had disappeared. 'On reaching the location,' Roque's statement reads, he and his colleague 'proceeded into the interior of the apartment . . . searched all parts of the residence and all the contents, in order to confirm the disappearance – effectively confirming that [the missing girl] was not in the interior.'

In the children's room, Roque noted that the bedclothes on Madeleine's bed seemed 'too tidy'. It appeared, he thought, 'that she had been picked up from or had left the bed with great care. There was a mark on the sheet that appeared to be made by a child's body.'

Roque and Costa also noted, as had nanny Amy Tierney, that the shutters of the children's bedroom were not totally closed. They were, Roque reported, 'raised up the space of the width of a hand.' The window, which nanny Tierney said was partially open when she saw it, was now closed. When Kate had found Madeleine gone, Gerry told him, both shutters and window had been open.

As did others, Costa thought it 'very strange' that, despite the tumult going on around them, the McCanns' twins were still fast asleep. The scene as he saw it, he would recall, did not suggest there had been a break-in. To him, it looked more like a 'normal disappearance where the child had left by her own means' than an abduction.

At about this time, a weeping Kate told Costa she wanted more policemen to come. 'She was worried by the fact,' she said on one of the calls to friends in the UK she and Gerry made that night, that 'there were only two police officers in the place, and thought that the police were not helping her with anything.' In fact, more police were already on their way.

On receiving a first report from the patrol officers, the duty sergeant at Lagos had decided to head for the Ocean Club himself. Antonio Duarte, a veteran, told his men to preserve the scene.

Too late, for they and many other people had by now been tramping in and out and around Apartment 5A for more than an hour.

Once at the scene, and briefed by Roque, Duarte decided there was nothing to be gained by him entering the apartment. He drove around Praia da Luz, focusing on swimming pools and open ground in the hope of finding the missing girl. Four more GNR officers, two of them off-duty men who volunteered, reached the scene within an hour of the first patrol. Two others arrived around 1 a.m.

In spite of the late hour, word of what had happened had spread around the apartment block and beyond. Paul and Susan Moyes, two floors above, had been woken by a knock on the door – perhaps by one of the McCann party. Told that a little girl had been abducted, they got up and joined in the search for about two hours.

Another neighbour offered a crumb of comfort. 'Don't worry,' Rachael remembered him saying, 'it will be all right . . . I went missing when I was a kid, and I came back.'

One objectionable visitor made for Apartment 5A. Fiona Payne, who was in and out all night trying to be supportive, remembered how 'a woman who worked in the bar in Praia da Luz . . . almost invited herself up on to the balcony and was just quite drunk.' Fiona and Gerry persuaded her to go away.

Sergeant Duarte, meanwhile, decided within ten minutes of arriving that this was too big for the GNR. The Guarda Nacional Republicana is a first-responder force concerned primarily with traffic control and public order. Detection of serious crime is usually handled by another force, the Polícia Judiciária, or PJ.

Whatever the views of his patrolman Costa, Duarte thought this episode at the Ocean Club might involve a crime.

So it was that not long after midnight, on Duarte's orders, a call went out to the PJ at Portimão. The head of the local Criminal Investigation unit, Gonçalo Amaral, was informed as he ate a late dinner. An inspector and an investigator were despatched to the Ocean Club's Apartment 5A.

From the point of view of the investigator – the man with initial responsibility for noting physical evidence – this incident scene was a disaster. 'The people in the apartment and close to it,' Specialist Joao Barreiras' notes observed, had 'entered and left the building and circulated in the whole apartment, completely freely . . . without there being any restriction or care in preserving the scene.'

The notes make clear that Barreiras thought the GNR responsible for the lack of care. One of the GNR officers told him, the report states, that they had earlier 'searched for the girl in the wardrobes and others places in the apartment, without having taken any care about leaving their own traces or about destroying or adulterating any traces of potential interest to the investigation.'

Around 2.00 a.m. or soon after, two more GNR officers arrived – with German shepherd dogs. Armed with a blanket from Madeleine's bed to identify her scent, they walked the animals around the immediate area, around the Ocean Club, then further afield. The lead dog appeared 'a little interested' at first, outside Apartment 5A, but nothing came of the search. The dogs' primary training was in public-order work, not tracking. Nevertheless, the officers were to work their dogs until the sun came up.

As the night wore on without news, Gerry and Kate McCann's anguish – and sense of impotence – mounted. Their family and friends have recalled how, hour by hour, they had striven to think of ways to help locate Madeleine. Russ O'Brien had got one of the nannies, Amy Tierney, to print up twenty or thirty photographs of the missing girl. Some of the photos were given to the GNR's Sergeant Duarte, who handed them out to the men he had searching the area.

After the PJ officers arrived, and when things quietened down, one of the investigating officers sat with Gerry and Russ O'Brien as they tried to reconstruct the events of the catastrophic evening – with the approval of the PJ man. O'Brien tore off the back of a child's sticker book that was lying in the living room – it had belonged to Madeleine – took a pen and scribbled down the salient events.

The scrawled note began:

> 8.45 – pool
> Matt returned 9.00–9.05 – listened at all 3.
> – all shutters down

Then, after listing the checks made in the course of the evening, it ended with:

> 9.55 – Kate realises Madeleine s [sic]
> 10pm – Alarm raised

Dr O'Brien, who thought the first draft so badly written that it was not 'going to be useful to hand to anyone to read', soon after did a second, similar draft on the inside front cover of Madeleine's book. Both chronologies wound up in Portuguese police files.

O'Brien noticed as they worked up the timeline that Gerry 'was just staring at the table . . . very quiet, very, very low.' He was weary now, certainly, but also frustrated. Earlier, on the phone to his sister Patricia in the UK, he had complained about the police 'not taking the situation seriously'. Why, he wanted to know, had the borders not been closed?

Earlier, they had managed to raise a British consulate employee, who responded by calling the Ocean Club and talking on the phone with the GNR's Officer Roque. From the UK, Gerry's sister and her husband contacted the British Embassy in Lisbon.

Ocean Club services manager Silvia Batista, who translated for the McCanns far into the night, gathered – as members of the group moved in and out – that they were 'anxious to tell the press what had happened'. David Payne thought they should alert the media, while O'Brien urged holding off and leaving things to the police. PJ officer Barreiras exclaimed firmly, 'No media!' but Gerry told him they had already made contact with Sky News.

There had been an effort to alert Sky News by email. At the request of one of the McCann group, upstairs neighbour Paul Moyes had used his laptop to try to email Sky. In fact that initial message did not reach the newsroom. Rachael Oldfield, for her part, rang a friend who was married to James Landale, a BBC journalist, in the hope of getting the attention of BBC News 24. A string of calls did spark the initial interest of the BBC's round-the-clock news service. Around 3 a.m., Kate got through to her best friend, whose partner Jon Corner ran a video production company and had press contacts. Corner would be circulating pictures of Madeleine to the BBC and other media outlets by the morning.

As late as 7 a.m., however, the story was still not being carried on the air. Then Kate got through to Jill Renwick, a friend from the early days of her medical career. Renwick phoned GMTV, then providing breakfast television for ITV, and Sky News picked it up around 7.30. Thus began a news story that was to last for years.

Even as they tried to be practical in those first hours, it was constantly apparent that Kate and Gerry were in extreme emotional distress – expressed in a way that Officer Roque thought 'unusual'. Not long after he and his GNR colleague arrived, the patrolman reported that 'the girl's parents knelt down on the floor of their bedroom and placed their heads on the bed, just crying.'

They were praying. Both the McCanns are Roman Catholics, and Kate is especially devout. 'Kate was desperate to have a priest,' Fiona Payne recalled, 'from almost immediately after Madeleine's disappearance, which people find weird. But I think that was just her way of thinking, "At least I can pray for Madeleine," her way of feeling that she was doing something. But she wasn't functioning . . . She kept praying, kept kneeling everywhere, just praying and praying and praying and asking for a priest. And wanted everybody to be praying for Madeleine for her to be safe.'

Separately, Kate and Gerry called Father Paul Seddon, the priest in Liverpool who had married them eight years earlier and who had baptised Madeleine. 'I phoned Paul,' Gerry would remember, 'and he asked, "What can I do?" And I said, "Just pray, please, pray."' They prayed together over the phone – and Seddon offered the hope that 'Madeleine could have had a bout of sleepwalking and would be all right.'

For Kate, however, long-distance spiritual counsel did not suffice. At 3 a.m., when she and Gerry again asked to have contact with a local priest, Officer Roque tried and failed to locate one. Later still, Gerry asked for directions to a nearby church. Silvia Batista, who was still acting as translator, was surprised by the McCanns' persistence. 'They didn't explain why they wanted a priest . . . There was no indication that the little girl was dead, and that is normally the circumstance in which one asks for a priest.'

Towards 4 a.m., the McCanns were moved out of Apartment 5A. The detectives from the PJ wanted the place sealed off, however belatedly. The Ocean Club nannies and the policemen helped carry the twins – astonishingly, still fast asleep – up to the Paynes' nearby apartment. Even then, Kate was still complaining angrily about the lack of a priest. 'I won't say what her language was,' recalled Fiona Payne's mother Dianne. 'But, you know [she was saying]: "Portugal's a Catholic country – and no priest?"'

'We made Kate and Gerry up a mattress on the floor,' Fiona Payne said, 'and by about half-four we all decided to just try and lay down, and at least to get a rest if not sleep.'

Before they lay down, however, Gerry and David Payne went out once more in search of Madeleine. They 'went down past the Ocean Club reception, down to the beach,' Payne remembered, and Gerry 'broke down with me on the front, just very obviously a broken man. I was trying my best to console him.'

What Gerry knew – though at that point Kate did not – was information their friend Jane Tanner had shared earlier, something that now seemed highly suspicious.

At the time Kate raised the alarm, Tanner had no longer been in the restaurant with the rest of the party but – because their younger child was poorly and wakeful – back in the apartment in which she and her partner Russ O'Brien were staying. On hearing shouting and going out to see what was going on, the first member of the party she had encountered was Rachael Oldfield. And when Oldfield told her the reason for the hulla-baloo, that Madeleine had disappeared, that the window of the children's room had been open and the shutters up, Tanner remembered something she had seen an hour earlier – something that had not seemed significant at the time.

On her way back to check on her own children – Tanner guessed it had been around 9.15–9.20, about forty minutes before Madeleine was missed – she had seen a man cross the road just yards from the McCanns' apartment. It had not yet been completely dark and she had been able to see him fairly well. He had been carrying a child who seemed to be asleep, a child in what appeared to be pyjamas.

Now, when Rachael Oldfield told her that Madeleine was gone, Jane Tanner 'made the connection'. As she was to remember it later, she felt: 'Oh, that person was a bit odd.' And then: 'It couldn't have been . . . ' Earlier, she had thought little of it – that the man had merely been 'some father carrying their own child . . . from the crèche maybe . . . Never in a million years would I have thought, "That's Madeleine."'

What, in hindsight, had seemed odd? 'The thing that really struck me,' she said, 'was the bare feet.' The child the man had been carrying in his arms had had bare feet – on a very chilly night. The man, for his part, had on reflection not been 'dressed quite touristy' – his clothing had suggested he was 'prepared for the weather'. And he had been striding 'purposefully', even – as Tanner said on another occasion – 'in a rush'.

Tanner looked 'shocked' as she talked with Rachael Oldfield minutes after the discovery that Madeleine had vanished. Fiona Payne, whom she told soon afterwards, noted that she was 'shaking', horrified by what she thought she had seen. They agreed that they should tell the police, and they did – both the GNR and later one of the Polícia Judiciária investigators.

That night, Tanner baulked at the thought of telling Madeleine's mother what she had seen, or might have seen. She could not avoid telling Gerry McCann, however, because he was in the room when she talked with the PJ investigator. As she described what she had seen, Gerry looked 'absolutely horrified'.

On the phone to his sister Patricia in the UK, as he talked of Madeleine's disappearance, Gerry had 'mentioned the possibility that she could have been taken by a paedophile'.

3

In the little that was left of the night, Kate and Gerry McCann soon gave up trying to sleep. 'It was starting to get vaguely light,' said Fiona Payne, and 'Kate and Gerry, wrapped up warm, went out on the streets looking for Madeleine.'

It was a dismal time for them. The couple today known worldwide for their abiding hope that their daughter has survived, were at dawn on May 4th, implicitly admitting that she might be dead. They did what others would do later that day and peered into rubbish bins.

'We were saying over and over again,' Gerry remembered, "'Just let her be found, just let her be found."' At that hour, between 5 and 7 a.m., those police officers still around did not appear to be doing anything. The couple felt abandoned.

The parents' resentment of what they saw as the failing of the Portuguese police, which had begun in the first frenzy of losing Madeleine, was to persist. In time there would be mutual, corrosive distrust between them and the police. It seems, though, that the officers who responded to the initial alert did not lack in personal commitment. One of them, Sergeant Duarte, would recall having stayed at the scene until after 5 a.m. that first night, taking a brief break, then returning at 7.00. There was a yawning gap, all the same, between the expectations of the parents – based on their concept of British urban law enforcement – and the ability of the Portuguese force to respond swiftly.

As late as 2012, a report by the GNR officers' staff association would be protesting about serious understaffing, poor facilities and deplorable conditions in police stations across the Algarve. This was especially so, it noted, in an area where – during the tourist season – the population tripled, rising from around 400,000 people in winter to 1.5 million.

A GNR report would later describe its officers' early efforts in the McCann case as having been 'titanic'. The reality was that the group who searched during the first night hours numbered nine officers – and these involved some who were off duty and had been called at home. A few more officers were corralled to search the beach in the morning. Handlers with four dogs trained in search and rescue, as distinct from crowd control, had to be called from their base – more than a hundred miles away – to drive through the night to Praia da Luz. More colleagues, and more dogs, joined them later. Only during the following afternoon would the GNR call in a helicopter and ask the local authorities for assistance.

Ocean Club manager John Hill, who thought there were some twenty policemen on the ground that first day, agreed that, had he been in the McCanns' situation, he too would have been 'frustrated as hell'. He added, however, that 'If there were a hundred police here I'd want more.'

Hill's staff helped a great deal, some of them tirelessly. Nanny Emma Knight, who had stayed the course until around 4 a.m., was back on the scene by 8.00. She would still be there in mid-afternoon, minding the McCanns' twins and pointing the helicopter out to them. The Club's Portuguese cleaning staff were all recruited to join in the search when they arrived for work that day. With the benefit of daylight, others again searched the swimming pools and grassy areas. 'Missing child' leaflets were printed off and distributed, both at the Club and – in Portuguese – around the village of Praia da Luz.

Some locals were concerned about points where roads had been opened for drainage and cable-laying operations. A British resident, John Ballinger, had a special interest in major roadworks being done along Rua Direta, on a corner two hundred yards from the McCanns' apartment, because it ran past his home (see photo 5). A trench five yards long and some four or five feet deep had been left open on the night Madeleine vanished, protected by only a flimsy barrier and with loose rubble above the hole. So concerned was Ballinger, when he heard the news about Madeleine, that he walked up to Apartment 5A to report the matter to a police officer.

Another British citizen, Rex Morgan, would report having seen a manhole with a cover removed in the same general area. 'The road is lit by street lighting,' Morgan said, 'but anyone could have fallen in.' The police files contain a report showing that municipal workers were much later questioned about these hazards, but said they carefully checked the roadworks on May 4th. Nothing had been found.

Back at the apartments after their dawn search, Madeleine's parents had unexpected visitors. Len Port, a Northern Irish freelance journalist who lived locally and had heard the news of the disappearance on Sky News, arrived expecting Praia da Luz to be buzzing with activity but found it 'so peaceful, quiet. There was nothing happening.' Then he spotted a police officer standing near the parking lot in front of Apartment 5A and thus became, almost certainly, the first reporter on the scene of what would soon become a media circus.

Port saw two women talking in the car park that serves the apartment. One of them was crying, and he realised she must be the mother of the missing girl. This was indeed Kate, who had been approached by an Englishwoman named Yvonne Martin. Martin, whose background was in child protection, was asking questions she thought pertinent. David Payne, who like Kate apparently thought her intrusive, asked her to leave.

A fellow Club guest brought along a Praia da Luz resident named Robert Murat, whose father had been half Portuguese, half British by birth, and who spoke both languages fluently. 'He appeared to be a very useful kind of person to be able to contact should we need him,' Russ O'Brien recalled, and put the man's number into his mobile phone. The police would use Murat as a translator in the days that followed.

Kate, meanwhile, had not let go of her urgent desire to see a priest. On her behalf, O'Brien spent time trying to reach first the local Roman Catholic priest – who turned out to be temporarily away – then, as a fallback, the Anglican minister. He and his wife would visit later that day, praying with Madeleine's parents and reading the passage in the New Testament that begins 'Suffer the little children . . . ' The local church, Nossa Senhora da Luz, a medieval building used by Catholics and Protestants alike, was to become a focal point for the McCanns in the weeks that followed.

When that morning Inspector João Carlos asked the McCann party to come to Portimão to make statements, Kate sat listening – on a mobile phone – as a friend in the UK prayed at the other end of the line. Waiting for her and Gerry at the police station in Portimão was the British consul, Bill Henderson, who knew of the McCanns' plight thanks to their overnight calls. The police were not well pleased, the investigation's chief Amaral would write later, to overhear Henderson 'saying on the phone that the Polícia Judiciária are doing nothing'.

While the inspector was taking her statement, Kate later recalled, he asked whether this was her first visit to Portugal. It was indeed, she said, adding that it would also be her last. It was the comment of a very weary woman, and one she would later regret. Relations with the Portuguese police had not started well.

The reports of the questioning that day make clear that both Gerry and Kate spoke of their friend Jane Tanner's sighting of a man carrying a small child near Apartment 5A – Kate had been told about it by this time – and Gerry ended his statement by calling for the arrest and prosecution of the person who had snatched his daughter. The parents had no doubt this had been an abduction. The police, as events would show, drew no such conclusion.

The efforts of the McCanns and their friends on the phone over the past twenty-four hours had paid off, as they discovered when the police car carrying them back to Praia da Luz pulled up outside the apartments. Waiting for them was a horde of journalists, television crews and photographers, notebooks poised, klieg lights blazing – a first taste of the media attention they felt they needed and would come to curse.

The couple sought shelter in their apartment. Inside, they found Kate's mother and father who had hurried to Portugal from Liverpool, advisers brought in by their holiday tour company and some British diplomats. Though food was on offer, Gerry thought they should go out to speak with the press.

Kate took with her Cuddle Cat, the favourite stuffed toy left lying in the children's bedroom when Madeleine vanished. She clutched it to her as they faced the press for the first time that night, would be seen with it again and again until it became world-famous.

The couple looked shattered and Kate stood with head bowed. Her husband put his arm around her as, close to tears, in his strong Scots accent, he read a note he had scrawled minutes earlier:

Words cannot describe the anguish and despair that we are feeling as the parents of our beautiful daughter . . . We request that anyone who may have any information . . . no matter how trivial, contact the Portuguese police and help us get her back safely. Please, if you have Madeleine, let her come home to her mummy, daddy, brother and sister.

The disappearance of the little British girl had suddenly become a massive international media event, and one not to the liking of the Portuguese investigators. The provisions of the Portuguese constitution and penal code severely limit what the police may reveal about an ongoing investigation. Even to let the press know of Madeleine's disappearance had involved formally requesting government permission. Now here were the McCanns suggesting to a vast audience that their daughter had been taken by an abductor.

This 'huge, unprecedented media presence' rankled with the PJ's Inspector Carlos. He would still be fulminating about it months later, complaining that all the police work had to be done in parallel with the press 'speculating and imagining scenarios, some possible, some fantasy'. To his chief Gonçalo Amaral, the scene in Praia da Luz was an 'astonishing invasion by the press'. It appeared, he later wrote sourly in a book on the case, 'that the McCanns' friends have reported Maddie's disappearance to the press before informing the police'.

The PJ thought, though, that there should be immediate dissemination of information within law enforcement. An initial alert had gone out to Interpol headquarters at 11.05 that first morning. A further message was transmitted before Gerry and Kate were driven home that night, though a 'VERY URGENT' Yellow Alert – a missing person's notice – would not be issued until early the following week.

Madeleine McCann had become an entry in the bureaucratic system. Corporal Roque, the initial GNR officer at the scene, logged a 'Report of Disappearance' of:

Name: Madeleine Beth Mccann [*sic*]
Female sex, white
Date of birth: 12-05-2003
Height: about 0.90 mt. Colour of eyes, blue left eye, greenish right eye with brown.
Blond hair with chestnut tips touching the shoulders
Daughter of Gerald Patrick McCann and Kate Healy
Single, Identity Doc. No. [deleted] issued on 04-08-2003
Born: Leicester. UK.
Residence: [deleted by authors] and temporarily since April 28th, in apartment 5A, Ocean Club, Rua Dr Agostinho da Silva, Vila da Luz
Tel:
Profession:
Place of Work:
Personal markings: small chestnut birthmark on left leg
Date of Disappearance: 03-05-07 between 21.30 and 22.00.
Probable Causes: from apartment 5A, Ocean Club, Rua

Dr Agostinho da Silva, Vila da Luz, when she was sleeping in one of the bedrooms whose window faced the parking area of the block in question together with her two-year-old twin siblings. The possibility of abduction was raised by the parents, given that Jane Tanner, a temporary resident of apartment D5, Ocean Club, Rua Agostinho da Silva is said to have seen an individual aged between 30 and 40, about 1.78 m in height, with dark hair, wearing light-coloured trousers and a dark upper garment, who was carrying a child who appeared to be wearing pyjamas; and also because of the fact that the shutters of the bedroom in question were raised and the window open. The Portimão PJ were contacted, two inspectors arrived at the scene and proceeded to make inspections.

OBSERVATIONS
On the left leg she has a small chestnut birthmark, she was wearing light-coloured pyjamas (top and bottom) with a pink donkey design on the bottoms with the letters ON [sic] and she was barefoot.

Signed in Lagos, May 4th, 2007
José M. B. Roque

While Roque mentioned only one possibility in his report – the explanation the McCanns had believed since the previous night – that of abduction, PJ officers were not so sure. A Portuguese online news service, citing a PJ source, said that there was as yet 'no evidence' of abduction. Ocean Club manager Hill, who had been talking with police at the scene, called the abduction theory 'questionable'.

For local chief investigator Amaral, as he would write later in a controversial book, the theory was questionable because he had had the feeling from the start that 'something isn't right in the account of events'. By midday, he would claim, he was concerned about what he saw as 'contradictions and inconsistencies' in the statements heard thus far from members of the McCann party. By late evening, after a long debate by his team, he said, there was concern about uncertainties that were 'perhaps convenient for the witnesses, but suspicious for the investigators'. At this early stage, one of his officers countered, such suspicions were unfounded.

The McCanns thought so too and would eventually sue Amaral for libel in connection with his book. Judgement was pending as this book went to press.

Earlier in the day, Amaral said, he had asked the British police liaison officer in Lisbon for background information on the McCanns and their friends. The response, he seems to have thought, was slow in coming.

The first day of the investigation ended in the early hours, Amaral recalled, with his men sprawled around the improvised 'crisis unit' they had set up in Praia da Luz, trying to grab some sleep. Already, his own local authority was being undermined. From then on, operations would be directed by senior officers sent in from Lisbon. The local team, Amaral reflected, would simply have to do their best.

Even as the investigator and his team conferred that night, a member of the McCann party was doing something that the Portuguese police team would certainly have seen as interference. David Payne, one of the McCanns' closest friends in the holiday party, put in a call to the Metropolitan Police in London. He had earlier talked with his sister and asked her to make the initial contact, because of 'the difficulties we were having,' the fact that they were 'in a strange country, [and didn't] know what was going on.' He wanted to 'do anything to help [bring] Madeleine back.'

So it was, shortly after 11 p.m., that Payne telephoned the Met's Specialist Crime Directorate, the department that at that time dealt with sex crime, including paedophilia, and kidnapping. Nothing came of the call at the time, according to Payne, but it reflected the frustration of the group, their determination to go on reaching out beyond Praia da Luz, to take control of events.

At midnight Kate was badgering the Polícia Judiciária, asking to be put through to the head of investigation in the Algarve with whom she had spoken earlier and who had promised to take her calls. She was fobbed off. There came a point, she has conceded, that she lost control of herself, began to scream and swear. She kicked a bed, damaging it badly, then fell sobbing to the floor.

Also about that time, she dialled the UK number of Nicky Gill, a friend she had known since their first day at primary school thirty-six years earlier. Gill would long remember the call. 'Kate,' she said, 'was devastated and appeared lost. She said that judging from the actions of the local police, one would think that she had merely "lost a dog".'

4

The initial search was better than that. Investigations chief Gonçalo Amaral, for his part, would remember how the walls of his crisis unit soon became 'covered in analytical charts, timelines, flow charts, assignments done and pending, photographs and other important items, with at its centre Madeleine's photograph – to remind us always of our mission's objective'.

Though Amaral would eventually be removed from the case amidst controversy, the many thousands of pages of Portuguese police records released in 2008 reflect the PJ's view that the force made a major effort.

'This case had special attention from the start,' Fernando Pinto Monteiro, Portugal's then Attorney General, told the authors, 'the same as would any other case of the disappearance of a child . . . This sort of crime must always be investigated as a priority.'

The ground search in and around Praia da Luz resumed the following day and would continue for a further week. As the investigation continued it was extended far beyond the immediate area of the Ocean Club, to cover at first twenty-nine and eventually ninety-six square miles. According to the Portuguese records, eighty officers were involved early on, many roped in from other units in the region. Six were from a sniffer-dog unit. Leave was cancelled for locally based officers.

Additional personnel were borrowed from the fire brigade and other emergency services. In the wider area, in the wilderness of scrub not far from Praia da Luz, personnel trained in forest-fire-fighting operations were used. Divers searched the water near the Bravura Dam, nine miles north of Praia da Luz. All-terrain vehicles and motorbikes – even horses – were used. Four light aircraft from the Lagos aero club flew low passes over the search areas.

British residents, who had volunteered their help from the start, were asked to cover the ground once again after it had first been searched by police. Specified areas were marked out and a supervising officer allocated to each area.

Police stopped and checked traffic on nearby highways 'to control access routes to Praia da Luz and the immediate area', doing so sporadically to create uncertainty, 'in case the girl had been taken by someone within this zone, [who] . . . intended to remove her from the area'.

Gerry McCann had been upset, on the night of the disappearance, because his understanding was that Portugal's nearby borders had not been closed. PJ investigation chief Amaral was to say he had in fact promptly ordered an alert both at the Guadiana road crossing – on the Spanish frontier just twenty-five miles away – and at Faro Airport. Former senior Portuguese and British law-enforcement sources told the authors it would have been unrealistic to have hoped to seal Portugal's extensive borders.

In Praia da Luz, the beach was searched. Metal probes were pushed into the sand without result. Taxi drivers in the village were questioned. At the Ocean Club, two maintenance men who had been in Apartment 5A two days before Madeleine vanished

– to explain how the washing machine worked and examine a broken shutter (not in the children's room) – were questioned and cleared. A report suggesting one of the gardeners might be involved in the disappearance proved to be false. In all, according to the police, more than seven hundred people would be questioned formally or informally. More than four hundred apartments and houses were searched, according to one police report, and checks were made on yachts and cruisers along the coast.

There was further forensic examination of Apartment 5A. One usable fingerprint was lifted from the edge of the apartment's patio doors, and nine unusable prints from the doors themselves. Three unusable prints were lifted from the outside of the shutters on the window of the children's bedroom. Identifiable prints were found on the inside of the children's bedroom window.

One hundred and forty-six hair samplings were also collected. A stain observed on the coverlet of one of the beds – not Madeleine's – was sent for analysis, on the suspicion that it might be semen. For DNA purposes, mouth swabs were taken from Kate and Gerry McCann and the rest of their group. Photographs were also taken in and outside the apartment.

Some of the hair would later be linked forensically to those known to have been in the apartment legitimately. There were seventeen different hair samples, PJ analysts found, that were not a match for any of the known people who had been in the apartment legitimately. Numerous other hairs were inadequate for forensic analysis. The stain suspected to be semen would eventually turn out to be the saliva of a child of the family that had stayed in Apartment 5A the week before the McCanns.

The prints found on the inside of the children's bedroom window turned out to match the palm and a finger of Kate's left hand. The fingerprint on the edge of the patio doors turned out to belong to – this was an embarrassment to the Portuguese police – one of the GNR officers who had first arrived on the scene.

Claims that the Portuguese police had run an efficient operation would draw scepticism, even derision, from some of the foreigners who took part in the searches. 'I never saw any police involvement in the operations carried out by civilians,' said Peter Patterson, a friend of the McCanns'. 'I felt dispirited because there appeared to be no coordination or leadership.' Kate McCann, for her part, doubted whether house-to-house searches were ever completed. She would caustically suggest, too, that the Portuguese forensic specialist who dusted the outside shutters of the children's room for prints did so with her hand unprotected by a glove. A photograph (see photo 10) indicates that Kate was correct.

The police looked in vain for what information CCTV cameras might have picked up. The Ocean Club itself had no such equipment. 'Most of the resort,' managing director Robin Crosland said in an interview, 'is spread throughout the village. The units are accessed via public roads and paths, and in Portugal it is illegal to have security video cameras in public places . . . On private property we don't need them, as we have manned receptions.'

Attempts were made to obtain surveillance tapes from petrol stations on the main roads serving Praia da Luz. Those that had been kept proved not to have useful information, others had been wiped, and a number of stations simply had no cameras.

Early on, investigations chief Amaral had formally requested British police assistance, asking for further information on the McCann party and for a criminal analyst to be sent to Portugal. A British liaison officer had arrived in Praia da Luz from his base in Lisbon within two days of Madeleine's disappearance.

The first officers to fly out from the UK had been family liaison officers – or FLOs – from Leicestershire. They had arrived within twenty-four hours of Madeleine having gone missing, to support the troubled parents.

In England, the wheels of law enforcement had not moved at lightning speed. Though the Foreign and Commonwealth Office had been contacted during the night hours after the disappearance, no call went out to the head of the UK's Child Exploitation and Online Protection Centre (CEOP) – at that time affiliated to the Serious Organised Crime Agency (SOCA) – until the weekend. This was Jim Gamble, a former head of Northern Ireland's anti-terrorism unit, who recalled in a 2014 interview with the authors how things developed. 'There was that urge that everyone wanted to help,' he said. 'What we agreed in consultation with the FCO was that we would send two of our behavioural analysts out.'

A profusion of British police and government agencies were to become involved. At an early meeting in London, however, it was agreed that the force from Leicestershire, where the McCanns lived, would take the lead. A 'Gold' group, comprising staff from Leicestershire, CEOP, SOCA, and the National Policing Improvement Agency, was formed to coordinate the British role. Representatives from most of these agencies would at some point arrive in Praia da Luz.

'The national directorate of the PJ had authorised the arrival of these police officers in the spirit of international cooperation,' Amaral was to write. 'We placed at their disposal a room next to our crisis unit, that they called Task Force Portugal [In fact entitled Operation Task] . . . They produced giant summary boards that covered the walls of the room. They took part in meetings of the Portuguese team and took part in the decision-making.'

The collegiate atmosphere somewhat withered, however,

according to Amaral, writing of the arrival later in May of Detective Chief Superintendent Bob Small. 'We wanted to be sure what these Englishmen wanted to do in our country, and where they would go,' Amaral recalled. 'So I gave firm orders to one of the Portuguese investigators to shadow the British Superintendent. I wanted to know what [the British officers] learned, what they did, and with whom they spoke.'

Amaral, moreover, declared himself less than impressed by his first British visitors. According to him, 'the information coming from the Leicestershire police was so much that the local police had difficulty analysing and screening it all.'

Criticism would become a two-way street. 'All the information coming in,' CEOP's Jim Gamble later learned from officers who went out to Portugal, 'ended up in boxes piled up on a table. In the UK you have the computerised HOLMES – the Home Office Large Enquiry System – collating everything. We couldn't be sure whether the material that was being sent through from the UK was being accurately collated in Portugal, properly analysed and actioned.

'Their system was so alien to us. That caused frustration. Their system was to a degree driven by magistrates' – prosecutors' – decisions. They're used to waiting. Our Portuguese colleagues' lack of operational autonomy was debilitating. We sometimes felt quite sorry for them.'

British frustration led to Portuguese resentment, the sense among some officers that they were – as Gamble put it – 'being condescended to'. There was a simmering feeling that the British were acting 'like a colonial power'.

Competent or not, the early Portuguese police search for any sign of Madeleine in or around Praia da Luz proved fruitless.

One faint hope of a breakthrough, the police file solemnly chronicles, came on the third day when a German citizen returned from a boat outing to report that he had seen a 'dark-coloured bag on the cliff' near Lagos – five miles from Praia da Luz. After a difficult retrieval operation, the bag was found to contain rubbish.

Meanwhile, from the very start, there were myriad reports of possible sightings of Madeleine in the company of adults. A petrol station manager in Albufeira, thirty-nine miles from Praia da Luz, thought he might have seen her the day after her disappearance in the company of a man and woman. A cab driver thought she was 'probably' the little girl he saw – that same day – more than three hundred miles to the north in the company of a man with an English accent who said he had 'just arrived from the Algarve'.

Another citizen wondered whether Madeleine had been the little girl her friend had seen, also on May 4th, 'held by the hand by a male individual, in a state of complete desperation (she was shouting and trying to free her hand)' – in Lisbon. Was she the girl seen that day in a Vodafone store in a Lisbon shopping centre? Or one of two girls being carried by a couple elsewhere in Lisbon?

There was a torrent of such reports: the possible Madeleine seen at a toll booth in a 'possibly Dutch- or English-' registered car driven by a couple who were 'quite unpleasant'; the 'Madeleine' – she had blonde hair and seemed to be the right age – who seized the arm of a customer at a snack bar and seemed to want help; the 'Madeleine' who was 'not wearing any clothing on her lower half' seen in the company of a man of Asian appearance who handed her to another man; and the 'Madeleine' picked up by a woman at a hotel after she was heard to say, 'I want to see my mummy.'

Meanwhile, from the start – and far into the future – 'possible' Madeleine sightings were reported in countries far from Portugal. There was the little girl in the pink cardigan who flew into Gatwick Airport accompanied by a man and a woman the very morning after the disappearance. The person reporting had thought it strange, given that it was only 11 a.m., that girl had looked 'very tired'. And the girl who, later that day on another flight into Gatwick, seemed 'very fretful' and whose hair appeared to have been cut 'without due care and attention'.

Soon, following a broadcast on either Sky News or the BBC, there came information that a child like Madeleine had been seen, wearing a floppy hat and holding the hand of a man, at a shopping plaza on Spain's Costa del Sol. The following day, Madeleine's 'double' was seen on the Costa Blanca. A week or so later, a Greek missing children's group reported that 'Madeleines' had been sighted at no fewer than seven different locations across the country: outside Athens, near Thessaloníki and on three different islands. Others thought they might have seen her in Geneva, Switzerland, on a ferry from Troon, Scotland, to Northern Ireland, on a flight from Frankfurt to the US city of Boston – and at a book fair in Brazil.

That was only the beginning. In the year that followed, there would be thousands of reports of possible Madeleine sightings from no less than forty-two countries on five continents – with Antarctica the only exception. Some sightings seemed potentially credible, others hopelessly contradictory – a Portuguese report notes an instance of the little girl having been 'seen' on the same day in places two thousand five hundred miles apart. Some, perhaps most, of the people who reported such sightings were well meaning. Others were fanciful, as is often the case following massive publicity about missing people – especially when the missing person is a child. Only a small fraction of the reports deserved to be – or could be – followed up.

There seemed to be virtually no leads to go on. No clues of any substance at the scene of the crime – if there had been a crime. Virtually no leads from the public, seemingly nothing to follow up. From the start and in the months and years to come, that would be the problem. The perceived problem, anyway.

The policemen at the top of the initial investigation considered what might have led to the disappearance. Gonçalo Amaral remembered weighing the possibilities: 'The child could have woken in the bed and, not seeing her parents, left the house in search of them; accidental death and concealment of the body; physical abuse causing death; killing, whether accidental or premeditated; an act of vengeance; kidnap for ransom; abduction by a paedophile . . . kidnapping or killing by a would-be robber, who had been surprised by the child.'

The regional head of the PJ in the Algarve, Guilhermino Encarnação, had told Kate after she and Gerry had given their statements that this could have been a burglary gone wrong. He had also echoed Amaral's thought that Madeleine might simply have wandered off.

At that early stage, and from a law-enforcement point of view, such alternative explanations were not unreasonable, according to a British authority speaking as late as 2013. 'These things at the beginning can be very difficult to deal with,' said Metropolitan Police Commissioner Sir Bernard Hogan-Howe. 'You don't know exactly if the child has just wandered off. It can be very difficult to know if you've got a serious crime.'

Nevertheless, in Portugal in May 2007, Amaral and Encarnação were more than open to the theory held by the McCanns both then and ever afterwards, that their daughter had been abducted. Amaral resolved at once that it was necessary 'to locate and identify all paedophiles who live in or have spent holidays in the Algarve'.

Notes in the released Portuguese police files refer to documentation, not yet made public, that indicates there were such offenders in the Algarve. Withheld are 'a list of individuals connected to sex crimes with minors and adolescents', as well as references to individuals 'with a past linked to crimes of a sexual nature with children' or 'acts of paedophilia' and to 'foreign nationals linked with child sex abuse and paedophilia'.

By May 5th, two days after the disappearance, Encarnação – very probably referring to Jane Tanner's statement that she had seen a man carrying a child near Apartment 5A – was telling reporters: 'We have evidence that indicates a kidnap.' Police were working, he added, 'on the assumption Madeleine was being held about three to five kilometres [two to three miles]' from Praia da Luz.

Of early interest to the police, according to press reports long afterwards, was a local man named Joaquim Marques. Together with another man, Marques, who lived five miles away in the village of Barão de São João, had one night in 1995 raped two holidaying British teenage girls on a local beach. He was now at liberty after serving a five-year prison sentence. Marques' female partner would reportedly be questioned as to his whereabouts on the night Madeleine vanished. The man was subsequently eliminated from the Madeleine investigation.

Another lead obtained while taking statements from Ocean Club staff, according to Amaral, was information on a British citizen suspected of sexual interest in a minor 'with links to a bar 150 metres from the location of [Madeleine's] disappearance'.

This man, research indicates, was in Iraq by May 2007 and thus became irrelevant to the investigation.

Another lead that led nowhere involved a forty-six-year-old British man who had lived in Zavial, on the coast some twelve miles west of Praia da Luz. It turned out that the man had no criminal record. Nevertheless, the tracking of Portuguese and foreign paedophiles in the region – 'the majority English', according to Amaral – continued.

Another development seemed very promising. A Portuguese man reported how, while he was with his wife and two children on the beach at Sagres, also near Praia da Luz, four days before Madeleine disappeared, he had: 'noticed a male individual holding a small silver-coloured camera who was covertly taking photographs of [the witness's] children . . . The individual, instead of holding the camera to his face, was taking pictures from the abdominal area of his body . . . After having taken pictures of his children . . . the individual took more photos of two male children, nine- and five-year-olds.'

The witness said he suspected at the time that the man snapping the pictures might be a child abuser. Later, when the stranger behaved as though he might be trying to approach his four-year-old daughter, the witness became thoroughly rattled and tried to photograph the man with his mobile phone. He did get a photo of the man, and the woman with him, in their car.

Diligent detective work identified the couple who had behaved so oddly, only to be disappointed again. They turned out to be a Polish couple who had left the Algarve, flying out of Faro Airport en route back to Poland, two days after Madeleine vanished. The woman did have a record in the files, for driving under the influence and being connected with 'obtaining property by deception'. There was no evidence, though, to link the pair to the Madeleine case.

Neither the apartment they had rented in Portugal nor the car they had hired threw up any incriminating evidence. No matches to Madeleine were found when spots of blood lifted from a kitchen unit were eventually analysed. Witnesses and other evidence established that no child had been with the couple on their journey back to Warsaw. Interviewed by police in Poland, they denied all knowledge of Madeleine.

The press, meanwhile, had excitedly reported that the McCann family themselves had visited Sagres during their stay in the area – fuelling the possibility that Madeleine was one of the children who had interested the suspect photographer. The story was false, however, for the McCanns never left Praia da Luz prior to Madeleine's disappearance.

Did the two Poles visit Praia da Luz? There is no way of knowing, for the photographs they took on holiday never surfaced. An account of one witness who encountered them, meanwhile, suggests that they may simply have been 'snap-happy' – obsessively keen to take pictures, of adults as much as of children. The story of the covert child-photographer, it seems, was an investigative red herring.

Even as the lead in Sagres was still being followed, on May 7th, a Portuguese police spokesman said the case remained a complete mystery. 'I do not have the facts to say that the child is alive or not,' PJ Chief Inspector Olegário de Sousa told the press. 'We're searching for the child, and until the moment she appears we can say nothing more – because we are not magicians.'

In 2014, Portugal's former Attorney General Pinto Monteiro, who was ultimately responsible for oversight of the case, recalled the almost total lack of evidence in the case. 'They didn't find anything,' he said, spreading his hands in frustration, 'nothing, nothing.'

Today, however, now that there has been time for analysis, some of the information that flowed in early on seems relevant and potentially valuable. Take the accounts by reputable witnesses of visits they received from a charity collector – or collectors – for a charity that apparently did not exist.

5

In the late afternoon of April 20th, thirteen days before Madeleine went missing, a tourist named Gail Cooper had been watching her grandchildren at play when the doorbell rang. She had opened the door to find herself facing an 'olive-skinned male, roughly 40–45 years of age, 6' to 6'2" tall, and slim to medium build . . . He had a Mexican-looking moustache which was thick and bushy and drooped down the sides of his mouth . . . He appeared to be Mediterranean. However, due to his appearance and mannerism, I did not feel he was Portuguese.'

Speaking English, but 'with an accent that did not sound Portuguese', the man told Mrs Cooper that he was 'collecting for a local orphanage in a nearby village, Espiche'. He flashed a leaflet and photo ID, but not so that she could read it, and said the orphanage was allowed to solicit contributions once each year. Though Mrs Cooper said she had no cash on her, the visitor continued – for up to fifteen minutes – trying to persuade her to come up with a donation.

She had found him 'pushy', somewhat 'intimidating', and he made her feel 'very uncomfortable'. He had made enough of an impression, she was to say, that she thought she remembered having seen him on two other occasions – both times on the beach at Praia da Luz. On the second occasion, she said, he was walking behind a group of young children as, escorted by adults, they approached a play area. The adults, she thought, had been wearing the T-shirts worn by crèche workers at the Ocean Club.

Two or three days after the encounter at Mrs Cooper's holiday villa, a very similar event occurred some four hundred yards away – at the very apartment that would shortly be used by the McCann family. British tourist Paul Gordon, who rented Apartment 5A during the week immediately prior to the McCanns' arrival on April 28th, remembered how – on either the 25th or 26th – he too had had an afternoon visitor.

'The children were sleeping,' Gordon remembered, 'when I heard a male voice say, "Hello."' The voice, he realised, was coming from the little gate at the bottom of the flight of steps leading down from the apartment to the road. He stood up and 'went to the man, who asked me if I would be interested in making a donation to an orphanage in the hills away from the coast'. Gordon gave him ten euros.

Like the man at Gail Cooper's door, the man at the gate had shown a badge and some sort of leaflet and said he had permission to collect for the charity once a year. Unlike Mrs Cooper's visitor, he was polite, not aggressive or persistent. Gordon remembered that he was clean-cut – no drooping moustache (see e-fit, photo 24, left) – and had no noticeable non-Portuguese accent. Going by Gordon's description, he was a different man altogether.

As many as four more such efforts to collect money are reported to have occurred – all of them in the late afternoon of the very day, May 3rd, that Madeleine was to vanish. One occurred at a villa in Praia da Luz owned by British couple Rex and Iris Morgan. The two men – not one – who turned up at their home said they were soliciting funds for a 'hostel' or 'hospice'. One of them, whom Mr Morgan recalled as having been in his mid to late twenties, seemed Portuguese but spoke English well. The other looked 'like a local country boy'. The money, one of the men told Mr Morgan, was 'so that he could help get young boys off the street and keep young girls away from prostitution'. (See e-fit of one of the men, photo 24, right.)

The men had produced photographs of the supposed hostel, and Mrs Morgan remembered something else. The institution they said, was 'at a place called something similar to "Baro St Hoa," which is beyond the town or village of Espiche'. Espiche was the same village mentioned thirteen days earlier by the man who had come to Mrs Cooper's door.

The men's appearance at the Morgans' home occurred around 4 p.m. At 5 p.m. or soon after, they – or two associates – showed up at the home in Praia da Luz of another British citizen, Denise Ashton. Both men were clean-cut, as she remembered, and both looked about forty. The one who did the talking, she noted, wore spectacles with thick lenses. The scenario and the pitch were as in the preceding visits: identity card, leaflet, photographs of a supposed orphanage – they featured children – and a reference to the village of Espiche.

Espiche is less than two miles from Praia da Luz, a tiny place of some two thousand inhabitants. Tiny Barão de São João, about four miles to the north – which must be the place Iris Morgan remembered as 'Baro St Hoa' – is even smaller.

What makes the charity-collector incidents significant to this story is that there was no orphanage or similar institution in Espiche, Barão de São João or anywhere in the area. The authors visited both small communities, and contacted local people who knew the area well. They, and the head of a foundation that raises funds for orphanages, have said that no such 'orphanage' existed.

The men who came trying to get money out of Mrs Cooper, Paul Gordon at Apartment 5A, the Morgans and Mrs Ashton, were all – at best – phoney charity collectors trying to obtain money under false pretences. What, though, if the people targeted had not been in when the men called? A reasonable speculation is that, if they learned a home or residence was unoccupied, they would have proceeded with the real business at hand – a robbery.

The known background more than supports that notion. 'We had to take account of the petty crimes committed in the seaside resort and the tourist complex,' chief investigator Amaral was to write. 'During the holidays, burglaries are not rare . . . The theory of a burglary gone wrong could not be excluded.' Following Madeleine's disappearance, the speculation prompted Amaral to send detectives to the local prison to question a young man held following a series of local break-ins. The man proved 'very reticent', and the detectives got nothing out of him.

There was in fact a veritable epidemic of burglary in Praia da Luz in 2007, although, in an area totally dependent on tourism, publicity on the subject was limited. In the first four months of 2007, according to a briefing issued during the later British probe into the Madeleine case, there was a fourfold increase in burglaries in the area.

Residents' concern was reflected by postings like this on the Expatforum website:

Mar. 23, Luz area . . . Sitting in the lounge watching *Deal or No Deal* (around 4.30 p.m.) while burglar got in the kitchen, took handbag left on table and we did not hear a thing. Only one shutter was open, door was locked, window was closed . . . No signs of break-in. Second villa to be burgled this week.

In their statements to the police after Madeleine disappeared, a dozen Ocean Club staff spoke of break-ins at the resort. Nuno Conceição, a maintenance man, said, 'break-ins to the apartments are common, especially for burglary, and some result from clients leaving their doors open.' Most common, said barman Tiago Freitas, were burglaries in apartments on the lower floors.

There had been recent break-ins at apartments close to the one rented to the McCanns. In February, three months before Madeleine's disappearance, an apartment a hundred yards away had been raided. Money, a camera and mobile phones were taken. The owner, Ian Robertson, learned afterwards that two of his neighbours with ground-floor flats had also been burgled.

Three weeks before the disappearance, £500 in cash and personal belongings were reportedly taken from an apartment in the same block as Apartment 5A. On April 16th, a man came to the door of another flat in the same block asking the British occupants for 'the German family'. Then, while they were out at dinner, the apartment was robbed. According to reports quoting police sources, there was yet another break-in at the Ocean Club that month. Though a child was disturbed, the intruders fled when the parents came in.

One day the week before Madeleine vanished, a burglar was surprised in the act of burgling the flat of Pamela Fenn, directly above Apartment 5A. 'She was sitting watching TV,' a friend said, 'when she heard a noise in her bedroom . . . The man must have heard her coming and was scrambling out of the window. She just saw the back of his head.'

Indeed, Apartment 5A itself may have been a target. Not only was it on the ground floor of its block but, with doors and windows on two sides providing access to the street, it was especially vulnerable. Two weeks before the McCanns were due to arrive, moreover, the front-door light had been dangling, out of order. Intruders may have been interested in 5A long before the incident that would make it infamous. A babysitter, Margaret Hall, was to recall an incident that had occurred while minding a little girl in the apartment one night in late summer 2006.

Hall's statement to the police recounts how she heard a noise, then ventured out of the apartment's front door to investigate. Something in the shadows moved and she thought at first – because there had recently been problems with rodents – that it must be a rat. She was shocked, moments later, to realise 'it was the brown shoe of a man. She shouted, and the man came out of the darkness, activating motion-sensor lighting. He came towards her, saying, "No, no."' The man seemed to Hall to be about thirty and probably Portuguese. Frightened, she retreated into Apartment 5A and reported the matter to the management the following day.

Information given to Kate McCann the night after her daughter vanished – by the British consul in the Algarve, Bill Henderson – indicated that there had recently been instances of an intruder getting into children's beds. No details were forthcoming at the time, but the fact that there had been break-ins with an apparent sexual motive would eventually become a serious focus for investigators. That line of inquiry, potentially highly significant, will be covered later.

Compelling testimony, indicating that someone was watching Apartment 5A during the McCanns' 2007 stay, comes from a young British girl named Tasmin Sillence. Tasmin, a twelve-year-old who lived nearby, had reason to notice what went on in the vicinity of the flat – it had once belonged to her grandmother and she had lived there for a time. She was to tell the police, just days after Madeleine's disappearance, that she had twice seen a man near 5A. He had seemed to be hanging around, watching the place.

The first time Tasmin saw the man had been shortly after 8 a.m. on April 30th, the third day of the McCanns' ill-fated trip, as she walked with her mother to catch the school bus. Mother and daughter had been on the left side of Rua Dr Francisco Gentil Martins (see street plan in photo section) when she noticed him. He had been leaning against the wall in the lane – on the pool side of the apartment block – 'staring intently at the balcony' of Apartment 5A.

On Wednesday, May 2nd, the eve of Madeleine's disappearance, Tasmin saw the man again. She had not gone to school that morning because she was not feeling well, but ventured out around noon to go to the pharmacy and the supermarket. It was about half an hour later, on the way home, that he again got her attention. This time he was not in the lane but standing in front of the Ocean Club entrance that led to the Tapas restaurant. Hands in pockets, the man was again gazing in the direction of Apartment 5A, perhaps at the adjoining apartments to its left as well.

In the afternoon of the same day, a British tourist staying in an apartment close to the McCanns' saw a man in more or less the same spot who also appeared to be 'watching' 5A. The woman – who has asked not to be identified – had seen him several days earlier, too, loitering nearby.

There was one further account of a suspicious sighting, and it occurred only hours before Madeleine went missing. It comes from Carole Tranmer, the fifty-nine-year-old niece of Mrs Fenn, the elderly woman who lived directly above 5A and who days earlier had confronted an intruder in her own apartment. Tranmer, a former secretary at Windsor Castle, was visiting her aunt while house-hunting in Portugal. In the latter part of the afternoon of May 3rd, while she and her husband were sitting on the terrace, talking, she saw something that even at the time seemed suspicious.

'I saw someone,' she would remember, 'come out of the ground-floor apartment, closing the gate very carefully and quietly. It looked very strange to me. He looked to one side and the other, shut the gate and walked very quickly below [us].' The man, Tranmer made clear, was in the same lane or alley in which young Tasmin had observed a man in the early morning three days earlier.*

Moments after seeing the man in the laneway, Tranmer said, she tried to bring up the oddity of what she had seen with her aunt and husband, but they were deep in conversation. The moment passed, but the incident stuck in her mind. Back in England a few days later, she read of Madeleine's apparent abduction and promptly telephoned the police. What had struck her as so peculiar, she was to repeat, was the way the man had closed the gate, as though he was 'ensuring it did not make a noise . . . he closed it with both his hands, several times . . . It was his furtiveness that got my attention.' The man had moved 'stealthily, as if he did not want anyone to know he was coming and going'.

---

* The transcript of Tranmer's later statement reads as though the person she saw acting suspiciously might have been at the gate of the apartment next to 5A, occupied that week by the McCanns' friends the Oldfields. The Oldfields and their one-year-old daughter had gone out by late afternoon, to the beach or sailing. Neither they nor Tranmer could later recall specific times.

According to testimony cited much later by the police, there may not have been only one man involved.

There are both similarities and discrepancies between the witnesses' descriptions of the person they saw. Carole Tranmer and Tasmin Sillence each remembered the man they saw as having been Caucasian, light-skinned, in the thirty-to-forty age range, with cropped fair or light-coloured hair. Their estimates of height – hard to judge from above, as in Tranmer's situation – varied between 5' 10", 'not short' (Tranmer) and 5' 11" (Tasmin). The female British tourist mentioned earlier has reportedly said the individual she saw was 5' 10" and, she thought, looked 'Portuguese'.

The descriptions by Tasmin and the British tourist of the facial appearance of the man each of them saw are very similar. Tasmin remembered him as having been 'ugly, even disgusting', with 'small pimples on the face'. The British tourist said the face of the man she saw had been 'very ugly, with pitted skin'.*

If there was illicit activity going on around Apartment 5A during those few days, it may have involved more than one man. According to testimony cited years later – on the basis of briefings by British police – *two* men were seen 'on the balcony of a nearby empty apartment, believed to be 5C, two doors down from the McCanns', on the afternoon of May 3rd.

It was some five hours after Carole Tranmer's sighting of the man in the lane that Madeleine McCann vanished.

---

* See images at photo 25. Left, based on Sillence's description; centre, based on tourist's description; right, based on Tranmer's description.

6

'Where's Madeleine, Mummy?'

The McCanns' two-year-old twins had astonished everyone by sleeping through the frenzied hours after their elder sister went missing. When they did finally awake, they seemed for a while to be oblivious to her absence. It was only on the second day that little Sean finally asked the question. His mother paused for a long moment, then told the twins the truth in the gentlest way she could muster. Madeleine was missing, she said, and must be found.

It was Kate and Gerry McCann, not their remaining children, who were in need of help. They had more family around them by now, as well as advisers brought in by the tour company. The atmosphere was one of desperation all the same. 'Really early on,' Gerry was to say, 'there was a time when I was worried because Kate said she wanted to go into the ocean and keep swimming and swimming and swimming. That obviously caused great distress.'

Kate recalled: 'I used to have thoughts like maybe we'll all get wiped out in a car on the motorway. So it would just happen, we'd all be gone and the pain would be away . . . It was just so painful and it's just so hard to describe, that heavy suffocating feeling day in day out, that pain of missing Madeleine and anxiety for her. There were times when I did want it to end. I wouldn't have done anything . . . '

A prominent feature to the east of Praia da Luz is a volcanic outcrop named Rocha Negra, the Black Rock. The morning after Madeleine's disappearance, a woman had told Kate that the previous night she had been aware of a car being driven up the track leading up to the Rock – a track where no one usually ventured. A day later, Kate contemplated forcing herself to run up the track to the outcrop, to punish her body with pain in an effort to extinguish the pain she felt inside.

In the days after Madeleine vanished, Kate recalled: 'I was tormented with a macabre slideshow of images that no sane human being would want in their head. I would see her lying cold and mottled on a big grey stone slab, and awful pictures of her being torn apart scrolled through my mind. I was desperate to talk to someone about them, and when Gerry and I took a walk on the beach in Portugal, I confided in him. Of course, he'd had similar thoughts.'

'Early on,' Gerry said, 'we couldn't think of anything else but the worst case, where everything was negative. That she'd been taken, abused and killed and dumped.'

For a long time only extreme fatigue brought a few hours' sleep. Kate recoiled from the very idea of eating and began to lose weight. The arrival at last of a Roman Catholic priest, which Kate had earlier demanded time and again without success, had brought some comfort. Father José Pacheco had been away, but, as he told the police, now went to the apartment to find the McCanns in a state, he judged, of 'great suffering'.

Pacheco, known locally as Father Zé, repeatedly came to

pray with them. That first Sunday, and for many Sundays afterwards, they attended Mass in the village church, Nossa Senhora da Luz. The following evening, a group of local women and children came to the apartment to say the rosary. Within days, Father Pacheco gave them a key to the church so that they could have access at any time, to seek solace and privacy.

On an impulse, as they left the church on the first occasion, a weeping Kate paused to thank the community for its support. 'Please,' she asked, 'continue to pray for Madeleine. She's lovely.'

That Kate managed this was an achievement in itself. By then, she and Gerry had for twenty-four hours had the advice of crisis counsellor Alan Pike, one of the consultants flown in by the Mark Warner tour company. On arrival in Praia da Luz, he would recall, he had found them both to be 'exhausted, anguished, confused and angry', even 'catatonic'. Pike, who had worked with people in tragic situations on dozens of previous occasions, thought the state they were in exactly 'what one would expect of parents whose daughter was taken from them'.

His view accords well with a report published in the USA in the year that Madeleine vanished by the National Center for Missing and Exploited Children. Children go missing at various ages and for differing reasons, but their parents' reactions are similar. They may, the report says, feel 'isolated, unsupported, vulnerable, angry, and impotent'. They suffer emotional shock that 'is not consistent and may be characterized by constant interjection of intense feelings followed by periods of numbing'.

Some readers may find Kate McCann's need for a priest, her prayers and repeated churchgoing, unusual or extreme. In fact, according to the American report, 'Involvement in a faith community can be supportive.' No surprise then, that in spite of the dreadful reality of her situation the first time she attended Sunday

Mass after Madeleine's disappearance, she felt somehow comforted.

Turning to her and Gerry during the service, Father Pacheco told them the congregation was with them. He urged them to have 'esperança, força, coragem' – 'hope, strength, courage'. For the McCanns, those three words would become a kind of mantra to be murmured, in Portuguese, in their darkest moments.

Alan Pike heard from the McCanns what they would barely ever concede publicly. In those first days, he said in a later interview, they were certain their daughter was dead. He reminded them of the evidence: 'There is nothing yet to demonstrate that Madeleine has died.'

Pike was to have almost daily contact with the McCanns for months to come, see them regularly for two years and still be available after that. One of his first pieces of advice seemed on the face of it contrary, yet proved sensible. Almost from the first they had been surrounded by family members, all sincerely eager to help, all in fact ineffectual.

Pike, Gerry would say, enabled them 'to look forward, to try to put speculation out of our heads, channel everything into looking forward'. He said their emotional needs were more urgent at this time than those of others, suggested that – in a way – the visiting family contingent might be too numerous. It was agreed that Kate's parents and her aunt, and Gerry's mother and his brother, would soon return to the UK.

The disoriented Kate, meanwhile, grasped at straws. When a friend of a friend of a relative in the UK reported having had a 'vision' that Madeleine had been on a boat moored locally, the police were duly informed. When the vessel was searched, predictably enough nothing was found.

It was a visionary moment, though, that transformed Gerry's stance in the crisis. While the couple were praying at the local church, he would recall, he 'started thinking . . . I was feeling really very down and not sure which way to proceed. I had this mental image of being in a tunnel, and instead of the light at the end of the tunnel being an extremely narrow and a distant spot, the light opened up and the tunnel got wider and wider . . . It was almost like something – I am not saying it was the Holy Spirit – came into me and gave me that image . . . I can't say it was a vision because I am not clear what a vision is. But I had a mental image, and it certainly helped me decide. I became a man possessed that night. The next day I was up at dawn, making phone calls.'

Crisis counsellor Pike, who had been urging the couple to 'take control of the things you can', may have been as influential as the vision. As a cardiologist of stature, Gerry McCann had always been a canny, determined, even driven man. He was to recall thinking, '"We can't cry our eyes out every day, because that's not helping." So, after three days I picked myself up, quicker than Kate could.' Emotionally wounded though he was, Gerry from now on showed that he did not intend to be a passive victim. He became, rather, an effective mover in what was already building into a unique global story.

The McCanns now had a media adviser and occasional spokesman who, like Pike, had been brought in by the tour company. Alex Woolfall, who was more usually co-opted to help companies respond to complex situations, observed that as the days passed Gerry 'behaved very much like a doctor would do. Doctors are analytical. He started to have more strategic conversations with me, about what they might do.'

Reporters, photographers and television crews were now on the scene in strength, most of them camped out as close as possible to the apartment the McCanns were using. They generated news, sometimes when there was none, and milked residents and tourists alike for quotes that amounted to little or nothing. One film crew got into the church, where Kate had imagined she had privacy. When for the first time she and Gerry ventured out for a walk, journalists tagged along behind.

Little more than a week after tucking their little girl into bed at night on a holiday in Portugal, the two doctors found themselves famous and their lives transformed – for the worst possible reason. They could not have known then that there would, quite soon, be poisonous rumours, bogus 'research' and lies about them. They could not know that elements of the media – Portuguese and British alike – now seemingly sympathetic, would come to libel them.

The McCanns' relationship with the Polícia Judiciária, which had been rocky from the start, took a turn for the worse. On May 10th, the couple and their friends Matt Oldfield, Russ O'Brien and Jane Tanner were asked to return for further interviews at the police station. Their experiences were at first promising, then frustrating, then downright weird. The officers seemed friendly and – more importantly – to be working hard on the case. Having waited for eight hours to be seen, however, Kate was told she could go home. Four months were to pass before the police would call her in again.

The McCanns' friend Matt Oldfield had a disquieting time at the station. Gerry, who was nearby while Oldfield was being interviewed, heard him shouting, sounding hysterical. It had been suggested to him, he said afterwards, that he had passed Madeleine out of the bedroom window to an accomplice. It sounded like some scene out of *Life on Mars.**

---

* The BBC science fiction/police television series that had run until April 2007.

Behind the scenes in Praia da Luz that week, away from all the commotion, the McCanns' companions had gathered to reconstruct once more – this time for the formal record – the events of the night Madeleine had disappeared. As reported earlier in these pages, Russ O'Brien had in the first hours of the crisis scribbled out two crude, very basic timelines. The police had said that those rough documents, written on the covers of a child's book, would not do. So it was, four or five days later, that they worked on the chronology again.

'We all felt when we came back from our initial interviews,' Russ O'Brien remembered, 'that there was probably a lot of detail that hadn't been got across about the evening. We were quite keen to get a timeline together before the facts started to become dim for us.' Using a laptop borrowed from one of the Ocean Club tennis coaches, O'Brien typed a first draft while Gerry and Kate were dealing with other business. When they returned, they added their comments. The result was a far longer, more detailed document, with minor adjustments to estimated times of group members' movements in the hour and a half before Madeleine was found to be missing. It was, the group agreed, the nearest thing to an accurate account they could produce.

Headed 'Sequence of Events: Thursday May 3rd 2007 – 2030 to 2200', the three-page document was transferred to a memory stick and handed to a British liaison officer who in turn formally handed it to a senior officer of the Polícia Judiciária. It remains the single most rounded summary, by those directly involved, of the critical events of the night and is reproduced here:

Sequence of Events: Thursday 3rd May 2007 – 2030 to 2200

As recalled by:

Gerry McCann – 5A
Kate McCann – 5A
David Payne – 5H (First floor)
Fiona Payne – 5H (First floor)
Dianne Webster – 5H (First floor)
Jane Tanner – 5D
Russell O'Brien – 5D
Matthew Oldfield – 5B
Rachael Oldfield – 5B

Times shown are approximate, but accurate to the best of our knowledge.

Prior to 2030, all couples and children were in their apartments preparing for bedtime.
-5A (Madeleine, Amelie and Sean McCann),
-5B (G   Oldfield),
-5D (E: and E   O'Brien) and
-5H (L: and Sc   tt Payne)

2030: Standard booking for meal at Tapas restaurant for group – same all week (Sun-Thur)

2035: Gerry McCann (GM) and Kate McCann (KC) arrive at table at Tapas Restaurant.

2040: Jane Tanner (JT) arrives, followed shortly by Matthew Oldfield (MO) and Rachael Mampilly Oldfield (RMO).

2045: Russell O'Brien (RJO) arrives at table.

2055: MO returns to apartments to check on ground floor flats, passing David Payne (DP), Fiona Payne (FP) and her mother Dianne Webster (DW) on their way down to the table.

2057: MO listens outside all ground floor flats' windows on the car park side of the apartment (5A, 5B and 5D) to make sure they were asleep. At this time, all the shutters were down on each window.

2100: MO return to the table. Starters were ordered.

2105: GM returns to his flat (5A) and enters via the patio gate entrance. This and a child gate at the top of the stairs were closed at the time. He enters the flat via the patio door which is closed but unlocked.

The door is slightly ajar (about 45 degrees) which is unusual. All the 3 children were present and asleep. GM believes the shutter was down. The room in which the children are asleep is completely dark. On leaving the room, GM shuts the door to approximately 5 degrees. He then goes to the toilet to urinate.

2115: JT leaves table, and sees GM talking with fellow resident ("Jez" Wilkins) outside the patio gate of 5A. The two were standing just up the hill from the gate towards Rua A. da Silva Road. She did not speak to GM as she passed.

As JT continued up the hill towards the junction with Rua A. da Silva, she sees a man carrying a child in his arms crossing left to right from the apartment side continuing east along Rua A. da Silva in the direction of the "Millennium Restaurant." He was on the same side of the road as JT 5-10 metres ahead of her.

Description of Man:

- Age 35 to 40.
- 1.7m tall approximately with a slim build.
- Good head of dark glossy hair, with possible flick of hair to the right. The hair was longer at the back (i.e not clippered or shaven).
- The central and the left side of the face were not seen.
- Full length trousers, casual, the material hanging without creases. The colour was possibly a browny mustard. They were not jeans.
- Long sleeved jacket, fastened at the front, possibly by a zipper. It had a gathered lower hem and was also possibly brownish in colour.
- Shoes may have been a semi-formal brogue.
- Whether he was wearing gloves or not could not be ascertained.
- He was not wearing a rucksack or any other identifiable objects.
- He was only carrying a child, with the head against the left upper chest away from JT and the feet to the right – i.e. cradling the child like a baby.
- He appeared to be walking in a rush to get somewhere.
- He was not someone JT recognised from the week.
- He was not dressed typically for a "tourist," or at least his clothing did not seem to be of UK origin and may well have been purchased in Portugal.

Description of Child:

- The child appeared to be a Caucasian girl about the ages of 3-4.
- She was seen to lie motionless/limp in the man's arms consistent with her sleeping or possibly drugged.
- She did not seem to be wrapped up well for the time of night wearing only pyjamas; the trousers were lightly coloured with a floral element, possibly with turn-ups. The top was not well seen though there was thought to be another colour involved possibly pink.
- She was not wearing shoes.

JT checked only 5D entering via the deadlocked door on the car park side of the apartment. Both children inside were asleep. She did not check 5A or 5B.

2120: JT then returns to the restaurant, by which time GM had also returned. The entire party then begins eating their starters which have arrived.

2125: After starters, MO and RJO go back to the apartments via the car park entrance to check all flats. They go first to 5D where RJO's daughter Evie is heard crying. RJO enters flat, whilst MO checks inside 5B, and then returns to 5D.

2130: RJO remains in 5D as daughter has vomited. MO goes to check on 5A via the patio gate entrance. The outside gate is probably shut, but the child gate on the stairs up to the patio is possibly open. The patio door is closed but unlocked.
MO enters flat, hears a sound in the children's bedroom that is probably one of the twins rolling over in their cot. He does not enter the bedroom but can see through a now quite open door (greater than 45 degrees) into the room.
He sees the two twins in their cot, but does not check Madeleine formally as no sounds and twins asleep. He recalls the room did seem lighter than expected, perhaps suggesting the shutter had been raised or the curtains opened?

2135: MO returns to restaurant table, by which time main courses are arriving or being eaten. MO tells JT that Evie unwell.

2140: JT returns to 5D to take over care of Evie from RJO.

2145: RJO returns to table to eat main course leaving JT in 5D.

2155: RMO asked time at table. RJO's main course arrives.

2200: (approx): KM leaves table to check children in 5A. The patio gate is closed and the child gate is also probably closed. She enters through the closed patio entrance, with the curtains closed. She crosses the living area, and there is no noise from the children's bedroom. She is about to leave, when she notices the bedroom door was open (approximately 60 degrees).
She starts to close it and it slams. Considering the patio doors had caused a draft, she checks these doors but they are closed. KM returns to the bedroom and opens the door to check the children were not disturbed by the noise.
At this point, she notices that Madeleine is missing. She checks the other single bed in the room and also Kate and Gerry's beds. Then she double checks that Madeleine was not in her bedroom again. At this point, she notices the curtains blowing forward with a gust of wind. She runs over, pulls open the curtain and notices the shutter was completely raised, and the window pushed open to the left as far as possible.
She then completes a check of the bathroom, kitchen and wardrobes.
On failing to find Madeleine, she runs to the entrance of the restaurant, shouting from the path leading to the restaurant area raising the alarm that Madeleine was missing.

By the time she contributed to this new timeline, Jane Tanner was even more persuaded that the child she had seen being carried across the road – while checking on her own children at about 9.15 on the fateful night – had been Madeleine. Her confidence that this was so had to do with the colour of the pyjamas the child had seemed to be wearing.

In her statement to the police on the morning after Madeleine went missing, Tanner had said she thought the child she saw being carried had been wearing 'what appeared to be cotton pyjamas of a light colour (possibly white or light pink)'. Although she was not certain, she said she had the feeling there had been 'a design on the pyjamas, possibly a floral pattern'.

The following day, though, while she was sitting with Fiona Payne, she had seen a report in the *Daily Telegraph* that described Madeleine's pyjamas simply as 'white' – no mention of either pink or a floral pattern. When she read that, Fiona was to recall, Tanner had reacted immediately. 'Maybe it wasn't Madeleine I saw then,' she said, 'if she was wearing white pyjamas. Because they weren't white pyjamas . . . They had, I'm sure they had, some sort of pattern on them, and a roll-up or some detail at the bottom.'

Fiona was stunned. 'At that point,' she was to say later, 'my blood ran cold.' For unlike Tanner, Fiona already knew – from Kate – the colour and design of the pyjamas Madeleine had been wearing when put to bed. They had indeed been very much as Tanner was describing the colour and design of the pyjama bottoms – all that had been visible to her – of the child she had seen the man carrying.

The pyjama pants, as Kate had told the police within hours of the disappearance, had indeed been white, but with a pink floral design, a motif of *Winnie-the-Pooh*'s Eeyore, and a small frill at the bottom of each leg (see photograph). She had purchased them at Marks & Spencer the previous year.

As the significance of what she had seen sunk in, as Tanner realised she might well have seen an abductor in the act of making off with Madeleine, she was appalled. 'I just felt so awful,' she would say many months later. 'I felt I could have stopped this from happening. I think of that every day.'

How important to the investigation Tanner's sighting was – or was not – would remain a question for years to come.

Kate McCann, for her part, would reproach herself time and again over something else – a little thing that had been bothering her even *before* she discovered that her daughter had disappeared. At dinner on the last night, as reported earlier, she had mentioned the moment that morning when Madeleine had asked why her mother had not come to her the previous night 'when me and Sean were crying'.

Madeleine had not responded when her mother had asked her to say more. As children will, she had just moved on to something else. After she vanished, the incident nagged at Kate's mind – enough to tell the Portuguese police she thought Madeleine's question 'strange'. She mentioned it again to British police officers when they spoke with her in Praia da Luz two days later.

Had Madeleine's question indicated, she and Gerry wondered, that an intruder had been inside Apartment 5A the night *before* the disappearance? 'When we discovered she'd gone,' she would still be saying years later, 'it seemed very likely to me that maybe somebody had tried to do the same thing the night before and had been disturbed. Maybe, when the children started screaming, they'd panicked and fled.'

There was another thing. The fact that, through all the commotion on the long night of May 3rd – through their father's howls and their mother's hysterics – the twins had slept on and on. 'They didn't stir,' Fiona would recall. 'That was odd . . . [Kate] kept putting her hands on the twins to check they were breathing. She was very much concerned in checking that they were okay . . . it did seem weird . . . they didn't so much as blink.'

Even when they were eventually carried off to another apartment, Fiona and her mother Dianne recalled, the twins still did not wake. The child Jane Tanner had seen being carried close to Apartment 5A, moreover, had been 'motionless/limp' – not, she thought, the way it would be likely for a child to look if it had just been taken out of its bed.

Could it be, Kate would be asking British police within two days, that the evidence that her children remained deeply asleep pointed to sedatives having been administered – to any or all of the children – by an abductor? Could that have accounted for the extreme weariness she had noticed in Madeleine that evening? Had she been given something during the day, or even the previous night?

Kate's speculation was fuelled by the recollection that she had noticed a brown stain on Madeleine's pyjama top on the morning of May 3rd, when her daughter mentioned that she had cried the previous night. Kate had thought at the time that it was probably a tea stain, but later she was not so sure. Years later, the matter nagged at her still.

One drug that can be used as a sedative, paraldehyde, does leave a brown discolouration on the skin following injection. It does not, however, leave such a mark on material, and cannot explain the mark on Madeleine's pyjama top. What looked like a tea stain may have been just that.

Forensic tests on an individual's hair can sometimes indicate whether a drug has been administered, and such tests were later conducted on the twins' hair. They were negative, but that may mean nothing. Months passed before the tests were carried out, and relevant hair may have been cut off in the intervening period. Hair analysis, moreover, is an imprecise science.

Whether or not the twins were sedated, how might an abductor have rendered Madeleine unconscious before removing her from Apartment 5A? Consultation of experts in the fields of anaesthesia and toxicology have produced no simple answer. Several drugs mentioned would have involved administration either by injection or by mouth, and neither method seem likely to have been used on May 3rd 2007. Even had a would-be abductor possessed the skill and equipment to give an injection, there was the risk that a child would wake and cry out before the drug could take effect. To have attempted to administer a drug to a sleeping child by mouth would have posed the same hazard.

One after another – surprisingly to the authors – the experts consulted referred to the potential of chloroform, a drug the authors had thought belonged only in Sherlock Holmes mysteries. A cloth or pad can be indeed used to administer chloroform, as venerable crime fiction suggests. It works fast and can render a person unconscious in less than two minutes. In the hands of someone who knows what they are doing, chloroform can be very effective in drugging a sleeping child. Doctors used it in that way in the Victorian era, to avoid frightening children before surgical operations.

That said, there are serious downsides to chloroform – not least for the hypothetical child-abduction scenario of the Madeleine case. The drug has a pungent smell that can be noticeable as much as an hour later – depending on the size of a room and the ventilation. Though it may be significant that Kate McCann said the window was open when she returned to find Madeleine gone, neither she nor any of the other people who then entered Apartment 5A noticed an odour.

Of the several other anaesthetic agents that can be applied soaked in a cloth, like chloroform – one is sevoflurane, which can render a small child unconscious within a couple of minutes. Sevoflurane, though, also leaves behind a noticeable odour. Other possible agents available to a lay person are industrial solvents benzene, xylene and toluene, which are used in cleaning products and paint strippers. They too, however, may for an indeterminate amount of time leave a significant odour.

Most of the sedative agents mentioned have been used in what are known as DFSAs – Drug Facilitated Sexual Assaults. To keep a subject asleep for any amount of time, however, as an abductor would almost certainly have required, one must keep on administering the sedative agent while keeping the airways clear. If administration of the drug is stopped, the subject wakes. Should a drug be inexpertly handled – or should a patient or victim, perhaps resisting, draw a deep breath and inhale too great a concentration of the drug – cardiac arrest may occur. Amateur anaesthesia can kill.

Saturday, May 12th marked four years to the day since Madeleine's birth. Yellow ribbons had been tied to the railings in the square in her home village of Rothley, Leicestershire, for days. Now, to mark her birthday, balloons were released into the sky. In Glasgow, Gerry McCann's hometown, fans at a Scottish Premier League match wore yellow wristbands and held up posters reading 'HELP FIND MADELEINE'.

In Praia da Luz, spokesman Alex Woolfall read a statement from the McCanns. 'Today is our daughter Madeleine's fourth birthday,' it read. 'We would like to mark today by asking people to redouble their efforts to help find Madeleine . . . Please keep looking, please keep praying, please bring Madeleine home.'

Gerry and Kate spent the day away from the press, at a private villa put at their disposal by the Ocean Club. Wine and beer had been brought, and Gerry tried to make a birthday toast to his daughter but was too upset to go on.

In the evening, the couple joined a congregation of more than three hundred at the church for a special service for Madeleine. People in the congregation were linked with green rope, to symbolise togetherness. Some carried branches sprouting green spring shoots – for growth, hope and new life.

Two days later, on Monday the 14th, Kate McCann went for a run (both she and her husband were runners), the first time she had had the heart to do so since the disappearance. As she ran, she recited a decade of the rosary.

At 9.36 that evening, Sky News broke the story that a man was being questioned by Portuguese police in connection with the Madeleine case. His name, it would swiftly emerge, was Robert Murat.

Cue now a tangled tale.

7

So far as one can tell from the record, the Murat episode began early on May 4th, the morning after Madeleine disappeared. Between 8 and 9 a.m. that day, Stephen Carpenter, a British tourist staying in an apartment about one hundred and fifty yards from Apartment 5A, heard a man's voice call, 'What is going on?'

The voice was English, and it was coming from the other side of a hedge that separated the apartment block from an adjoining property. Carpenter, who had met the McCanns during the week, explained that he had just learned that their daughter was missing. The unseen speaker in the next-door garden then walked around to say, 'I have lived here for fourteen years. I speak Portuguese fluently, and I can help translate.' His name, he said, was Robert, and he added that he had a daughter in the UK the same age as Madeleine. He understood what her parents must be going through.

This was Robert Murat, the thirty-three-year-old son of an Anglo-Portuguese father and a British mother. He had grown up in Praia da Luz, but had worked in both Portugal and the UK. He was separated from his British wife, who lived in England with their four-year-old daughter. Murat's fluency in Portuguese had on occasion given him translation work, locally and in the UK.

Carpenter realised at once, he said, that the encounter with Murat could be useful. Without delay, he walked his new acquaintance over to the Ocean Club to introduce him to Gerry and Kate McCann. The GNR's Sergeant Duarte, back on the scene now after a short break, would recall that Murat 'offered his help to translate'. He was already there, standing by to assist, when a PJ inspector arrived at 9.30 a.m. When *Daily Telegraph* correspondent Fiona Govan arrived at Apartment 5A, Murat was her 'first point of contact'. They subsequently met on several occasions, and he would say that he was working closely with the police.

By early afternoon, along with an accompanying Ocean Club supervisor, Murat was working with officers who were interviewing British guests. The police were to list him as 'interpreter' on reports of several interviews with witnesses – including one of those conducted with Dianne Webster, Fiona Payne's mother.

Murat rapidly became a familiar face to British journalists crowding into Praia da Luz. The work with the police aside, he helped his mother – with whom he shared a house – run an improvised information booth about Madeleine on the seafront. He several times offered his opinion, the *Telegraph*'s Govan reported, that Madeleine 'had been taken by someone from outside the area and that he believed she was no longer in Portugal and may never be found'.

'I'm just a local guy who's doing all he can to help out,' Murat told *Daily Mail* reporter Neil Sears. Three days into the investigation, however, on Sunday, May 6th, some of the journalists became leery of him. That day, Polícia Judiciária Inspector Manuel Pinho was 'contacted by some of the journalists, who said they thought the behaviour of [Murat] appeared very suspicious in his contacts with them, especially because he always seemed extremely curious . . . When they tried to take photographs of him, he appeared quite alarmed and flatly refused because, he said, he had a daughter the same age as the missing girl and was going through a divorce.'

Then, on May 8th, an anonymous caller – a woman speaking fluent Portuguese – phoned the Polícia Judiciária. She poured out a torrent of malicious accusations, none of them substantiated by the facts but clearly aimed at Murat – and hard to ignore.

Five days later, on the evening of May 13th, the Portuguese police – working through British police liaison officers – had the McCanns' friend Jane Tanner take part in a covert identification experiment. They wanted to know whether she thought Murat was one and the same as the man she had seen carrying a child near Apartment 5A some forty-five minutes before it was realised Madeleine had vanished.

There is no reliable, cogent record of the identification procedure, or what its outcome was. It apparently involved Tanner and the police covertly watching – from inside a van disguised as a commercial vehicle – as Robert Murat and two dissimilar men crossed a road. According to then chief investigator Gonçalo Amaral, Tanner did recognise Murat as the man she had seen carrying a child on the night Madeleine went missing – 'from the way he walked'. In confusing answers during a much later interview, Tanner said both that she did not think it was Murat she saw from the van and – it seems – that she thought at the time that it might have been. According to Kate McCann, the Portuguese police accompanying Tanner told her it was not necessary for her to sign a statement as to what she thought.

Before the identification exercise with Tanner, Murat had rented a car and temporarily left the area. He told a British reporter covering the story that he had become concerned about the attention he was getting. He appeared, nevertheless, to have sufficient sense of humour to go along with the in-joke journalists were making – that he was the 'prime suspect'. He even took to introducing himself as the principal suspect.

On May 14th, the day after the identification exercise with Tanner, no one was joking. At 7.00 that morning, police descended on the house near the Ocean Club where Murat lived with his seventy-one-year-old mother. They sealed it off with tape, and white-suited officers in face masks were seen coming and going and working in the garden. Two large water tanks were drained. Computers, mobile phones and videotapes were taken away, the BBC reported.

Gerry and Kate McCann learned of the development from television news coverage. They stood watching, petrified that the next thing the news would show would be a policeman coming out with a small body bag.

There would be no such dread discovery, however, that day or in the days that followed. PJ Chief Inspector Olegário de Sousa said the search at the villa was a 'normal development'. Robert Murat, meanwhile, had been taken to a police station for questioning and formally declared an *arguido*, a status routinely invoked under the Portuguese justice system.

An approximate translation of the word *arguido* is 'named' or 'formal' suspect. It is important to understand the word's meaning, not least because the McCanns themselves were eventually to be designated *arguidos*. The term formally denotes a person who, it is suspected, may have committed an offence. When declared *arguido*, a person's situation is similar to that of being 'questioned under caution' in the UK or – in the United States – being read one's Miranda rights.

Accusatory questions may be put to someone who has been

declared *arguido*, and the answers become part of the record. Along with the discomfiture of becoming *arguido* at all, however, come certain rights. A person may have a lawyer present when questioned, has the right to remain silent, cannot be prosecuted for lying, and must be informed of all evidence against him or her.

Following some nineteen hours of questioning, and now publicly labelled a suspect, Robert Murat was released without charge. What he could now say publicly was severely limited by law, but – in an exclusive interview with Sky News' crime correspondent Martin Brunt – he declared he 'had been made a scapegoat for something I did not do . . . This has ruined my life and made things difficult for my family here and in Britain.'

In the UK, at her home in a Norfolk village, Murat's estranged wife Dawn declared her belief that her husband was 'totally innocent'. He was, she said, 'the most helpful and genuine person I have ever met'. She and others put up posters proclaiming as much. Murat's uncle Ralph said he was 'so sweet and goodnatured. He was just trying to help.' His cousin Sally said there was absolutely 'no way' Murat could be involved in Madeleine's disappearance. He had just been 'overenthusiastic trying to help people as he always does'. An English friend and former colleague, Gareth Bailey, said he was just 'a laidback guy'.

There were supportive people, too, in Praia da Luz. Veronica Fennel, who had worked with Murat, said he was 'a nice guy', if also a 'try hard' who 'wanted to be the focus of attention'. A family friend, Tuck Price, said Murat was 'very distressed' by the allegations and 'desperate to come out and speak to clear his name'.

Robert Murat's predicament was to last for many months and engulf three other people, including a German woman, Michaela

Walczuch, with whom he was romantically involved. They were making plans to work together in the property business, saw each other almost daily and were in frequent touch on the phone. Detectives now grilled Walczuch on her movements and her contacts with Murat at critical times. Just as they had searched Murat's home, they searched hers.

Also targeted was a twenty-two-year-old Russian named Sergei Malinka, who worked in computers. Murat and Michaela Walczuch had asked him to create a website and were in touch with him in that connection. So it was that he in turn was questioned and his home also searched.

Aspersions of one sort or another would swirl about the trio. The day after Madeleine vanished, a truck driver was to report, he had seen a blonde woman beside a car passing a 'bundle wrapped in a blanket' – the driver suggested it contained a child – over a fence to a man in another vehicle. Shown photographs, the witness thought one of them perhaps resembled Michaela Walczuch. The lead went nowhere. Complex checks on their mobile-phone records, and the position of their phones when calls were made, established that Walczuch, Malinka and Murat had all been many miles away at the time of the supposedly mysterious bundle exchange.

Malinka declared publicly that he had no criminal record and was completely innocent – and nothing relevant to the Madeleine McCann case was discovered at his home or in his possessions. The police did not make him a suspect. Nevertheless, he was to say, the furore around him meant that the time he had spent trying to succeed in Portugal had "suddenly, in one hour, fallen apart."

As for Robert Murat, the damaging assertions had not ended with the anonymous call to the police that had been made just before the storm broke around him. Other individuals made allegations about his sexual and psychological background. All the claims proved unfounded. One witness interviewed by the police, a childhood acquaintance named Lyndon Pollard, thought the allegation he was asked about "ridiculous".

The most compromising items the search of Murat's home turned up were a vibrator – such as could be found in the bottom drawers of millions of people – and a page from an old copy of the *Daily Telegraph* featuring a review of a book entitled *Casanova's Women*. A Portuguese prosecutor's office report would eventually note that analysis of Murat's computer – and indeed Malinka's – 'produced nothing that could compromise them as having taken part in any illicit activity'.

Poisonous allegation and titillating rumour aside, what really mattered evidentially was whether and how Murat, his girlfriend Walczuch and Sergei Malinka could account for their activity on May 3rd, the night Madeleine had vanished.

Walczuch said she and her daughter had been at a Bible meeting – she was a Jehovah's Witness – had stayed on afterwards, got home around 11 p.m., then gone to bed. Malinka said he dined with his family at home that evening, then worked on his computers in his room. Nothing in the record indicates that the police were less than satisfied with their alibis.

Unfortunately for Robert Murat, the facts about his whereabouts during the critical night hours were blurred by a degree of perceived doubt. He said from the first that he got home that evening around 7.30 p.m. – after his mother Jenny got home from walking the dogs, he thought – then spent the evening watching television, eating, and talking with his mother in the kitchen. Around '10.30 p.m. or a little later', he said, he heard the sound of a siren. His mother Jenny, whose account matched

1. Madeleine McCann vanished on May 3rd, 2007,
nine days before her fourth birthday.

2. Apartment 5A is on the ground floor at right.
The archway, left, led to the Tapas restaurant.

3. The Ocean Club. Gerry and Kate McCann and their friends dined
each night beside the pool, sixty yards from the apartment.

4. Apartment 5A at night, after Madeleine disappeared. Did the small gate afford an abductor access to its unlocked patio door? Madeleine's empty bed, (below), as photographed by police.

5. An innocent explanation? There were open trenches like this, part of a new drainage system, near the McCann apartment. Did Madeleine wander?

6. 'Words cannot describe the anguish that we are feeling...' Gerry and Kate McCann face the media. The press descended on Praia da Luz – and stayed.

DESAPARECIDA
MISSING
Madeleine McCann

VISTA PELA ÚLTIMA VEZ NA PRAIA DA LUZ NO DIA 3 DE MAIO
LAST SEEN IN PRAIA DA LUZ ON THURSDAY MAY 3
Se tiver informações telefone
If you have any information please call
Portimão PJ 282 405 400 | Faro PJ 289 884 500

7. The hue and cry was unprecedented. The McCanns (below) display pink and white Eeyore pyjamas like those Madeleine had worn.

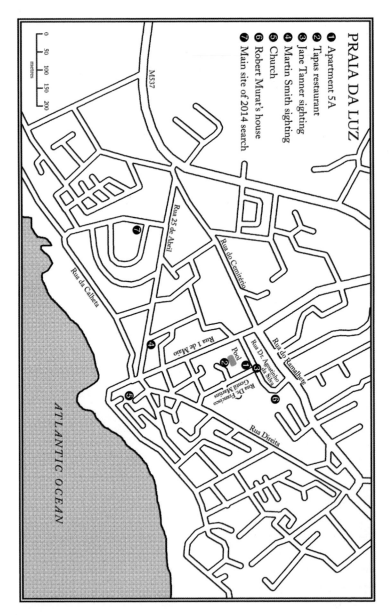

PRAIA DA LUZ

❶ Apartment 5A
❷ Tapas restaurant
❸ Jane Tanner sighting
❹ Martin Smith sighting
❺ Church
❻ Robert Murat's house
❼ Main site of 2014 search

0 50 100 150 200
metres

M537

Rua 25 de Abril

Rua do Cemitério

Rua da Calheta

Rua 1 de Maio

Pool

Rua Dr. Agostinho da Silva

Rua da Ramalhete

Rua DR. Francisco Gentil Martins

Rua Direita

ATLANTIC OCEAN

8.

9. Gonçalo Amaral of the Polícia Judiciária, who led the early investigation but was removed from his post, would suggest the McCanns had something to hide.

10. A Portuguese detective dusted the window shutter of Apartment 5A for fingerprints – without wearing gloves. The British press would accuse the local force of incompetence.

11. Robert Murat, who lived near the apartment, became the first suspect. No evidence was found against him, and he said later he had felt the police 'were trying to set me up.'

12. Kate McCann with Cuddle Cat, her daughter's favourite toy. A British sniffer dog (below) trained to hunt for human remains, 'alerted' to the toy.

13. During operations in Apartment 5A, the dog also alerted to an area behind a sofa in the lounge. So did a second dog, trained to scent blood.

14. Both dogs also indicated interest in a Renault car the McCanns had rented about a month after their daughter went missing. There was no evidence to support the dogs' response.

her son's, also said she heard a siren. If they did, what they heard may have been the sound of the first police car hurrying to the Ocean Club in response to calls reporting Madeleine's disappearance – it arrived around 11 p.m.

According to Murat, he made some remark to his mother on hearing the siren but 'did not leave the house to investigate . . . went to bed around midnight, and did not leave the house until morning'.

Questions were raised initially as to that timetable, because some members of the McCann party, and others, told police they thought they had seen Murat – or a man who resembled him – near Apartment 5A on the night of Madeleine's disappearance. Three business people who knew Murat, however, and seven policemen, stated that they had not seen him there. Members of the McCann group would later concede that their recollections of having seen him near the apartment were less than reliable.

Finally, there is something to be learned from the police analysis of the traffic on Murat's phones the night Madeleine vanished. It shows that he talked with his girlfriend Michaela Walczuch three times, using his mobile phone, between 11.20 p.m. and 11.48 p.m. During this sequence of calls, there was also a brief, thirty-second mobile-phone call to Sergei Malinka at 11.39 p.m. The last of the calls to Walczuch that night lasted from 11.53 p.m. to a minute after midnight, and was made from the landline at Murat's home. Assuming it was not made by his mother, it would indicate Robert Murat was at home at that time.

The ordeal was not over, though, for either Murat or Malinka. As late as the spring of 2008, Malinka's car was destroyed by flames while parked near his home. Nearby, on the pavement, someone had daubed the word 'FALA' – 'TALK'. He was, Malinka said, 'living a bad dream that never ends'.

Nor was Murat's own torment over. He was still officially an *arguido*.

Murat became a prisoner of the Madeleine story. Leery of putting his nose outside, he soon became 'desperate . . . pacing up and down', his mother reported. He told a British caller: 'I did absolutely nothing. I have nothing to hide . . . And my family are all being crucified.'

He was still being treated as a suspect two months later when police arrived to search the grounds around his home for the second time. Undergrowth was cleared, trees felled, the ground probed – and he again found himself besieged by reporters. By October, when nothing had changed, he would be telling the BBC: 'It's been five months. My savings have gone. Mum's doing what she can, and it's just very, very difficult.'

This predicament was to continue, as it turned out, for more than a year. By June 2008, however, a report shows, the Portuguese police had concluded that, 'Despite the exhaustive and methodical investigation into Murat and the persons close to him, no elements whatsoever were collected to connect him to the crime that was under investigation.' The following month, it was announced that his *arguido* status had at last been lifted.

Murat brought libel actions against eleven British newspapers and Sky News over their reports of his situation the previous year. They apologised and paid some £600,000 in damages. Sergei Malinka and Michaela Walczuch, who also sued, received apologies and a total of £200,000 in damages.

Perusal of the Portuguese police files by the authors confirmed that there is nothing whatsoever to indicate that Robert Murat, Walczuch or Malinka, had anything to do with the disappearance of Madeleine McCann. Former 'named suspect' Murat would eventually have an opportunity to describe on a public platform what he had endured. As the key speaker at a Cambridge Union debate on the tabloid press, he told how – for month after month – he had felt 'like a fox being pursued by a pack of hounds. Often I felt like I was somewhere between a Kafka novel and the Will Smith movie *Enemy of the State*.'

Looking back at how the ordeal began, he was to say, the interrogation by the police reminded him of 'a KGB movie. I felt they were trying to set me up.' His life, he said, had been shattered. The only way he could truly recover, he had said at the very start of it all, back in the spring of 2007, 'is if they catch Madeleine's abductor'.

That, for Robert Murat, is probably still the reality of the situation.

8

Though the focus during the second half of May 2007 was on the 'named suspect', the larger Madeleine story had become a journalistic juggernaut. By the 16th of the month, the BBC had reported that 'the huge media interest has turned a sleepy Algarve resort upside down.'

At the beginning there had been a mainly British posse of reporters waiting around for anything that might be a new development, waiting for any statement there might be from the McCanns, looking for a photo opportunity, trying – usually – to behave compassionately. London editors had withdrawn some of the British contingent after the first ten days or so – only hastily to resume their coverage when the Murat story broke. 'We were here for a week then went back on Sunday,' *Sunday Telegraph* photographer Justin Sutcliffe recalled. 'But then on Tuesday they decided to send us out again. I just about had time to do my laundry.'

Other European newspapers and broadcasters had followed. First among them were reporters from neighbouring Spain, then Germans, French, Scandinavians and – for the United States – the Associated Press. This was the kind of 'emotional impact' story,

German TV reporter Sabine Michel said in what would turn out to be an understatement, that 'crosses borders'.

Starting on the very first day with coverage by the *Algarve Resident*, the English-language paper in the Algarve, Madeleine's disappearance had brought Portugal's own media to Praia da Luz in force. During the week the press in the UK was temporarily diverted by Prime Minister Blair's announcement that he was to step down, the Portuguese paid the Madeleine story more attention than did the British.

The kinder explanation of that circumstance was that – as may well be the case – the Portuguese nation has a special fondness for children. Less generously, the Inter Press news agency suggested, the Madeleine story was a prime example of the Portuguese idiom '*Para o inglês ver*'. This translates as 'For the English to see' – or, put another way, as putting on a front to impress outsiders and ward off criticism.

Praia da Luz was jolted out of its tranquillity by the media feeding frenzy. The first helicopters had been part of the search for Madeleine. Those seen now were platforms for cameramen. Residents' sleep was disturbed by the hum of generators powering the satellite trucks. Photographs taken at the time tell their own story. The McCanns, venturing out as they did most days to speak to the press, found themselves staring down the barrels of myriad microphones and camera lenses (see photo 6).

In a statement on May 14th, for example – the day Murat was named as a suspect – Gerry McCann stepped out to articulate the position he and Kate were to take far into the future. Absent evidence to the contrary, he said, 'We believe Madeleine is safe and is being looked after.' Until she had been found, he said, they had no thought of leaving Portugal.

Sometimes there was, on the face of it, not much to tell the press about. The McCanns had difficulty, Gerry would say shortly afterwards, dealing with what he called the 'information void'. Under the Portuguese system, as reported earlier, police are not permitted to share information on an investigation – even with the victims of the crime.

British reporters, too, found it hard to operate under these rules. 'Sky sources,' wrote the news channel's crime correspondent Martin Brunt, 'are a bit thin on the ground. There's no sidling up to a friendly cop for a quick natter away from the cameras. I'm having to rely for information on the local Portuguese press, whose accuracy is sometimes highly questionable.'

Gerry McCann had early on seen major press coverage as essential, a way to enlist public help in the hunt for Madeleine. He had not, though, thought it would last, saying at first that the case might turn out to be 'a weekend story: "British Girl taken from Portuguese Resort," a terrible story and then that's it.' Even weeks later, asked whether he was worried people might lose interest, he would still be predicting that media coverage was 'not going to last a long time'. He added, though: 'We have been much, much more successful in driving a message out there than we could ever have possibly imagined.'

The most striking imagery, for the television-watching public, was coming from Praia da Luz itself and the McCanns' home village of Rothley. The railings near the Ocean Club were bedecked with yellow ribbons and flowers. Soft toys, deposited by adults and children alike, included a furry Winnie-the-Pooh – whose friend Eeyore, everyone knew by now, had adorned Madeleine's pyjamas the night she vanished.

More than a thousand miles away in the UK, the jumble of offerings on the Rothley war memorial had multiplied and spread to nearby benches, even the bus stop. Ribbons, flowers and toys

aside, there were children's drawings, a basket with cash dona-
tions, religious votives and image after image of Madeleine. 'Maddy,
we didn't even know you,' read one message, 'but you are with
us in our hearts.' Another card, with an image of hands clasped
in prayer, asked the onlooker to 'Expect a miracle.'

Comments posted on the BBC children's channel included:

I really feel sorry for her parents and her . . . I always wear
a yellow ribbon pinned on my shirt and yellow ribbon in
my hair. Most of the time I wear yellow clothes too. I hope
she's OK!

Jazmine, 12

I can't sleep because I am having nightmares of being abducted.
Keep my eyes open to see if anyone comes in my bedroom.

James, 11

It's made me feel really unsafe. When I'm alone I'm really
cautious, even if it is just when I'm walking home. I think
it's evil . . . Come Home Soon Maddie xxxx

Lizzie, 11

The case of one missing child had become a daily smorgasbord
of news (even when there was none to report), a prodigious
European-wide event, a potent, infectious mix of international
fellow feeling, grief and hope, though sometimes over sentimental
and mawkish.

The key to the story's phenomenal rise and rise was the Internet.
A hectic telephone blitz by Gerry on May 9th, the day after he
had his revelation in church, his realisation that he should take
positive action, had reaped rapid results. An old friend of Kate's
mother, Pat Perkins, who was a project manager for the NHS,

sent an email appeal and picture of Madeleine to NHS colleagues, asking them to forward it to friends and contacts. The message went viral.

Most influential of all though, for months to come, was a website set up in the north of Scotland at the suggestion of Gerry McCann's older sister Philomena, a Modern Studies teacher. Philomena – 'Phil' to family and friends – took the initiative of asking an eighteen-year-old former pupil, Calum MacRae, to set up the site. MacRae, a computer whizz-kid, had it up and running within twenty-four hours, originally as www.bringmadeleinehome. com and then as www.findmadeleine.com. From a storeroom in a garage on an industrial estate, he and five other former pupils would eventually run an operation that, along with the site itself, involved speaking with Gerry McCann daily, passing incoming information to the police and stuffing 'Look for Madeleine' wrist-bands, badges and posters into envelopes for circulation around the world.

The website received sixty million hits within forty-eight hours. In little more than a week, 7,500 people posted messages of support from countries as varied as Holland, Australia, South Africa, Malaysia, Singapore and even Kazakhstan and Azerbaijan. Gerry McCann's blog, launched on the site in mid-May, was to register a billion hits from eighty million different visitors in the first three months.

The word going out from Praia da Luz about one little girl had set a vast information mill turning. More than thirty Facebook groups sprouted, their twenty-three-thousand membership keen to help find her. Madeleine's image was everywhere on YouTube. Suddenly, her blonde fringe and her eyes – one with its unusual, streaked iris – were familiar worldwide.

Madeleine's Aunt Phil started a chain email reading, 'We don't think she is in Portugal any more and need to get her picture and the story across Europe.' Within days, people were receiving her appeal in a form that initially looked like spam, having been forwarded by so many others.

In the UK, television channels offered airtime for advertisements designed to help the campaign to find Madeleine. Advertising agencies donated expertise and content that would also be available online – in six languages. Mobile-phone operators Vodafone, O2 and Telefónica ran a text campaign.

The age-old 'Missing Person' poster system was also exploited to the full. There were posters of a smiling Madeleine at check-in desks at Stansted Airport that serviced flights to Portugal; posters in cars and shop widows in Gibraltar; twenty thousand adhesive posters, paid for by a British businessman, that could be stuck on cars and trucks heading off across Europe; a giant inflatable billboard installed on the beach at Praia da Luz, featuring a massive *News of the World* headline with the words 'FIND MADDIE'; a poster to be screened during the Eurovision Song Contest, designed by Gerry's sister Philomena; and an A4-size poster, available online, targeting both Portuguese and English speakers in the Algarve. Complete with the familiar appealing picture, it read:

DESAPARECIDA
MISSING
Madeleine McCann
VISTA PELA ÚLTIMA VEZ NA PRAIA DA LUZ NO DIA 3 DE MAIO
LAST SEEN IN PRAIA DA LUZ ON THURSDAY MAY 3
Se Tiver Informações Telefone
If you have any information please call
Portimão PJ 282 405 400 Faro PJ 289 854 500

In the third week of May in Portugal, after circulation of a
chain email, some – including senior detectives working on the
Madeleine investigation – stood in silence for a minute in soli-
darity with the McCann family. In Northern Ireland, a hundred-
strong crowd held a candlelit prayer vigil.

A record producer named Stuart Epps wrote and recorded the
first of numerous songs for Madeleine:

>   I was thinking, how can the earth be round,
>   With people crying 'When will this girl be found?'
>   Where's the meaning in all the suffering and pain,
>   Madeleine?
>   Hoping you'll be home again, Madeleine.

On the same morning as the vigil, two hundred commercial
radio stations across Britain played the song 'Don't You Forget
About Me' by the group Simple Minds. It would become the
theme song at events for Madeleine, and later for missing children
everywhere, for years to come. Another candidate for a theme
song at an early stage was Bryan Adams' 1991 hit 'Everything I
Do', and Adams later dedicated a concert to her.

In Leicestershire, where the McCanns lived, ten thousand people
bought awareness wristbands in yellow and green – in Portugal,
they are the colours that symbolise hope – with proceeds going
to the fund to help find the missing girl.

There were individual demonstrations of sympathy. One man
cycled three hundred miles over two days, from Derry in Northern
Ireland to Rothley, to raise money for the Madeleine fund. Seven
schoolgirls in Cheshire collected money by selling yellow ribbons
to other pupils. Two former soldiers from Yorkshire, one of whom
had previously lost a daughter in a fatal car accident, travelled

to Portugal to mount their own search mission around Praia da Luz. Dressed in army-surplus clothing and equipped with maps, compasses and binoculars, they scoured wasteland and derelict buildings near the village.

Highly effective, for the British public, were the appeals made by sportsmen – especially footballers. Their appeals for Madeleine's safe return had come one after another: Manchester United's Cristiano Ronaldo, himself Portuguese; Chelsea's John Terry with Portuguese teammate Paulo Ferreira; and the ubiquitous David Beckham. When a photograph of Madeleine wearing the Everton strip appeared – Kate McCann was of course originally from Liverpool – Everton players Nuno Valente and Manuel Fernandes, both also Portuguese, appealed for information.

Every sporting event in the calendar seemed to feature a call to help Madeleine. In Glasgow, Gerry's hometown, a video was played to Spanish fans attending the 2007 European Champions League Cup Final. Another film was shown at half-time during the FA Cup Final. In mid-May at Lord's, when England's cricketers played the West Indies, they wore yellow 'awareness' ribbons for Madeleine. Leicestershire and Lancashire cricketers would wear the wristbands. Jockeys riding in the Epsom Derby, an event seen by millions of television viewers, were to wear yellow ribbons.

Famous political names associated themselves with the case. Kate McCann received a call from Cherie Blair, wife of outgoing prime minister Tony Blair, who mentioned that her friend Lady Catherine Meyer was the founder of two missing children's organisations – a cause she had pursued since a former husband had kept her two sons away from her. This would become a significant ongoing connection to the Blairs.

Probably as the result of a call Gerry McCann made to Britain's ambassador in Portugal, John Buck, the then Foreign Secretary

Margaret Beckett placed a call to Gerry at the Ocean Club. He used it to ask for pressure to ensure that the Portuguese push their investigation harder, more efficiently – an expression of the doubt and distrust that had begun within an hour of the disappearance and would never go away.

In Portugal, even years later, some would suggest the British government brought inappropriate pressure on the government in Lisbon. 'It was never just a case of a criminal investigation,' Carlos Anjos, the then president of the Polícia Judiciária's union, told the authors. 'I don't remember any other case where the diplomats of one country brought such pressure on the authorities of another country.' Rumours would even circulate, and still do to this day, that such pressure was exerted because of some connection between the McCanns and UK intelligence.

Former Portuguese Attorney General Monteiro Pinto, however, recalled no abnormal pressure – from either his own government or the UK. 'No member of the government ever raised the case with me,' he said in 2014. 'Neither the Prime Minister nor the President can give the Attorney General orders . . . The British ambassador did at one point invite me to lunch – his wife was Portuguese – and we exchanged some thoughts. He merely asked me to give the [Madeleine McCann] case priority. I assured him that everything was already in place.'

Politicians aside, many other celebrities showed support for the rolling campaign in one way or another. Zoë Wanamaker, the award-winning actress who had appeared in *Harry Potter and the Philosopher's Stone*, did the voice-over for one of the online Madeleine campaign advertisements. Former Spice Girl Victoria Beckham, herself at the time the mother of three children and living in Spain, wore the yellow ribbon for Madeleine on her

Hermès Birkin handbag. Given the blanket coverage of her by the media, this was high visibility indeed.

Another kind of support – crucial support – came in from famous names. In their apartment in Praia da Luz, the McCanns had confronted the fact that their family tragedy raised serious financial questions. The first donor, according to Kate, was a medical colleague in the UK, who pledged £100,000 towards a reward leading to Madeleine's recovery. Within less than two weeks, it was announced that as much as £2.5 million was on offer.

Those promising contributions included Virgin's Sir Richard Branson, British Home Stores boss Sir Philip Green, *Harry Potter* creator J. K. Rowling, Everton Football Club chairman Bill Kenwright, Manchester United's Wayne Rooney – and Rupert Murdoch's then still flourishing *News of the World* newspaper. These were the smaller contributors. Scots health-spa owner Stephen Winyard on his own pledged a full million. The McCanns had to sit down with lawyers to discuss how reward money and a 'fighting fund' should be properly set up and administered. 'Madeleine's Fund: Leaving No Stone Unturned' was established with the stated aims of finding Madeleine, supporting the family and bringing anyone criminally involved to justice.

On May 22nd, the McCanns announced that their commitment to the hunt for their daughter had no limits. 'We will travel wherever is necessary,' Gerry told reporters, 'to ensure people across Europe recognise Madeleine's picture . . . All we're doing is starting to spread the net far and wide.'

What they did the following day ensured a further wave of international publicity – and a greater awareness of their religious commitment. They made the four-hour journey by car to the Roman Catholic shrine at Fátima, north of Lisbon, where in 1917

– according to the account credited by believers – three shepherd
children had six times seen an apparition of the Virgin Mary in
the foliage of a tree.

In the church at Praia da Luz ten days earlier, the day after
the McCanns had marked Madeleine's fourth birthday, the priest
who had baptised her – just arrived from the UK – had concele-
brated a special Mass on the anniversary of the miracle. Now, in
Fátima, Gerry and Kate prayed beside the marble pillar that marks
the spot where the apparitions of Mary are believed to have been
seen. Kate, who was, as so often, holding Madeleine's toy Cuddle
Cat, wore yellow and green ribbons in her hair.

Kate prayed that the Virgin would protect her daughter. The
rector of the shrine prayed 'for all the children that are away
from their homes, especially little Madeleine, so that Our Lady
can keep these children in Her care.'

In a remarkable development, the McCanns now had an official
British liaison. This was Clarence Mitchell, a former BBC newsman
whose usual job was with the Media Monitoring Unit at the Cabinet
Office in London. He had been seconded to the Foreign Office with
instructions to fly out to Portugal to deal with the press. The same
week, and surely not by coincidence, Prime Minister-in-waiting
Gordon Brown phoned Gerry and Foreign Secretary Margaret Beckett
discussed the case with her Portuguese counterpart.

During the three weeks he stayed with them, Mitchell became
close to the McCanns. He would eventually quit his government
job to work with them, and would still be acting as their spokesman
as late as 2014. It was Mitchell who told the couple, on May
27th, that a visit to the Vatican was in the offing.

To the Vatican, and a meeting with Pope Benedict XVI, they
duly went. Aboard a private jet provided by Sir Philip Green,
and accompanied by a gaggle of reporters, the McCanns flew to

Rome. They were welcomed by the British ambassador and other diplomats to the Holy See, spent the night at the ambassador's residence and the next day found themselves waiting in the Prima Fila, special reserved seating, to meet the Pope.

For a Roman Catholic, as Kate was to recall, this was 'incredibly important. I mean, I truly believed that would make a difference for Madeleine . . . The closest you can get to kind of meeting God in some way. And I just thought, all my prayers, etc., would be channelled more quickly to God.'

The encounter was brief but moving. An aide directed Pope Benedict to the McCanns and Kate asked him to pray for her missing daughter. He held both their hands, and then – using his thumb – blessed a photograph of Madeleine. At a press conference afterwards, Gerry said their Catholic faith had given them strength, that the outpouring of goodwill generated by the abduction had restored his faith in humanity.

There followed thirteen days of helter-skelter travel that achieved little or nothing but kept the story in the news. Not twenty-four hours after their return from Rome, the McCanns flew to Madrid. Five days later, they headed off on a series of whistle-stop trips to Germany and Holland, then back to Portugal.

More plane flights, some of them again by private jet courtesy of another businessman, more welcomes by polite British diplomats, more media interviews. Meetings, too, with government ministers and – for the first time – with representatives of organisations that worked with missing and abused children. There were eye-opening conversations about child trafficking and about the disquieting rise in the distribution of images of child sex abuse.

The first cruel encounter, too, with a hoaxer. At the British Embassy in Berlin, they were told there had been a call from a man – he called himself 'Walter' – who claimed he had information about Madeleine. He would speak only, he insisted, with Gerry or Kate. The call had come in to the Spanish police and was being taken as serious until proven otherwise. Briefed on how to handle the call, the McCanns waited – and waited. There was no further contact with 'Walter'.

A sixty-one-year-old Italian and his Portuguese woman friend would be arrested – in Spain – because of allegations that they had tried to extract money from the McCanns by offering false information. The case never came to trial.

The weeks that followed brought similar, more drawn-out torment. There was this unsigned email on June 14th:

> To: M McCann
> Subject: kidnapping of maddie
> THIS MESSAGE IS FOR THE FAMILY MCCANN
> I SPOKE YESTERDAY A POLICE OFFICER AND TOLD HIM I WILL SEND A MESSAGE
> I HOPE THAT POLICE WILL HAND THIS OVER TO GERRI
> If he wants to get the kidnappers it will take one day and the case is over. I think this is the last weekend for your daughter without her family.
> It depends on mr mccann

In one of a series of exchanges, an email from Gerry said:

> We need to know the information is genuine. Can you give me proof that you know where Madeleine is and that she is well?

Another message from the person who initiated the contact read:

Hello gerri or . . .

I don't know if you are gerri or a policeofficer or a spokesman of the family. But i can tell you that i really know these people because i grew up with them . . . I know the hideout, name, address, everything of the kidnappers. I will be honest with you and the whole team of investigators.

I want a reward and that will be in total 2.000.000 (2 mill. Euro).

For this reward I want an advance of 500.000 (500K).

The advance you must bring to me in Holland by yourself . . . After receiving this amount I will send you all details of the hideout . . .

You must know that i am a crook too but i only do this for the money.

The author of the emails was traced to Eindhoven in Holland, where he had hoped to avoid detection by sending his messages from an Internet café and an unemployment office. He was charged with attempted fraud.

There would be six extortion attempts significant enough to be taken seriously. Another deception brought the couple real distress. The newspaper *De Telegraaf* in Amsterdam received and published a letter and map pinpointing an area near the Portuguese village of Arão, just nine miles from Praia da Luz. The map was marked with crosses and the words '*vermoedelijke vindplaats* Madeleine' – 'place where Madeleine can possibly be found'. The missing girl's body, the letter said, was buried 'north of the road under branches and rocks, about six to seven metres off the road'.

The letter somewhat resembled one received the previous year that had suggested where two missing Belgian girls – killed by a paedophile – might be buried. In Portugal, the police took it seriously. Officers with sniffer dogs cordoned off a wide area, concentrated on a patch of rocky ground – and found nothing.

Gerry said: 'When you have something like this, put together as a credible letter, giving information, the immediate reaction, is "Is there something to this?" The thought of a very public search, with Madeleine coming out of it dead, was very upsetting. Kate was not good.'

For the McCanns, life seesawed between hope, disillusion and despair. Weeks earlier, news had come of the rescue just eighty-six miles from Praia da Luz, near the border with Spain, of an eleven-year-old girl who had been abducted. A dramatic car chase had ended in the arrest of the abductor – he turned out to be a drunk known to the family – and the return of the girl to her parents.

Joy for one couple, kudos for the Portuguese police and continuing anguish for the McCanns. As the hunt for Madeleine continued, the police inspired no such confidence in them.

And there was, always, the waiting.

9

The McCanns' relationship with the Portuguese police was to go from strained cordiality to eventual terminal rift. Their negative feelings on the very first night, when they were hysterical with worry, had perhaps been somewhat over the top. The following day, though, they had been less than impressed by the atmosphere at the police station, by the sight of police officers lounging around in jeans and T-shirts. The impersonal way they were treated that day, Kate would recall, had rankled.

Gerry was to tell the press that he and Kate had 'never' criticised the Portuguese police. That was true of their public utterances, but did not reflect what they had been feeling and saying in private. For public consumption, Gerry limited himself to observing that the time for 'learning lessons' would come much later.

In fact, there was little to lead them to feel confident about the police in the weeks after Madeleine's disappearance. The insensitivity continued. Worst was the feeling that they were being excluded, told nothing of how the investigation was progressing. Only three weeks after their daughter vanished, in response to repeated requests, was it agreed that two senior officers would meet with them.

Those who briefed them were top echelon, regional Polícia Judiciária chief Guilhermino Encarnação and Luís Neves, who headed the national agency that dealt with serious crime. Though they shared little of substance, the McCanns felt an effort was being made.

There were to be a total of eight such private sessions. After the initial one, PJ spokesman Olegário de Sousa expressed optimism that Madeleine would be 'recovered alive' and said the investigation was continuing. The McCanns, for their part, issued public praise for the 'great, determined work of the PJ'.

Portuguese police records show that they had kept busy, if with little result. There had been the Robert Murat lead to deal with, a second round of interviews with several members of the McCann party, forensic follow-up, witness statements and myriad 'sightings' of potential relevance and none. Madeleine, or a child people thought resembled her, had been seen in the Algarve, in Spain – multiple reports – in North Wales, in Ireland and Scotland, in Egypt and in Mallorca. The police were receiving, as one inspector put it, a 'Babel' of information.

Though the search in and around Praia da Luz had been wound down from May 10th, sporadic work on the ground continued. Police dogs had been brought in to reconnoitre an abandoned house two miles from the Ocean Club. A police frogman had been lowered into a well in a nearby field. All without result. 'An investigation,' spokesman de Sousa reminded the press, 'is not a police novel in which the author of the crime is always unmasked in the end.'

The following day, an unnamed police source said bleakly: 'The truth is that up to now we don't have the slightest idea of the whereabouts of the victim. It is painful to say this, but we have to be realistic. The chances of finding the girl alive are less likely every day.'

The investigation was being scaled back, it was reported, and many detectives who had been drafted in from Lisbon were returning to the capital. A core team of thirty remained active.

To the puzzlement and frustration of the McCann party, the police had for three weeks not issued a description of the man the couple's friend Jane Tanner said she had seen crossing the road with a child in his arms – right outside Apartment 5A – at 9.15 p.m., before it was discovered that Madeleine was missing. When they did so at last, on May 25th, they muddled the key matter of the man's height.

As recorded in a report by the police officer who had spoken with Tanner the night Madeleine vanished, she had reckoned the possible suspect was 5' 10", which the officer rendered as 1.78 metres. The next day at the police station, when she spoke with a different officer, the height was noted as 'cerca de 1.70' – 'about 5 foot 7'. Tanner would say later that the shorter height resulted from mistranslation and difficulty in converting imperial measurement to metric. The significantly shorter height was the measurement given out on May 25th to the Portuguese press, while the English-language media were given the 5' 10" version. Confusion all round.

A couple of weeks later, the McCanns let it be known publicly that they were 'dismayed' by a new comment from police spokesman de Sousa. Years later, when there was no longer a need to be diplomatic, Kate acknowledged that she had in fact been furious. De Sousa had said that the presence of many people in Apartment 5A after Madeleine's disappearance 'may at least have complicated the work of the forensic team. At the worst they may have destroyed all the evidence. This could prove to be fatal for the investigation.'

The police files show that the officers who responded to the apartment that night and should have secured the potential crime scene, had failed to do so. They themselves had been careless in Apartment 5A, had even allowed in dogs. The inference drawn from de Sousa's comments, however, was that the McCanns were to blame for contaminating the scene. That, a source speaking for the parents said, was 'insensitive at the very least. Of course the family are going to search the apartment. If your child goes missing, you search under the beds, in the wardrobes, behind the doors, everywhere. It's inevitable.'

There was something else, something disquieting. Within twenty-four hours, on May 4th, chief investigator Gonçalo Amaral had himself been declared a formal suspect – an *arguido* – in court proceedings that had to do with another missing-girl probe and which were to sully his reputation as a police officer.

The case related to the 2004 disappearance, fourteen miles from Praia da Luz, of an eight-year-old Portuguese girl named Joana Cipriano. Her mother and uncle had been convicted of murdering her, though no body was ever found. Then, from prison, the mother claimed she had been tortured into confessing by three of Amaral's detectives. While the detectives would eventually be cleared, in 2009 Amaral would be handed a suspended sentence for making a false statement.

In 2007, when the charges against Amaral in the Cipriano case were announced just over a month into the Madeleine McCann investigation, the McCanns said through their spokesman that they were 'naturally very concerned'. It does seem remarkable that Amaral should have been allowed to play a leading role in a major investigation – one into the disappearance of another missing girl – while the odour of possible professional misconduct was in the air.

Asked about this years later, the man who served as president of the PJ union in 2007, Carlos Anjos, demurred. 'That's not correct,' he said of Amaral. 'He was overall boss, chief of the department, but uninvolved in the actual investigation . . . in the one case or the other . . . The British police never understood that.'

Just before Amaral was charged in connection with the Cipriano case, the British press ran a story suggesting that he was not taking the McCann case seriously. He had been observed taking lunch in a Portimão fish restaurant in the company of Chief Inspector de Sousa. The report stated that there had been wine and a bottle of Johnny Walker Black Label on the table, and the officers had appeared to be enjoying themselves. They had asked for the television to be turned on to catch the news – this was when the McCanns were in Berlin giving a press conference – and, a fellow diner said, were 'laughing and joking amongst themselves while it was on . . . [they] seemed to be sharing some sort of in-joke.'

Asked whether he thought this scenario acceptable, de Sousa offered a stout defence. The Madeleine probe was 'very, very sad,' he said, 'but a person's free time is for lunch . . . they must eat and drink. It is normal.' Former PJ union president Anjos agreed. 'Amaral,' he said recently, 'started to be pressured by the media, so they learned all the details about his life . . . The British police officers sent out were seen having four-hour lunches, but there was no mention of that.' Amaral himself joked: 'I don't drink whisky. I drink beer at lunchtime. Had they written that, that would have been correct.'

Depending what exactly the laughing and joking had been about, it was indeed normal enough – and the Portuguese had by no means quit the investigation. Even as they reduced the number of men working the case on the ground, the Portuguese had reached out to their British counterparts for specialist assistance.

Responding to a request from Lisbon, the UK's Child Exploitation and Online Protection Centre had early on made an Internet appeal for any information that could help find Madeleine. Behavioural analysts from CEOP had been assisting with the enquiry, and the agency was to maintain its commitment to the case for the long haul.

Specifically, CEOP asked tourists who had been in Praia da Luz weeks before Madeleine went missing to send in any holiday photographs taken in the area of the Ocean Club. Images of people in the background of photographs were compared with those of known British paedophiles and other criminals, using modern facial recognition techniques. None led to any dramatic breakthrough.

Where an offender on a British list could not be ruled out, however, information on the individual was sent to Portugal. 'We did have a list,' said CEOP's Jim Gamble. 'You're going to get expats across the continent who go to live in the sun. You're going to have some who have a sexual interest in children. In a holiday environment, where you have children who are scantily clad – that kind of man is going to be interested. We put together a list of sex offenders who were in the general area of the Algarve, and it was passed to the Portuguese.'

British telecommunications specialists arrived in the Algarve to assist in analysis of mobile-telephone activity in the area of the Ocean Club at the relevant time. When switched on, even if it is not being used for conversation, texting or other activity, a mobile sends a signal to a mast in the area and a timed log is preserved that shows the approximate location of the telephone – 'within give or take maybe a hundred yards', Gamble told the authors. 'There was a wealth of phone data.'

'On its own initiative,' Gamble said, 'one major telecom

provider had captured data relating to the time Madeleine disappeared. That's sounds like a needle-in-a-haystack problem, but it really isn't.'

In the Madeleine case, the hope was twofold. Phone analysis could make it possible for law enforcement to verify the accounts of their movements given by people interviewed. By tracking unrecognised mobile signals, meanwhile, the specialists could try to map the movements of possible abductors. Such signal tracking data had been used five years earlier to convict Ian Huntley for the murder of two little girls in Soham.

A common feature of media coverage of major criminal cases is to ask former police officers to opine on the progress and direction of an investigation. Sometimes a former officer talks on the basis of a briefing by insiders, sometimes based merely on his own background knowledge. The Madeleine McCann case has been no exception. A former Scotland Yard commander, John O'Connor, gave his views in mid-May.

The record, O'Connor suggested, showed that abductions like Madeleine's 'only ever happen in quiet or remote places'. Though many would not agree, he appeared to mean that Praia da Luz was such a place. 'It's more than likely,' he went on, 'that her abductor has her in quarters very close to the crime scene, and cannot escape due to the high profile and activity surrounding her disappearance.' Backtracking, he then pointed out that – contrary to the common assumption – there was still no certainty Madeleine had in fact been taken by anyone. It remained a possibility, he thought, that the child had just wandered off into the night.

In a line suggesting that his purpose was to get across a diplomatic message, O'Connor dismissed criticisms of the Portuguese police. He believed they would solve the case.

About two weeks into the investigation, and whatever their competence, some information of great potential importance reached the local detectives.

On the evening Madeleine disappeared, a large family from Ireland had been out and about in Praia da Luz. Martin Smith, a retired Unilever executive in his late fifties, was there with his wife Mary, son and daughter-in-law Peter and Síle, daughter Aoife and four small children. It was the last night of the holiday for Peter and Síle, and the whole group had been out to dinner and drinks at a local bar. Then they headed back towards the apartment the Smiths owned in a development near the Ocean Club.

While on the way there, all of them except the small children would later remember, they had encountered a man carrying a small child. As Peter Smith put it later, 'It was a common enough sight in a holiday resort, and we didn't think much of it.' Some two weeks later back in Ireland, however, and with Madeleine's disappearance still headline news, Peter and his father woke up to the fact that what they had seen might be important. Martin then called the Portuguese police, who – liaising through the Irish police – asked him and other family members to attend for interview.

So it was that on May 26th, Martin Smith, son Peter and daughter Aoife returned to Portugal to provide formal accounts of what they had seen of the man with the child. They had seen him as he came towards them from a distance of a little over two yards. According to Smith and his son, he had been white, aged perhaps in his mid-thirties, of average build and between 5' 9" and 5' 11". All three Smiths thought he had short, brown hair.

The child the man had been carrying was a girl – about four

years old, Martin Smith and his daughter thought. (Peter Smith reckoned she might have been somewhat younger.) She was white and – all three agreed – had blonde or fair hair. Aoife recalled the hair as having been long. She and her father said she had been wearing what appeared to be pyjama pants – Aoife thought they were 'white or light pink'. She was not wrapped in a blanket. When the family looked back on it, trying to remember, some thought the little girl had been barefoot. Her arms had been dangling and she appeared to be asleep. To Martin Smith, the man had seemed to be carrying the child awkwardly – as though he was not used to doing so.

The nine members of the Smith family were not bunched together when they encountered the man with the child but in different positions on the road. Peter thought his speed had been normal enough, 'with a fairly quick step because he was coming downhill'. Aoife said he had come towards them at 'between a fast walk and a run'. Peter Smith did not recall the man having made an effort to hide his face or avoid their gaze. His father Martin thought otherwise. 'The one thing we noted afterwards was that he gave no greeting,' he said. 'My wife Mary remembered afterwards that she asked him, "Is she asleep?" But he never acknowledged her one way or another. He just put his head down and averted his eyes.'

The Smiths had seen the man at or near the junction of Rua de Escola Primária and Rua 25 de Abril. Study of the Praia da Luz street map suggests he had come from the general direction of the McCanns' apartment and the point at which Jane Tanner had also seen a man carrying a child – about four or five minutes' walk away.

The time of the encounter, according to the Smiths, was about 10 p.m., which would mean it occurred about forty-five minutes after the Jane Tanner sighting, and at exactly the time Kate McCann discovered that Madeleine was missing. Investigators would debate the possible significance of both sightings for years to come.

Were the Tanner and Smith sightings both of an abductor – the same man in both cases – making off with Madeleine? While the descriptions of the individual Tanner saw and the man the Smiths saw have striking similarities, they differ on his hairstyle. Tanner's man, as she remembered it, had hair 'long to the neck'. Aoife Smith recalled the man she saw as having hair that was 'short at the back'.

Witness recollections of details after the event can be notoriously faulty. If Tanner and the Smiths saw different individuals, though, was one of them an abductor and the other merely an innocent parent walking home with his child? If so, which was which? If the person the Smiths saw at 10 p.m. was an abductor – and if the person Tanner saw forty-five minutes earlier was not – that would substantially alter the timeline of the evening's events. But – and it remained a large but – is it possible that neither Tanner nor the Smiths saw a person of significance? Were both their sightings of some innocent parent? In 2007, in a case virtually devoid of substantial leads of any sort, it was best to keep an open mind.

Had the recordings made on a CCTV camera near the scene of the Smiths' encounter been examined in timely fashion, chief investigator Amaral was to say, he thought film of the man they saw would have been found. That was not done, however. 'I asked my officers to gather all the CCTV camera footage in Luz,' Amaral said ruefully, 'but by the time they got to this [location] the film from this camera had been wiped. It was a mistake and I shall always regret it. I do feel Madeleine was let down.'

Martin Smith, for his part, has said he 'found the Portuguese

cops not to be the most efficient bunch'. He thought they failed
to take his information seriously. Justifiably or not, other English
people touched by the case would echo that feeling. One was a
supermarket owner named George Brooks, who said he promptly
reported an odd incident that occurred just before 6 a.m. on May
4th, the very morning after Madeleine's disappearance.

Brooks had been up before dawn that day to drop his son off
at the train station in Lagos, some five miles from Praia da Luz.
It was still pitch-dark, he recalled later, when as he left for home
he caught a man and a woman in his headlights. Like the two
men seen late the previous evening not far from the McCanns'
apartment, they were carrying a child.

Though it was hard to see them clearly, Brooks said, he thought
the couple were both in their thirties. The man was 'less than 6
foot tall', had 'shoulder-length hair and looked quite tanned'. The
woman was 'dark-haired and slim'. To him, they did not look
British, or like tourists. What struck him as odd was the way
they were handling the child. 'You could tell from their posture,'
he said, 'that they were trying to carry the child without anyone
seeing it, and they were extremely disturbed when I caught them
in my headlights.'

Brooks thought they had looked 'very suspicious' and called
the police when he got home. However, the record quotes him
as saying that it was decided the episode 'would not be of interest
to the investigation'. Another document states that the matter
had been looked into at the time – an assertion that does not
accord with a report reflecting an effort to follow up months
later.

There is no way now of knowing whether Brooks really saw
something suspicious or whether he merely startled an innocent
couple hurrying along with their child. The spot at which he saw

them, he pointed out at the time, was close not only to the railway station but to Lagos marina. The proximity of the marina, with its dozens of boats, may be of relevance. Detectives spent time at the harbour early on in the investigation and seized records of vessels that came and went in the period just before Madeleine went missing and just afterwards. The possibility that she had been taken out of Portugal by sea, some two hundred miles across the Straits of Gibraltar to Morocco, loomed large in May 2007.

Six days after the disappearance, a Norwegian woman named Mari Olli walked into the shop at a petrol station in the Moroccan city of Marrakesh. It was there, as she was waiting at the cash desk, that she noticed a girl aged about three or four standing beside a man. 'I looked at her because she was very sweet,' Olli would recall. 'It's unusual to see a small blonde girl standing alone [in Morocco] . . . she looked sad. I looked at her, she looked at me. Then she turned to the man and said something that sounded like, "Can we see Mummy soon?" I am not sure whether he replied.'

Something about the situation had struck her as strange at the time, Olli was to say. She had meant to say something to her husband when she got back to their car, but did not – the couple were preoccupied with finding the route back to the ferry port to leave Morocco for their home in Spain. She had not been paying attention to the news while on holiday and did not know that a little blonde girl had gone missing, knew nothing of the hunt for her. It was only the following day, when she did watch the news, heard about Madeleine and saw her picture, that she woke up to what she might have seen. She was, she said, 'Ninety-nine per cent convinced of the similarity.' She called the police.

The wheels moved slowly. The Spanish police, Olli said, did

not even want to take her call. She called the UK and spoke to an officer at Scotland Yard. No one called her back. She phoned again on May 23rd. The record indicates that it was not until June 6th, more than three weeks after her first report of what she had seen, that Olli was contacted by the Portuguese police.

Just back in Portugal from their trips to Germany and Holland, Gerry and Kate McCann flew to Morocco, were shown a filmed television interview Olli had done and emerged from the viewing despondent. Though the lead was a strong one, or so it seemed to them, it had not been followed up in a timely fashion. It was not only the delay in interviewing Olli that troubled them. There had been a CCTV camera in the shop where the witness had seen the girl she thought likely to have been Madeleine. By the time police asked to see the relevant day's footage, however, it had been routinely wiped.

Fragile hope dashed, the McCanns returned to Praia da Luz. There was to be a veritable cascade of further reported Madeleine sightings in Morocco, the police record shows, over the weeks and months that followed. Not a jot of tangible evidence, though, indicates that there was substance to any of it. There would be excitement, in September, when a woman produced a photograph – taken while visiting Morocco – that showed a little blonde girl being carried on the back of a dark-haired Moroccan peasant woman. The press set off in full cry and – more seriously – CEOP applied computer techniques to examine the photograph.

The girl in the picture turned out not to be Madeleine but the daughter of the woman seen carrying her. It had looked as though she was Caucasian, and about the right age, build and complexion to have been Madeleine McCann. In Morocco, however, there is a higher incidence of fair-haired people than in other parts of the region.

Dr Robert Jenkins, a facial recognition expert consulted during the brief flurry of interest in the photograph, pointed out that the girl in the picture could be one of thousands of Moroccan children.

'Presumably,' he added drily, 'there is a good deal of wishful thinking here.'

Wishful thinking by many, and hope against desperate hope by Gerry and Kate McCann.

10

The McCanns had maintained their astonishing pace – and the highest possible profile. On the eve of the swing through Berlin, Amsterdam and Morocco, Gerry and Kate appeared on the BBC's *Crimewatch* programme to make another appeal for information. Looking exhausted, Kate held up pink and white pyjamas identical to those Madeleine had worn the night she went missing but noticeably smaller. They belonged to her two-year-old sister Amelie.

In a steady voice, she spoke of the good people – the majority – who had given such 'amazing' support over the weeks. Then she went on: 'There are a few bad people in the world, but also there are a few sad people. And I guess I'm hoping that it's someone sad who just wanted our daughter.'

'It's not too late,' Gerry said, 'to hand her over . . . It'd only take one phone call, and someone has a key bit of information. And it may be someone close to whoever has Madeleine – it may be the person themselves – they can phone and tell the police where Madeleine is.'

In the days that followed, the news about the McCanns kept coming. They intended to stay on in Portugal until the end of the summer, a spokesman said on June 9th – 'the place where mentally they make a connection . . . As far as they're concerned this is where Madeleine still is.' Then, while in Morocco, Gerry said they planned next to have a 'period of reflection'. The following weekend, Father's Day, the quote was: 'I can't think about anything other than how we can help try to get Madeleine back.'

Not a week later, there was a worldwide event for Madeleine. In fifty countries, at almost three hundred locations, batches of fifty yellow balloons were released to mark the fiftieth day since Madeleine had gone missing. The balloons in Ireland, launched by schoolchildren, bore phone numbers and email addresses that people could contact should they have useful information. In California, fifty white doves were released. In Afghanistan, fifty kites were flown – each bearing a picture of Madeleine. In Praia da Luz, Gerry and Kate were photographed sending the balloons into the air. The next phase of the campaign, Gerry said, would be 'event-based'.

Unhappy though life now was for the McCanns, it was taking on a pattern. Campaign planning was central to their routine, Gerry's blog for the final three weeks of June shows. There was now an emphasis on maintaining public awareness in Portugal, and on becoming increasingly involved in the international debate on children's issues. The couple met with police to keep up with developments – there were in truth not many at this stage – and to discuss how to handle people who thought they had seen Madeleine. Gerry was constantly struggling to deal with the avalanche of letters and emails their efforts had triggered.

Their friends of the disastrous holiday period, who had stayed on long after their original departure date, were gone now. Other friends and relatives, flying out to offer what solace they could, came and went. Family days, time with Sean and Amelie at the beach or swimming pool, were now especially important. Religious observance remained a constant and was much more than routine.

On June 12th, Gerry had noted in his blog that forty days and forty nights had passed since Madeleine's disappearance – an allusion to Jesus' ordeal in the wilderness – and that he and Kate had gone to the Praia da Luz church to ask that Madeleine was safe and would be found.

Kate was praying fervently every day. She alternated between beseeching the Lord to bring her daughter back and becoming irritated that He did not respond to her prayers. 'Would this make or break my faith?' she had asked herself, she told an interviewer from the Roman Catholic weekly *The Tablet*. She concluded that it had not broken it. 'It has done the opposite. It has given us hope and strength.'

Their Catholic faith aside, both Kate and Gerry had for some time in their desperation been considering the help offered by those wedded to a very different form of the spiritual – psychics.

Individuals of that ilk had dabbled in the Madeleine case from early on. They included: practitioners of reiki, who believe in their ability to transfer 'universal energy' through their palms and who answered an Internet appeal for positive thinking in aid of Madeleine's safe return; a dowser in Austria – dowsing involves locating an element or items, usually using some form of tool – who, using his pendulum, concluded that the missing girl was in a named village in Spain; a medium who told police in the UK she had obtained information on Madeleine while holding a picture of the little girl; a clairvoyant who asserted in late May that Madeleine was alive, in a crate aboard the Egyptian river cruise ship the MS *Andrea* and would disembark at a given time; and a Dutchman styling himself an 'angel-communicator' who had contacts with friends of Kate and Gerry (who had lived in Holland in 2005) and who claimed to have envisioned the kidnapper as a thirty-eight-year-old man with a female accomplice.

These particular claims may well not have reached the McCanns themselves. Kate and Gerry received thousands of communications from psychics, though, and devoted a good deal of time and effort to following up on some of them.

Five days after Madeleine's disappearance, according to a British police report, Kate McCann had been in touch to say that:

> A friend of her aunt and uncle from Leicester had a friend that had a strong vision that Madeleine was on a boat with a man in the marina in Lagos. This person arrived in Portugal and has spoken to Kate. They have visited the marina and identified the boat as 'Shearwater' . . . I spoke with Kate today and she has given me photographs of the boat. She has also given me a photograph of a man who had been on the boat. This is not the man that the woman had in her vision . . . This is very important to Kate . . . and she is very pleased that we are making enqs. into the matter . . . Once the enqs. have been completed can we please let her know the result?

The matter was followed up ten days later, Portuguese police records show. Three officers made their way to the Lagos marina, checked out the boat named *Shearwater*, photographed it, talked with the British citizen currently on-board and learned from harbour records that it had not left its moorings in the past two months. The senior police investigator involved filed a report noting that he had found 'nothing strange . . . or anything that aroused any interest'.

Three weeks after Madeleine's disappearance, the press reported that 'top psychic' Diane Lazarus was about to fly to Portugal 'to join the hunt'. Lazarus, who said she had been invited by a close friend of Gerry and Kate McCann and 'would never go to Portugal without the consent of the family', offered preliminary findings even before leaving.

According to her, Madeleine was alive in Spain, had been made to look like a boy by cutting her hair, was being well looked after and 'will be returned to her mummy and daddy'. She had been abducted, following surveillance, by a man 'with olive skin, dark hair and a drawn, skinny face'. Several culprits were involved, including a woman. They had 'felt [that] as the McCanns have two other children taking Maddie wouldn't be quite so bad'.

After a few days in Praia da Luz, and having visited Apartment 5A, Lazarus expanded on her assertions. She now claimed to be able to describe the male abductor in more detail, including his height – details that sounded very like Jane Tanner's description of the man she had seen carrying a child near the apartment. He had made his getaway in a 'large silver car'. She could 'actually see' Madeleine 'eating yoghurt from a pot'. She, two boys and the abductors were holed up 'in an old-fashioned stone building' near Madrid. 'The people who have got her,' she added darkly, 'have links to Sicily.'

In June, acting on another psychic's tip about Madeleine passed on by Interpol, police searched an area in the Republic of Ireland. Nothing was found. A Texan named Brian Ladd, meanwhile, who claims to be 'the world's most accurate psychic' – his speciality is dreaming – offered the Portuguese police sketches that he claimed had relevance.(This fellow was to stay at it, with a YouTube video entitled 'Madeleine is alive, and we know exactly where she is!')

By late July, Diane Lazarus would be back – this time with bad news. Now she could 'see' that Madeleine had not been treated very well. 'Now,' she said, 'I don't think things look too good for her . . . I don't like being the bearer of bad news.' She had, Lazarus added, told the police in the UK what she 'knew' and said that the UK police would liaise with their Portuguese counterparts.

In just the first month of their work, the Portuguese police accumulated two three-inch folders of messages from psychics of one sort or another. Their spokesman, Olegário de Sousa, said each claim was taken seriously – 'in case it might be from the kidnapper . . . If there is sufficient information to follow up, then we do. If not, we can't do anything.'

Chief investigator Amaral would say that he and his colleagues were 'men of facts . . . rather sceptical', but added that, during the Madeleine probe, the FBI had recommended bringing in a medium the agency sometimes consulted. The view of a former senior FBI agent, John Douglas, is that 'a psychic should be a last resort as an investigative tool'.

The US Department of Justice, meanwhile, has warned that many psychics are fraudulent or at best misguided individuals who 'want to help so much that they have self-induced visions . . . Keep an open mind – *and a closed pocket-book*.'

In spite of claims by psychics that they have in the past come up with key information and leads, British police also take their information with a large pinch of salt. 'I have consulted with all of my senior investigating officers,' David Mirfield, head of West Midlands Police Major Investigations Unit, responded to a question in 2006, 'and none can recall using such a person . . . I am not personally aware of any occasion where the use of a psychic has resulted in the detection of a murder.' London's Metropolitan

Police, while acknowledging that it welcomed 'any information', said in 2009 that it knew of no enquiries 'significantly progressed solely by information provided by a psychic medium'.

Psychics and the like would persist in producing theories on Madeleine for years to come. The McCanns, for their part, though increasingly disenchanted, were slow to give up on them. In 2008, when information came in from 'psychics' who had produced sketches of a supposed Madeleine abductor for a television show, they asked that they be shared with the private detectives they were by then using.

Kate McCann has explained very understandably, why the couple were long so receptive to psychics – to almost anything that might hold out hope. 'Not knowing where your child is, how she is, who she is with, and when you will see her again, is a glimpse of hell.'

That the McCanns were vulnerable in many ways, psychics or no psychics, had become very evident by early June 2007. There were ways, by then, in which the massive media response had started to go sour.

Gerry McCann was to make no bones about how they had deliberately courted publicity. That first day, when they had got back to their apartment to find a horde of reporters waiting for them, they had had to make a quick decision: 'Either we didn't interact with them, or we did – and there were two reasons: one, we thought it would help in the search for Madeleine, and – two – we thought it would be easier on us as well to interact and work with them rather than go away and hide . . . We have done everything I think that could have an effect on the outcome.'

They had – in spades. They had been praised in many quarters for their handling of the media, and for the most important reason of all. 'The media strategy of the family has been a huge success,' said the chief executive of the National Missing Persons Helpline, Paul Tuohy. 'We know publicity works because coverage we produce for other missing people helps us to directly find ten of them every week.'

Pre-empting possible criticism of the couple's high-profile tour of Europe, columnist Faith Eckersall put it simply: 'The McCanns understand the game.' The two medical doctors from Leicestershire – Gerry especially – had rapidly got the hang of the media machine; had given the press something to feed on virtually every day. What the couple had not understood, perhaps, were the ways in which playing the press could boomerang.

As June began, a Foreign Office official rang Clarence Mitchell, the emissary it had sent out to be the McCanns' spokesman, expressing concern that Mitchell himself was 'becoming the story'. He was withdrawn shortly afterwards, though he would later leave his government post and return of his own volition.

In the *Sunday Times* of June 3rd, the columnist India Knight noted that there was 'clearly a growing rumble of unease out there at the McCanns' omnipresence in the papers and on television. No aspect of their grief is deemed too private to share with the media . . . Enough, detractors say.' Personal tragedy, she was to write later, had become 'popular entertainment'.

In the *Guardian*, Simon Jenkins noted – not with approval – the fact that the Madeleine story had led the six o'clock news on the BBC, ahead of Gordon Brown's bid to become prime minister. 'To suggest that this might not be a good way of finding a missing child,' he thought, was 'clearly spitting in the wind. It is possible that publicity in the McCann case might have induced witnesses to come forward in the immediate aftermath of the girl's disappearance. It is equally possible that media hysteria could drive a cornered criminal to desperate measures to cover their tracks. Is it worth the risk?'

Jenkins also noted something else. An episode billed by the press as 'Every parent's nightmare,' he wrote, had become 'the nation's nightmare. Families closed their doors to the world, hugged their children close.' There was truth to that, for a mass of reports suggested that many parents in the UK were resorting to extraordinary measures to safeguard their offspring – as though there were not one child missing in Portugal but the imminent threat of paedophile attacks and abductions all over the place and all the time.

Some parents in Bournemouth set up a group called Parentally Aware Neighbourhood, members of which, wearing yellow bibs, escorted their children to school. Signs were erected warning that paedophiles were 'not welcome'. In Birchington in Kent, a group of mothers said the furthest they allowed their children to roam was to the garden gate.

In 1970, reportedly, 80 per cent of primary-school children walked to school on their own. This statistic had fallen to 9 per cent by 2007. Now, in the midst of the Madeleine furore, the Birchington mothers agreed that to allow their children the freedoms they once enjoyed would be irresponsible. Two eight-year-olds in the village told a reporter of their fear that if they went beyond the garden fence, they 'might get kidnapped or taken by a stranger,' and that 'In the park you might get raped.'

There were reports – difficult to know their accuracy – that some parents were resorting to all kinds of gadgets to protect their children. Devices on the market included: hidden cameras, mobile phones that made it possible to locate your child from the family computer, pay-as-you-go tracking services, electronic wristbands, 'toddler tag' bracelets and specially tagged pyjamas.

Implantable microchips, it was said, were about to come on the market.

Nothing suggested that such precautions were rational. 'You are more likely to be hit by lightning than have your child abducted,' said Michele Elliott, director of the child-protection charity Kidscape. 'We must be wary of sending our children the message that the world is such a dangerous place that they need to be tagged.' Nevertheless, it was reported that sales of child-monitoring and tracking devices had noticeably increased. According to a spokeswoman for the long-established company Kiddicare, the Madeleine case had 'frightened' parents.

A *Times* columnist noted not only the panicky trend but its causes. 'If I've heard one parent say that they're now holding their own child a bit tighter, a bit closer,' wrote David Aaronovitch, 'then I've heard a hundred . . . But it isn't our child. Our child is safe . . . We want to "learn lessons", but there are twin problems. First, such an abduction could happen to anyone, not just a child left alone in a room for twenty minutes. The second is that it hardly ever happens to anyone. In other words, there may be no lessons to learn, just the void of the child's disappearance and the pathology of the person who took her.'

Observations like this, in the 'serious' papers, were levelled at the nature of much of the media coverage and the symptoms of public panic, not at Gerry and Kate McCann for fuelling it. From early on, though, there was sniping at the couple themselves. Some early barbs were about who they were and the advantage their position in society gave them.

Several listeners expressed this view on a BBC radio programme. 'White middle-class families look better on the news,' one said. Another thought the Madeleine story got more airtime than other cases of missing children because 'this victim is cute and middle-class'. Another asked, 'Would a less fortunate family staying in a different, much cheaper resort have received the same attention and sympathy?'

Though both came from humble backgrounds, the McCanns were of course both doctors and quite affluent. Gerry was and is a cardiologist, and Kate had been working part-time as a GP. Their income bracket aside, however, the massive publicity they received was due to a combination of factors. The initiative and commitment that made Gerry what he was could be switched to the unfamiliar task of fighting for his lost daughter. There was also the fact that – in the very first hours, and even before the McCanns' fight got under way – the British press had flocked to cover the story. Finally, key to the phenomenon, was the fact that the case was an almost unheard-of event and that it broke in the age of the Internet.

Statistics on children going missing in Europe are woefully inadequate, uncoordinated between countries. However, it is clearly very, very rare for British children under ten to disappear while abroad. A trawl by the authors identified only four such cases – including Madeleine McCann – since 1981.

That year, a two-year-old girl named Katrice Lee vanished from a British NAAFI food store in Germany while her parents were shopping. Nine-year-old Rachel Charles disappeared in 1990 in Portugal after getting off the school bus near her home thirty miles from Praia da Luz. The following year, twenty-one-month-old Ben Needham disappeared while outside his grandparents' farmhouse on the Greek island of Kos. Rachel Charles was found dead, strangled, days after her disappearance. The fates of Katrice Lee and Ben Needham remain unknown.

While these cases had been reported – that of Ben Needham received extensive coverage at the time and since – they were obscure compared to that of Madeleine. Katrice's father, Richard Lee, and Ben's mother, now Kerry Grist, have both sympathised with the McCanns. Both, however, have expressed resentment that their children never received the official British support allotted to the Madeleine case.

A major criticism, one to which they were arguably vulnerable, was levelled at the McCanns from the start. Why, the *Daily Express* had asked within thirty-six hours, had they left their children alone in Apartment 5A while they dined with friends some distance away? Why had they not placed them in the care of the nannies at the Ocean Club crèche?

Some comments were gentle but uncomprehending. 'I am finding it hard to feel complete sympathy for her parents,' a woman in Scotland wrote, 'because I would never dream of leaving my own children on their own, especially abroad on holiday.'

Some were understanding. It had been a 'grave mistake', a writer in Northern Ireland thought, but 'in reality it's not unusual for tourists to lock their children in hotel rooms at night and adjourn to socialise.' In fact, of course, the McCanns had chosen not to lock the patio doors of their apartment.

Some did not reprove them at all. 'I have taken my family on a Mark Warner holiday,' an academic wrote. 'We did exactly what Kate and Gerry did; left the kids and checked them regularly when we ate . . . The McCanns did as countless thousands of other parents have done.'

Many others, however, were scathing – and in ways that reflected the social divide. 'Ponder what the media and public reaction would have been if these parents were non-professional, unreligious, working class,' a man wrote in to the BBC's *Newsnight* programme. 'It is likely they would be roundly condemned/

hounded and their other children taken into care on the grounds of culpable negligence.'

Versions of that sentiment were widespread. It was reported that an astonishing seventeen thousand people eventually signed an online petition to the prime minister demanding that social services 'investigate the circumstances which led to three-year-old Madeleine McCann and her younger siblings being left unattended in an unlocked, ground floor hotel room'. The petition was rejected.

In Portugal, newspaper after newspaper expressed the view that leaving the three small children alone had been – as one paper put it – 'pure irresponsibility'. (To the contrary, as reported earlier in these pages, the McCanns' friends said they had been the most conscientious of the group in checking on their children.)

The McCanns themselves openly acknowledged time and again, that they had been at fault on the night Madeleine vanished. 'No one,' Gerry told the BBC three weeks after Madeleine's disappearance, 'will ever feel as guilty as we do over the fact that we weren't with Madeleine at the time.'

Less than two weeks after Gerry's comment about blaming themselves, during their visit to Berlin, a German radio reporter named Sabine Mueller asked a question that went to the possibility of a very different sort of guilt – criminal guilt.

'How do you feel,' Mueller asked, 'about the fact that more and more people seem to be pointing the finger at you, saying the way you behave is not the way people would normally behave when their child is abducted, and they seem to imply that you might have something to do with it?'

Some of those who heard the reporter's full question audibly gasped. Kate McCann did not catch all of it and began saying

– yet again – that she and her husband were responsible parents, that she thought only a small minority were critical of them.

Gerry had heard the question. 'I have never heard before,' he said, 'that anyone considers us suspects in this. The Portuguese police certainly don't.'

But they would.

11

On July 3rd, Gerry and Kate openly sought to improve relations with their host country's police and press. Two months to the day after Madeleine's disappearance, they told Portuguese journalists they felt they had a 'good working relationship' with the Polícia Judiciária and were sustained by the support and goodwill of the Portuguese people. Kate used the moment to say – though privately she was by no means convinced – that she was absolutely sure the Portuguese police were '100 per cent committed to finding Madeleine'. She was grateful, she said, that relations with the force had improved.

The real situation was not healthy at all, and never had been. Officers of the Polícia Judiciária had been flouting the strict secrecy regulations by leaking information and – insidiously – innuendo. Within hours of taking the first statements from the McCanns and their friends, regional PJ chief Guilhermino Encarnação – speaking off the record – had told the *Diário de Notícias*, a major daily paper, that the depositions were 'confused', 'a very badly told story'. According to José Oliveira, the paper's crime reporter, the PJ 'didn't believe the theory that [Madeleine] had been kidnapped. The police started to suspect the parents from the word go.'

There was also slander. Within two weeks, former PJ Chief Inspector José Barra da Costa had gone on the national television channel Rádio e Televisão de Portugal – RTP – citing 'people who know' as having told him that the McCanns were 'a couple who practise "swinging", that is, sex relations between couples and then changing partners.' The waiters at the Tapas restaurant, a source has suggested, would have thought members of the McCann party leaving the table from time to time 'strange, mysterious'. (The toing and froing, of course, was in fact to check on their children.)

There was not an iota of evidence to support the 'swingers' claim and the police themselves publicly disowned it. Repetition of the slur in the British press would later become part of a successful libel suit by the McCanns.

The interview session to which the McCanns invited the Portuguese press had been an exercise in damage limitation. Just three days earlier, the weekly *Sol* had published a three-thousand-word article headlined 'The Madeleine Case – A Pact of Silence'. It again harped on about the notion that the accounts the McCanns and their friends had given of the night Madeleine vanished were not consistent. 'The account of that last dinner varies among the members of the group,' it said. It was 'a story that will change'. Kate's account of the circumstances of the moment she realised her daughter was missing was a 'highly unlikely scenario'. Gerry 'changes his version several times'.

For the *Sol* article, PJ regional chief Encarnação said on the record: 'We cannot rule out the hypothesis of the family and friends as suspects.'

Encarnação leavened this startling assertion by adding that other leads were of course never neglected, that 'everyone who was at the resort at the time are suspects'. *Sol*'s editors felt it safe, nevertheless, to open the article with a flat statement that

Madeleine's parents and their friends were 'suspects in the investigation'.

A reporter for Britain's *Sunday Times Magazine*, David James Smith, would later interview the article's co-author, Felicia Cabrita. He reported: 'The information had been handed to Cabrita by the police – she says she acquired the material through good journalism, which in a sense it was.'

Amaral, for his part, was also to place his own interpretation on a bizarre episode that took place a week after the McCanns' conciliatory press conference. The episode occurred with his officers' full knowledge and cooperation, yet he would use it to cast suspicion on the McCanns. In fact, there is no reason to doubt that it reflected the same combination of tragic resolve and suggestibility that led the couple to give psychics a hearing. Back in May, days after the saga began, a message from South Africa had reached Portuguese police. It referred them, without explanation, to a recent report on a long-running Johannesburg television programme, suggesting that doing so might lead 'to the appearance of little Madeleine'. The message was filed and forgotten.

Had the police bothered to check out the television report, they would probably still have ignored it. The programme had reported on the activities of one Danie Krügel, a former policeman who claimed to have invented a miraculous gadget that could locate precious metals – and missing individuals. Using just one hair from a missing person in the device, and taking readings from different vantage points, he could determine where the person was – whether alive or dead. He called his procedure the 'matter orientation system', or MOS. Asked how much success he had had with it, he replied: 'A lot, a lot, a lot.' The programme interviewed several people who corroborated his claim.

Asked by the programme's presenter whether he was a psychic, Krügel replied, 'I'm a Christian . . . This is science, science, science! That is what is so fantastic about it. It is tied to the science we hear but people didn't realise it . . . It's just science.' Given his gadget's 'massive potential', the programme noted, Krügel refused to divulge how it worked. From the little he did reveal, however, it supposedly married DNA science to GPS technology.

Krügel's interest in helping find Madeleine, Kate has recalled, had reached them early on. They became more interested, some-time later, when a woman friend of Krügel's appeared in Praia da Luz to sing his praises. He had references from South African police personnel, she said, and supposed backing from the coun-try's minister for justice.

Kate would nevertheless later wonder how it was that she and her husband had overlooked the fact that Krügel's marvellous inven-tion had not been tested or vouched for by any independent authority. After all, the couple were themselves doctors, trained in professional disciplines. What won them over, perhaps, was the fact that Krügel appeared to be a decent man. There was, too, the fact that he professed to be a fellow Christian. The overriding factor, though, was that they were by now at their wits' end.

And so the McCanns asked a relative in the UK to go to their home in Leicestershire and try to find specimens of Madeleine's hair. She came up with several – from inside the hood of a coat of Madeleine's – and they were duly sent off to Krügel in South Africa. Armed with these treasures, he soon told them, he found he could receive 'signals' pointing to Praia da Luz – even from five thousand miles away. Now, he said, he needed to meet them in person.

So it was that, at one of their meetings with the PJ's regional director Encarnação, the McCanns asked for police help in facilitating Krügel's arrival in Portugal – special precautions were necessary, he had said, to safeguard his miraculous device.

The former South African policeman flew in on July 15th, huddled with the McCanns, enlisted the cooperation of the police and asked for nothing to be said until he had completed his work. What he then did, according to chief investigator Amaral, was to move to different points of the compass in the proximity of Praia da Luz and – with one of Madeleine's hairs inserted into his secret gadget – trace lines on the map. Where the lines intersected, according to Krügel, there Madeleine was to be found. Then, after only a few days and having submitted a report to the PJ, he departed.

While Krügel's report remains unseen, we know something about it. His gadget, he asserted, had produced a 'static signal' in an area some three yards wide near the eastern end of Praia da Luz beach. If the implications of 'static signal' were not obvious, Krügel's report is said to have included the words: 'Madeleine's body is in this area.' 'I am convinced this is the place,' he would say months later, 'this is the place where Madeleine is buried.' Yet he also said: 'If I look at the area, there is a very, very slight possibility that she could be alive.' The slight possibility, he said the following year, was that she might be 'held hostage' in one of the houses in the area indicated.

The self-styled inventor was still holding forth as late as 2010, calling for a proper search of the area – and offering to train Scotland Yard officers in how to use his device. By that time, he had long since been claiming his device could also detect cancer in blood samples. A book he had written entitled *Light in Darkness* – the cover is emblazoned with a shimmering crucifix – features the words: 'The greatest discovery of all time.'

The authors asked the eminent scientist Professor Wolfram

Meier-Augenstein, a senior member of the British Association for Human Identification and an adviser to the UK's National Policing Improvement Agency (NPIA), about the claims Krügel had made for his gadget. 'Analysing and identifying a complex molecule such as DNA remotely by waving a handheld device through the air,' he wrote, 'is such a preposterous claim that words fail me. This alleged device could not detect DNA in hair even if such a device existed, for the simple reason that hair (as opposed to a hair's follicle) does not contain any DNA.

'How does Krügel's device establish a link between DNA and GPS coordinates? . . . None of the existing national DNA databases are connected to the GPS satellites orbiting the earth. Secondly, only the DNA of people charged with or convicted of a criminal offence is entered into these databases, which leaves out Madeleine McCann.' Krügel's claims, Professor Meier-Augenstein told the authors, are 'enough to cause my BS detector to go off the scale'.

To their lasting regret, Madeleine's parents failed to see through the South African's pretensions. A year later, by which time police suspicions of them had drastically surfaced, then waned and he himself had been removed as chief investigator, Gonçalo Amaral would weave that failure, and the couple's resorting to psychics, into a possible sinister scenario.

It was at the time of the Krügel episode, Amaral wrote in his 2008 book, that 'it seemed as though, suddenly, the McCann couple had awoken to the harsh reality – the strong possibility of their daughter being dead.'

To back up this assertion, Amaral told his readers that Kate had started to comment 'on information regarding the location of her daughter's body . . . provided to her by people with psychic or paranormal abilities . . . that the body could be in a sewage pipe that disgorges on to the beach at Luz, or in the cliffs at the beginning of that beach.' Just weeks later, Amaral pointed out, the McCanns had introduced Krügel, with his 'supposed cutting-edge technologies dedicated to locating bodies'.

'However naive we may have been,' Amaral told his readers, 'there was a time when we felt that Kate . . .was prepared to disclose the location of her daughter's body without committing herself to the information or compromising herself.'

It was at that time and in that atmosphere, according to Amaral, that his team thought it was necessary to go back to square one of the investigation and the 'starting point,' Apartment 5A. He reached out for 'the best in forensic investigation, with the help of specialised canine expertise,' that the British police could offer. The Polícia Judiciária formally requested assistance in determining 'the absence or presence of M. McCann's concealed remains'.

The request went to the National Policing Improvement Agency and Mark Harrison, then its national search adviser. Harrison, a twenty-year veteran who also held the post of visiting professor at Southampton University, specialised in the use of enhanced search techniques. His brief for the work on the McCann case included acting as 'critical friend' to the Portuguese officer in charge of the search for possible remains, assisting in the use of non-Portuguese assets and offering a view on unorthodox attempts to locate Madeleine. His reports would be dry and to the point, not at all like Amaral's.

Harrison's rejection of the claims in Danie Krügel's report was not understated: 'highly unlikely', 'poor quality', 'low value'. In preparation for the serious business at hand, 'the possibility that Madeleine McCann has been murdered and her body is concealed within the areas previously searched', he flew out to the Algarve, walked relevant areas by day and by night, flew over them by helicopter and ploughed through the case records. Then he suggested locations he thought might reward further sophisticated examination.

Unsurprisingly, he called for new work on the Praia da Luz beach and shoreline, with its high cliffs; an open area near the village that featured empty buildings, dense vegetation and wells; Robert Murat's house, garden and cars – Murat was still, on paper at least, a suspect, though that status would be lifted a year later – and both Apartment 5A and the apartments their friends had been using when Madeleine disappeared. More innovatively, he called for the use of ground-penetrating radar (GPR) and the introduction from the UK of specially trained dogs.

The background on police use of dogs – and the results of the work they were to do in the Madeleine case – is highly controversial.

During the two years prior to the request from the Portuguese police force, Harrison had worked with a fellow officer with many years of experience as a police dog handler, Martin Grime. Grime, who was also used by the FBI in its Canine Forensic Program, had been working with dogs for thirty-five years. By 2007, his team consisted of two springer spaniels, a breed first described in England almost five centuries ago. Once favourites of the aristocracy, spaniels have long been used by hunters to flush out and retrieve game birds. In modern times, their remarkable sense of smell has led them to be used as sniffer dogs for a variety of work.

It has been calculated that dogs have 200 million nasal receptors, compared with 5 million in humans. Springer spaniels have been recruited by the British army and by the police to locate weapons caches, sniff out explosives, search out illegal immigrants and even – in prisons – to locate illicit mobile phones. One celebrated dog was reportedly credited with being able to tell the difference between inmates' phones and those legitimately held by prison officers. In searching for missing people, and suspected victims of homicide, however, it is these canines' ability to detect the scent of blood and hidden corpses that counts.

One of the dogs Grime was using at the time of the Madeleine investigation was a three-year-old spaniel bitch named Keela, trained exclusively to search out human blood. In handler Grime's words, she could 'accurately locate human blood on items that have been subjected to "clean-up operations" or . . . been subjected to several washing machine cycles. In training, she has accurately located samples of blood on property up to thirty-six years old. In order for the dog to locate the source, the blood must have "dried" in situ . . . She will search for and locate blood in such small proportions that it is unlikely to be recovered by the forensic science procedures in place at this time.'

The other dog on Grime's team was a seven-year-old male named Eddie, who had been taught to sniff out 'human remains and body fluids, including blood, in any environment or terrain'. In the United States, in his work with the FBI, the dog had been able to target human remains. Because such training was not sanctioned in Britain, he and similar dogs were taught using human blood and decomposing piglets. According to Grime, research indicated that 'the scent of human and pig decomposing material is so similar that we are unable to "train" the dog to distinguish between the two.'

An important point, Grime emphasised, was that Eddie had been 'introduced to the scent of a decomposing body, *not foodstuff*. This ensures that the dog disregards the "bacon sandwich" and "kebab" etc. that is ever-present in the background environment.'

In six years' work, on more than two hundred cases, Grime told the Portuguese, Eddie had never 'alerted' – barked – in response to meat-based foodstuffs or roadkill.

Working either alone or with another dog, Grime wrote, Eddie had proved useful in the investigation of three murders of women in 2004. Attracta Harron, a librarian in Northern Ireland, had gone missing on her way back from church. During a search by Eddie of the rear footwell of a burnt-out car, the dog promptly alerted to the presence of human material – a sample that turned out to have the DNA of the victim. It later found Mrs Harron's body buried in a riverbank behind a suspect's home.

Amanda Edwards, a young nurse in Wiltshire, disappeared one morning after dropping off her boyfriend. The dog's search of a former boyfriend's house located bloodstains later identified as Edwards'. Then, after first alerting to heavy tools found in a suspect's van, Eddie located the spot on a building site where the suspect – a builder – had buried the body.

Charlotte Pinkney, a sixteen-year-old who disappeared in Devon, never was found. The dog alerted, however, to a place where her body had apparently initially lain. A suspect, known to have been with the girl the night she was last seen, was later convicted.

Such was handler Grime's confidence in Eddie, he told the Portuguese that the spaniel would 'locate [a] cadaver, whether in the whole or parts . . . deposited . . . to a depth of approximately 3 to 4 feet [from] shortly after death to the advanced stages of decomposition and putrefaction through to skeletal. This includes incinerated remains even if large quantities of accelerant have been involved. The dog will locate [a] human cadaver in water, either from the bank . . . or when deployed in a boat.'

Keela, the second dog to be assigned to the hunt for Madeleine, had distinguished herself following training by Grime and Harrison. Surrey police had called on her services after a young mother named Abigail Witchalls was stabbed and left paralysed while pushing her child in a pram. Weeks after the attack, Keela and other dogs established a 'pattern of scents' that placed the top suspect at the scene.

The spaniel had also been used to search a fishing boat on which a person was believed to have been killed. It was contaminated by rotting fish and blood. Keela alerted to a blood sample that, when analysed, was judged to be 'primate'. 'There are only two scenarios to suit this find,' Grime wrote. 'The blood was either human or a gorilla who went out in a boat fishing.'

The dogs were defined according to their specialities. Eddie was an Enhanced Victim Recovery Dog, or EVRD, Keela, a Crime Scene Investigation animal, or CSI.

When briefed by the NPIA's Mark Harrison, chief investigator Amaral was to recall having been won over by both what Harrison told him about the dogs' skills and the UK's 'databank on homicide of children under five years old'. He and colleagues were shown a videotape of the dogs in action 'to convince us of their capability and the extraordinary work carried out by these very special detectives'. Amaral thought them 'absolutely remarkable' and Harrison suggested they be used in the search for Madeleine. So it was, on July 31st, that Grime and the two spaniels were flown out aboard a British Airways flight and driven in an air-conditioned vehicle to special accommodation. A vet would be on hand during their stay.

Amaral had also been impressed by a document that, he would recall, Harrison provided. 'The figures quoted in the report,' he wrote, 'give us the shivers. The crimes [Amaral appears to have been referring to murder and abduction] are committed by the parents in 84 per cent of cases. 96 per cent are committed by friends and relatives. In only 4 per cent of them is the murderer or abductor a total stranger to the victim. In this roundabout way, Mark Harrison points out that the guilty party may be a person close to Madeleine and even her own parents. From now on, we have to explore this track.'

The Polícia Judiciára were soon to become committed to the notion that the McCanns were involved in the death of their daughter and the concealment of her body.

Soon after the search dogs arrived in Portugal, Kate – all unknowing of the way things were moving – would say she was 'really happy about the way things are going'.

Gonçalo Amaral thought that 'an operation in search of evidence, of a kind never before carried out in Portugal' was beginning.

12

The grey jeep carrying dog handler Martin Grime pulled up outside the Ocean Club around 8 p.m. on July 31st. His prized animals' first target was to be Apartment 5A, where the McCann family had been lodged until the night of Madeleine's disappearance. Eddie, the dog trained to detect the presence – past or present – of corpses, was first into the place.

'My observation,' Grime wrote later in his report, 'was that the dog's behaviour changed immediately upon opening the front door to the apartment. He will normally remain in the sit position until released and tasked to search. On this occasion he broke the stay and entered the apartment with an above average interest. His behaviour was such that I believed him to be "in scent", and I therefore allowed him to free search without direction.'

At first, Eddie gave a 'bark indication', or alert, in the bedroom on the terrace side of the apartment – apparently near the wardrobe – but without selecting a specific area. Then, after hunting around, he began paying attention to a sofa alongside a window in the lounge. 'He was quite interested in the sofa,' Grime noted, 'but he didn't have access to the back of the sofa.'

The sofa was then, it seems, pulled away from the wall. Once Eddie got behind it, Grime said, 'what I saw was that – approximately in the centre of the wall where the window is . . . between the tiles and the wall – he was scenting there a lot stronger than he had anywhere else . . . The second time, he'd decided, "Yes, that's what I'm looking for . . . " And that's when he gave me the bark indication.

'What we should understand with this dog is that he only barks when he finds something. He won't bark at any other time. He won't bark at other dogs, he won't bark at strangers, he won't bark when somebody knocks on the door.' Grime deemed the barking behind the sofa in the lounge 'a positive indication'.

Keela, the dog trained to scent human blood, was brought in a little later. She also headed behind the sofa and 'gave specific alert indications to specific areas on the tiles of the floor area behind the sofa and on the curtain in the area that was in contact with the floor behind the sofa. This would indicate to the likely presence of human blood.'

Under the guidance of a British adviser, the Polícia Judiciária later followed up by lifting numerous samples from the wall and from upholstery on the sofa. Tiles were removed from the floor, the curtains and curtain lining taken down and packaged up. So were parts of a climbing plant outside the apartment in which the blood dog Keela had also taken an interest. Most of the material was sent to the British government's Forensic Science Service laboratory in Birmingham.

The following day, the search effort shifted to areas near Apartment 5A, Praia da Luz beach and nearby scrub and wasteland. Following consultation with experts from the oceanographic department of the University of the Algarve, Mark Harrison had considered the possibility that Madeleine had been murdered and her body either hidden on the beach or disposed of in the sea. He appears not to have thought that a likely scenario – for several reasons.

Though digging on some parts of the beach would have been relatively easy, to have done so would have risked being seen. Wave action, moreover, might quickly have exposed the body. 'The wave energy,' Harrison thought, 'is not sufficient to "take a body" out to sea . . . Instead, the body would most likely continue in a re-circulating motion along the shoreline.' For the shoreline search, Harrison had the team probe the ground with metal bars at various points, in the hope – Amaral recalled – of bringing about 'possible release of gas emanating from a decomposing body'. The dogs were to be used on the beach and open ground on two occasions, but there were no alerts.

The developments during the examination at Apartment 5A had prompted the police to make other moves. 'The initial work with the dogs,' Inspector João Carlos wrote in a memo to Amaral, supported the hypothesis that 'Madeleine McCann may have died inside Apartment 5A.' He applied for warrants to search the accommodation the McCanns were currently using – a villa half a mile from the Ocean Club – and the rental car they had been using since late May, three weeks after their daughter had vanished. The applications were swiftly approved.

According to Amaral, writing later, his team saw the search of the villa as the moment when 'either we find evidence of [the McCanns'] responsibility, or they will once and for all be cleared of all suspicion in the disappearance.' In the event, Grime's report shows, there was only one positive response in the villa itself – by cadaver dog Eddie. 'The villa interior, garden, and all property within were searched [by Eddie],' he reported. 'The only alert indication given was when the dog located a pink cuddly toy in the villa's lounge. The [blood] dog did not alert to the toy when screened separately.'

The cuddly toy was Madeleine's Cuddle Cat, which Kate had carried with her virtually everywhere she went from the first, and which was by now familiar to millions. It 'smelled of suntan lotion' and was by now dirty, she would recall, and she had washed it. Whatever changes the washing might have made for the human nose, in Grime's view it was 'possible' that Eddie had alerted to 'cadaver scent contamination' on the toy.

When the detectives left the McCanns' villa, they took a carload of the family's possessions with them: Cuddle Cat – the police inventory listed it as 'one (01) pink cloth toy with yellow paws and ears and blue label, with a wooden rosary and a green ribbon alluding to Fatima' – boxes of clothing, suitcases, a pair of latex gloves, two diaries, a notepad and a Bible. When these items were taken to another location for examination, the dog Eddie alerted to clothing in one of the boxes. Again, Grime thought it possible that the cadaver dog was reacting to cadaver scent contamination.

Referring to the dog's reactions to both Cuddle Cat and the clothing, the handler cautioned: 'No evidential or intelligence reliability can be made . . . unless it can be confirmed with corroborating evidence.'

In his 2008 book, Amaral drew a far more definite conclusion. 'Eddie barked,' he wrote, 'to indicate that the soft toy had been in contact with a body. The toy had the odour of a dead body.' His descriptions of the villa were filled with innuendo:

Kate seemed to be in mourning . . . Numerous photos of Madeleine were pinned to the wall or framed on her bedside table. By each of them, as though watching over the little girl's soul – a crucifix, a saint or a rosary . . . In contrast, on the other side of the room [the side] occupied by Gerald, the walls are bare, cold, not a single photo of his daughter Madeleine.

In the room Gerry used as an office, the officers noted 'with amazement,' according to Amaral, police manuals and books that, he said, were restricted for the use of police services and government agencies. The publications Amaral listed included: *Missing and Abducted Children, A Law Enforcement Guide to Case Investigation and Program Management* (National Center for Missing and Exploited Children) and *Training Courses* (Serious Organized Crime Agency – Child Exploitation and Online Protection Centre).

There was in fact nothing remotely strange about Gerry's possession of this material – he had been in close touch with both the National Center and CEOP in the course of his quest for research information on missing children.

The Bible, found on Kate's bedside table, especially caught Amaral's eye. A bookmark in it, bearing the likeness of a saint, marked a page from the Old Testament's second Book of Samuel that told of the death of one of King David's children. The page is reproduced in full in the Polícia Judiciária's case records, and Amaral quoted it in his book. Lines in the passage include:

The son born to you will die.

The Lord struck the child that Uriah's wife had borne to David and he became ill. David pleaded with God for the child.

On the seventh day the child died. David's servants were afraid to tell him that the child was dead.

David noticed that his servants were whispering among themselves, and he realised that the child was dead. 'Is the child dead?' he asked. 'Yes,' they replied. 'He is dead.'

[David] answered . . . 'Can I bring him back again?'

In Amaral's book, he cited these verses at considerably greater length, as though the fact that they were flagged with a bookmark in the Bible at Kate's bedside had some dark significance.

Had Amaral asked, he would have learned – as would emerge much later when the seeming oddity was investigated – that the Bible had been loaned to Kate by two friends, Peter and Bridget Patterson, who had flown out to Portugal to support the McCanns. It was Bridget who had marked the passage from the Book of Samuel, in reference to a tragedy in their own family.

Four days after the detectives had trawled through the contents of the villa, the British dogs were used for another search – one that to many would seem, on the face of it, rather surprising. In his initial recommendations, Mark Harrison had suggested searching not only accommodation used by the McCanns and their companions but also 'any hired vehicles'. As the McCanns had not rented a car until three weeks after their daughter had gone missing, one might have thought it would have no evidential relevance. Nevertheless, on the afternoon of August 6th, the search team gathered in an underground parking lot on Praça 1 de Maio in Portimão, opposite police headquarters.

Ten cars were lined up on level 4 of the lot. Some of them were owned or used by others in whom the police had an interest, such as Robert Murat and people associated with him. One was thought to have been a rental car used at one point by the McCanns' friend Russell O'Brien. Another was a silver Renault

Scenic, rented from Budget, which Gerry McCann and his wife had picked up on May 27th and were still using.

'Ten vehicles were screened,' dog handler Grime would write in his report. 'The vehicles, of which I did not know the owner details, were parked on an empty floor with twenty–thirty feet between each . . . [Cadaver dog Eddie] was then tasked to search the area. When passing a vehicle I now know to be hired and in the possession of the McCann family, the dog's behaviour changed substantially. This then produced an alert indication at the lower part of the driver's door, where the dog was biting and barking. I recognise this behaviour as the dog indicating scent emitting from the inside of the vehicle through the seal around the door. This vehicle was then subjected to a full physical examination by the PJ and no human remains were found.'

As a result of their examination, police retrieved numerous strands of hair and nail fragments. A 'minutely detailed' search found no trace of blood. In the early hours of the following morning, however, blood dog Keela was put to work on the vehicle. In Grime's words, 'An alert indication was forthcoming from the rear driver's side of the boot area.' The Portuguese police report of the search specifies that the blood dog indicated 'an area of the lower right-hand side of the interior part of the baggage compartment of the car'. It states, too, that it then drew attention to the map pocket on the inside of the driver's door. This was found to contain the car's plastic electronic ignition key and Budget key ring.

To check the response to the key ring, the Renault's key was taken from the car and hidden beneath sand in a fire bucket some distance away. Then, at different intervals and on different levels of the parking lot, the dog twice indicated interest in the area in which the bucket had been placed.

The ignition key and a part of the Renault's luggage compartment were removed. All of the evidence taken from the car would
be sent for analysis at the Forensic Science Service laboratory in
the UK.

'It is my view,' handler Grime wrote at the end of the part of
his report that deals with the Renault, 'that it is possible that
[Eddie] is alerting to "cadaver scent" contaminant or human blood
scent. No evidential or intelligence reliability can be made from
this alert unless it can be confirmed with corroborating evidence.'

Rumours about the results of the search of the rental vehicle
would soon enough become ominous, so ominous that the
McCanns were at one point to consider having independent tests
done on the vehicle. The Renault would be kept for a while in
the garage of a villa near Praia da Luz, with that in mind.

Amaral's account of the day's events would be categorical. The
cadaver dog, he was to write months later, 'did not show any
interest in the other cars inspected, only showed interest in the
car used by the McCanns'. In its search at dawn, he asserted
flatly, the blood dog had found 'traces of human blood'. Things,
he was to say, had evolved. The McCanns 'were suspects until
we got to the work of the English dogs, and then the suspicions
became evidence'.

Even before the dog searches had been completed, but after
their work in Apartment 5A and the villa the McCanns were
currently using, Portuguese newspapers had begun running stories
that signalled a major development in the Madeleine investigation. *Sol*, the weekly that reportedly had access to Amaral, declared:

'There are strong signs' that Madeleine, the English child
that disappeared from Praia da Luz . . . 'is dead', police

sources have told *Sol*. The 180° turnaround that the investigation by the Polícia Judiciária from Portimão appears to have taken in the past few days, even led the Attorney General, Pinto Monteiro, to postpone the granting of an interview that had been requested by British broadcaster BBC . . . The moves by the PJ and some officers from the British police during these last days – accompanied by two dogs, in Praia da Luz – seem to indicate that the investigation is now centred on the McCann family and their group . . .

On Tuesday night, a black and white cocker [*sic*] spaniel that is trained to detect death, spent several hours in the apartment the McCann family occupied in the Ocean Club resort, and from which Maddie disappeared on May 3rd. According to sources within the investigation, the dog marked the death of the child inside the apartment.

The *Correio da Manhã*, the daily paper with the biggest circulation in Portugal, reported the following day that the PJ now:

. . . centres its investigation on the McCanns' close circle . . . The kidnapping theory is starting to be discarded after English dogs detected a trail that points to the existence of a corpse inside the holiday residence. The Polícia Judiciária believes that Madeleine may have been killed in the Algarve apartment.

A day later, another national daily, the *Jornal de Notícias*, referred to 'traces of blood from a dead person, presumably Madeleine' having been found on a wall in the McCanns' bedroom at Apartment 5A. This 'fact', it said, 'places the child's death inside the apartment'. Investigators 'do not take it as certain that this was a homicide', it went on, but 'somebody tried to clean up the traces'.

The day after that, the *Diário de Notícias* had it that the police had 'known for a month that Madeleine McCann was killed on the night of May 3rd, in the apartment . . . The suspicions that have always fallen on Maddie's parents, since she disappeared, are now growing stronger.' This was attributed to 'a source that is connected to the process'.

The same day, Lusa, the semi-state-owned news agency, had its source on the investigative team declaring that there was 'light at the end of the tunnel'. The *Correio da Manhã* had one of its sources saying the work with the dogs 'helped confirm the worst suspicions from the PJ: Maddie actually was killed inside the apartment.' 'Now,' an inspector had told the paper, 'there is no going back.' The PJ was 'close to the key to this crime'.

The Portuguese police were leaking details to the press of an incomplete investigation – long before knowing the findings of the Forensic Science Service on material sent to the UK for analysis.

13

Gerry and Kate McCann had no way of knowing, in early August, just how dark and serious were the suspicions harboured by the men at the top of the Portuguese inquiry. They were troubled, nevertheless, and not just by the press coverage. There were signs – barely perceptible but there all the same – that the police attitude to them was changing. An officer who liaised with them regularly had seemed to be behaving in an odd way. There was his throwaway remark that the investigation was taking a different tack. And there always, day after day, was the painful truth that their hopes of their daughter's return remained unrealised.

Kate's deeply held Christian faith was further shaken. She found herself asking, she was to tell the BBC's *Heaven and Earth* programme, 'Why do this to Madeleine? Why have You let this happen?' The 'darker moments', she added, though, were short-lived. 'You realise that God hasn't done this. Somebody else has done this.'

The McCanns had, meanwhile, been widening their focus. Gerry, ever the man of action, had flown to the United States for meetings at the National Center for Missing and Exploited Children. Established in the wake of prominent child-abduction cases, and partially funded by the US Justice Department, NCMEC had for years worked to help locate children missing for any reason – including abduction – and to raise awareness of child sex abuse and the spread of images of child sex abuse. In a whirl of meetings, Gerry talked with the organisation's director, met with the Bush administration's Attorney General and members of Congress – and appeared on *America's Most Wanted*, a programme similar to the UK's *Crimewatch*.

The knowledge Gerry gleaned about techniques in locating missing children aside, the trip had achieved what the McCanns had sought from the start: more publicity that might, just might, help find Madeleine. Following his return from the States, more-over, he and Kate appeared on a YouTube video to launch 'Don't You Forget About Me', a website promoted by NCMEC's inter-national wing, on which parents could post information about missing children.

During this same time there had been the unexpected – to the McCanns – police descent on the villa the couple were using. They had been told it involved forensics, and guessed the purpose was a belated check for any DNA an abductor might have left on their belongings. Only on August 8th, when the McCanns were summoned to the police station in Portimão, did the extent of the change in the Polícia Judiciária's posture dawn on them.

Two officers, one of them PJ regional director Encarnação, the other Luís Neves, head of Portugal's equivalent of the UK's Serious Organised Crime Agency, told the McCanns that they had moved away from the hope that Madeleine was alive. Gerry was asked to leave the room and they grilled Kate – yet again – on the events of the evening of May 3rd. They pushed and pushed, then told her they did not believe her. They suggested to her that her memory was at fault.

Kate broke down, sobbing and gasping for breath. When Gerry in turn had been re-interrogated, he had a question of his own: Was the case now a murder inquiry? He could probably guess, he was told, that it was.

Two days later, the PJ's Olegário de Sousa, its spokesman for public utterances – as distinct from the cascade of covert leaks – made an oblique comment. New evidence in the Madeleine case, the BBC reported him as having said, had given 'intensity' to the possibility that she had been killed, but her parents were not considered suspects.

This on August 11th, which marked one hundred days since the McCanns' daughter had gone missing. That day, one of the couple's Portuguese police liaison officers opened up a little to them. One of the dogs brought in from the UK, he said, had identified human blood in Apartment 5A. The actions of the other dog, moreover, had signalled that someone had died there. Being told this information, Kate recalled, left the couple both perplexed and distressed.

None of these insinuations against the McCanns would ever be supported by any evidence. In the month that followed, the tension only increased.

Just as their relationship with the Portuguese police was becoming increasingly strained, so too was the McCanns' relationship with the media. Towards the end of the month, Scots-born Gerry gave interviews at the Edinburgh Television Festival. With hindsight, and in the circumstances, his presence there resonates with a terrible irony. For appearing there on the same day, garbed in a tartan tracksuit and fronting a festival edition of *Jim'll Fix It*, was Sir Jimmy Savile – five years later, in death, to be exposed as having been a serial child abuser. There, too, was the *Newsnight* presenter Jeremy Paxman, who excoriated the media 'circus' over Madeleine as the sort that 'sucks good sense and consideration out of the brains of those involved'. Gerry McCann, for his part, complained of the 'absolutely wild speculation' by some in the media. His and Kate's intention now, he said, would be to try to withdraw from the glare of publicity – limiting themselves to what might help their daughter.

Before leaving for Edinburgh, the McCanns had let it be known that they intended to hit back at media slurs. According to a source speaking for them, a broadcaster on Portugal's national television channel RTP – which had previously carried an interview citing 'people who know' as having said the McCanns were 'swingers' – had implied Kate might have murdered Madeleine. The broadcaster denied it, but the couple threatened to bring suit. Two days later, while being pestered by an interviewer for Spain's Telecinco channel to discuss the investigation – which he had explained Portuguese law prevented him from doing – Gerry had torn off his microphone and left the room. 'Do you think it is remorse,' the show's presenter would ask when the programme was aired, 'that made Gerry leave?'

The following day, the front-page headline of the Portuguese weekly *Tal & Qual* – the title translates as *This & That* – shouted '*PJ ACREDITA QUE OS PAIS MATARAM MADDIE*', or 'PJ BELIEVES THAT THE PARENTS KILLED MADDIE'. In capitals, but in a smaller font, was the slightly less accusative, 'SUSPEITAS APONTAM PARA MORTE ACIDENTAL' – 'SUSPICIONS POINT TO ACCIDENTAL DEATH'. The article suggested the McCanns had either been responsible for a fatal accident or had sedated their daughter. It attributed the information to a 'source close to the investigation'. This story crossed the line, and the couple did issue a writ against *Tal &*

Qual. The suit was eventually aborted, when the newspaper went out of business.

There was no evidence at all that the McCanns ever gave Madeleine sedatives. The family's present GP and a former GP who had cared for them would both later tell British police in the UK they had never prescribed such medicine to the couple. Two witnesses who had babysat for them, and also a relative by marriage, would all say they never knew the couple to administer any drug to Madeleine other than Calpol (paracetamol), a medicine for childhood fever or pain.

The notion that PJ detectives thought Madeleine had died after her parents had given her sedatives, however, did not end with *Tal & Qual*. Five days on, also citing a 'source close to the investigation', *Correio da Manhã* alleged that the McCanns had kept 'a syringe with tranquillisers' in a chest of drawers in their bedroom in Apartment 5A. Their spokesman promptly responded by telling the *Daily Express*, which picked up the story in the UK, that they had had neither syringes nor sedatives with them on holiday. The story was 'absolute nonsense'.

Yet the British tabloid media, which had been doing so for weeks, would continue to piggyback on the Portuguese coverage. So would a good deal of the rest of the foreign press. The 'Madeleine sedated' story, drawing on Portuguese sources, was not about to go away. None of these insinuations against the McCanns would ever be supported by any evidence.

In the absence of any real information, Gerry and Kate McCann tried to get back to what had for months now been their ordinary daily routines – though of course none of their routines were now ordinary at all.

Kate had a dream one night that Madeleine turned up safe and well. 'It was very tangible . . . I think I got rung by the nursery [school] where she went and they said, "Madeleine's here". I went . . . it felt like I was holding her. And then I woke up and I was hysterical . . . it was horrible.'

Gerry, for his part, would reflect that his daughter should at this point have been about to start primary school. In the world of the Polícia Judiciária, there was no place for Madeleine's what-might-have-beens, only on driving the case – as they now saw it – forward. No results were yet in from the British government laboratory that had been sent the evidence gathered during the searches by the specialist dogs, but the contemporary PJ record indicates that senior officers had already made up their minds.

On September 3rd, the second in command of the investigation, Chief Inspector Tavares de Almeida, sent his boss Amaral a series of suggestions. His focus was on the dogs. The 'unique in the world' dogs ought now to be deployed in the UK to target what he termed the 'possible perpetrators/accomplices' in Madeleine's death – those who had been the McCanns' companions during their holiday.

Almeida asked for an 'inspection by the dogs of the clothing used by the group of friends of the McCann family', and seizure and forensic analysis of anything potentially useful. To discover more about the McCanns themselves, he wanted authority to examine the couple's home in Leicestershire – and, again, to seize and analyse material of possible significance. He wanted the teachers at Madeleine's nursery school, people employed at her home – any non-family members who had known her – to be questioned.

Chief Inspector Almeida requested these things because, he wrote, the police were now 'in a situation in which the death of the minor Madeleine Beth McCann occurred on May 3rd 2007, inside Apartment

5A . . . The work done by the dog team led us firmly towards this line of inquiry, not that it had been previously ignored but because the dogs may have determined where scientifically verifiable clues/ evidence could be recovered.'

Prior to the work done by the dogs, Almeida told his chief, there had already been a range of hypotheses as to what might have been involved in Madeleine's death – 'accident, negligence, or the crime of homicide'. Now, they had to consider also 'conceal-ment of a body' and 'the simulation of a crime [i.e. an abduction]'.

In an interview months later, Amaral would concur as to how important the dogs had been. 'It was the dogs' work,' he told the press. 'That was when we were most convinced.'

On the very day Almeida filed his request for further investi-gative moves, the police acted on their apparent convictions. Ricardo Paiva, a detective inspector who had acted as liaison with the McCanns for months, came by the villa ostensibly to get some routine signatures. That done, however, he then amazed and shocked them. They were to come to the station for 'interroga-tion' – Kate one day and Gerry the next – and they should come accompanied by their lawyer.

Knowing that witnesses were not normally required to attend interviews in the company of a lawyer, Gerry asked whether and how their status was to change. They were, Paiva said, to become *arguidos* – formal suspects, just as Robert Murat had been for months.

Kate would recall in her 2011 memoir that she had been dumbfounded, wept, asked Paiva whether the police were trying to destroy their family, had been utterly distraught. Known only to those who have perused the Portuguese police files, however, is the loaded way Inspector Paiva reported the McCanns' reaction in the report he hastened to file later that day:

When the undersigned went to the [McCanns'] temporary residence to notify them that they should present themselves at the police station to make statements . . . KATE McCANN immediately reacted in a negative manner, making comments such as, 'What are my parents going to think?', and 'What is the press going to say when they find out?' and that 'The Portuguese police is under pressure from the government to finish the investigation quickly'.

With regard to GERALD McCANN, he constantly insisted on giving the undersigned letters and emails that he was receiving, mostly from psychics and mediums whom he had selected, and which contained information without much credibility about the possible whereabouts of Madeleine and her presumed abductor.

More recently . . . during a telephone call between GERALD McCANN and the undersigned, he made a reference regarding the investigation, that he was certain that the police did not have any proof that could incriminate them with regard to the death of Madeleine McCann and he said that the police were wasting their time in targeting their investigation around the parents.

Earlier in his report, Inspector Paiva had referred to supposedly 'strange' behaviour by the McCanns he had observed during his recent liaison work. They had, he wrote:

. . . gradually begun to react in a very negative manner to the increased investigative activity carried out by this police force, especially during the use of the English sniffer dogs for detecting cadaver odour, when more evidence arose in the investigation for the hypothesis of the death of Madeleine

McCann. Several times, the McCann couple said that the attention of the police should maintain a focus on the abduction hypothesis, which in the couple's opinion was the only scenario . . . and that the police should not forget to continue to investigate the suspect Robert Murat.

Strangely, Kate also made several requests, three months after the disappearance of Madeleine, that the police should take blood, hair and nail tests of Madeleine's twin siblings, because, she said, she remembered that on the day of Madeleine's disappearance – in spite of all the commotion and noise made [in Apartment 5A] by the authorities and other persons who were looking for Madeleine, they remained asleep, due to which she now presumes that they were under the effect of some sedative drug that a presumed abductor had administered to the children to be able to abduct Madeleine – a situation that Kate refers to being plausible, according to what she had read in a criminal investigation manual given her by the British authorities, as having been the abductor's procedure if that were the actual situation of the child's abduction, rape and murder.

The day after Paiva told the McCanns of their impending *arguido* status, September 4th, the Polícia Judiciária received a preliminary report from John Lowe, the senior scientist who – following the dog searches – had been analysing material from Apartment 5A and the McCann rental car. His findings, he noted, had yet to be 'formalised in a final report'. Meanwhile, he reported on three samples he had received.

There was DNA on the swab allotted the number 3A, a specimen lifted from the floor in the lounge of the McCanns' former Ocean Club apartment, Lowe noted. The swab, which had produced an incomplete DNA result, contained 'low level indications of DNA from more than one person'. He then wrote: 'However, all of the confirmed DNA components within this result match the corresponding components in the DNA profile of Madeleine McCann.' It was not possible, though, in the scientist's view, to say what body fluid swab 3A represented. In other words, it might be not blood but some other human fluid.

Swab 3B, also from the floor in the lounge, was not useful. There was no evidence, Lowe flatly stated, 'to support the view that Madeleine McCann contributed DNA to the Swab 3B'.

The third sample, material taken from the boot of the McCanns' rental car – numbered 10(2) in this report – was a somewhat different matter.

The technique used by Lowe analyses 'regions' of DNA known as short tandem repeats (STRs), which vary from individual to individual. With the exception of identical twins, every person's DNA profile is unique.

British scientists use ten specific components of an STR region, each of which contains two alleles – one inherited from the mother and one from the father. Because they know the frequency with which each occurs in the population, scientists can calculate the likelihood of any two samples matching in all twenty of these alleles. The method the scientists use produces a 'peak' for each allele. There are *always* twenty alleles but, because we all have several alleles in common, an identical allele will sometimes be inherited from both parents, giving just one 'peak' at one or more locations. Because Madeleine's parents had one such identical allele, Madeleine's DNA profile shows a total of not twenty but nineteen unique peaks.

DNA profiling uses the technique of DNA amplification (repeated copying) to increase the quantity of DNA available for analysis. In the case of the specimen from the rental car boot numbered 10(2), Lowe used a variation of the technique called LCN (Low Copy Number), which further increases the number of amplification stages. This means that a DNA profile can be obtained from samples in which the amount of DNA initially recovered is too small for other methods of identification. Unfortunately, however, the Low Copy technique also amplifies degraded DNA or alleles that may originate from multiple contacts and is often difficult or impossible to interpret.

Comparing Madeleine's DNA with those of sample 10(2), Lowe found, 'Of these 19 components 15 are present within the result from this item.' Lowe's next words, though, dispelled the notion that any conclusion could be drawn from this fact. 'There are 37 components in total,' Lowe wrote. 'There are 37 components because there are at least three contributors.' He went on to caution that the 'individual components in Madeleine's DNA are not unique to her.'

'Elements of Madeleine's profile,' he noted, 'are also present within the profiles of many of the scientists here in Birmingham, myself included. It's important to stress that 50 per cent of Madeleine's profile will be shared with each parent.' In a sample made up of components from at least three individuals, Lowe wrote, the question 'Is the match genuine or is it a chance match?' was unanswerable.

The Portuguese police summary of this preliminary British forensic report, written a week later, made the information sound far more clear-cut. Written by Inspector João Carlos, who had requested the search of the villa and car, it stated that – in one sample – 'all of the confirmed DNA components coincide with corresponding components in the DNA profile of Madeleine McCann.'

Carlos was similarly definitive about specimen 10(2). 'In the sample collected in the boot area of the vehicle,' he wrote, '15 of the identified DNA components coincide with the corresponding components in the DNA profile of Madeleine McCann, this [having] 19 components.' If that is the baldly definitive way – devoid of the scientist's caution – that the police interpreted Lowe's initial report when they received it on September 4th, it surely made them even more convinced that they were right to be targeting the McCanns.

As late as the 5th, according to Kate, she and her husband still had some hope that they would not be declared *arguidos*. If so, they hoped in vain.

The following afternoon, Kate arrived at police headquarters in Portimão as arranged. A jostling throng of reporters and photographers were there to see her arrive, and it would be around midnight when she left. In the station, her lawyer at her side, she endured a lengthy re-interrogation – mostly by Inspector Carlos – on the details of the days before Madeleine's disappearance and the night itself. They also asked what medicines there had been in Apartment 5A. Kate responded there had been Calpol and Nurofen, in adult and children's dosages – to treat fever and pain – but that neither had been administered to the children during the holiday.

When they talked late that night, her lawyer was gloomy. He had been briefed on what the dog search of Apartment 5A had produced. He knew about the Bible that had been found next to her bed at the villa they were using, and the passage about a dead child that had been marked in it. In Portugal, the lawyer said, the sum of it all was enough to send her to jail.

Then, according to Kate, he said to the couple's astonishment that the police had proposed a plea bargain. Should Kate confess that Madeleine had met her death accidentally, and that she had concealed and then disposed of the body, she would be treated with leniency – perhaps go down for two years – and Gerry might be released. Should she not accept the deal, he said, and if the charge was instead murder, both she and Gerry might face life in prison.

Back at the police station the next morning, September 7th, Inspector Carlos began by telling her that she was now formally declared *arguido*. Then he and Ricardo Paiva laboured through a prepared list of more than forty questions. Following her lawyer's advice, and as a formal suspect has the legal right to do, on this occasion she declined to answer. The very nature of the questions, however, indicates what the police were driving at.

They wanted to know what had been in the bedroom cupboard when she returned to Apartment 5A on May 3rd; why she had said from the outset that Madeleine had been abducted; why she thought the twins had slept on during the commotion after Madeleine went missing; whether she was accustomed to giving her children medication; whether – as a mother – she had ever felt driven to despair or anger by her children. They showed her the videotape recorded during the searches of the apartment and the Renault by the dogs, told her the dogs – marvels both – had alerted to the odour of death and to blood.

As Kate – in public polite to a fault – sat through this, she was one day to recall, she found it comforting to keep repeating under her breath: 'Fucking tosser, fucking tosser . . . '

Gerry McCann was also re-interviewed for four hours that day. Though he, too, was informed that he was now an *arguido* and did not need to respond to questions, he chose to answer them. Routine points about the holiday aside, his interrogators wanted to know: whether he had played any part in Madeleine's disappearance – this question was apparently asked three times – whether his wife had suffered from depression; whether she had ever talked of giving Madeleine to another family member to look after. His answers were all in the negative.

Like Kate, Gerry was asked whether he could explain the twins having slumbered through the uproar on May 3rd, whether he had given any of the children any medicine while in Portugal. He had no explanation for the twins having remained asleep. He said he and Kate had brought with them on holiday several medicines, including Nurofen, Calpol, the antihistamine terfenadine, and Losec, a medicine he himself took occasionally for gastric problems. As well as using Calpol for fever and pain in children, some parents give their children Calpol to bring on sleep. He and Kate, Gerry said, had not given any of their children Calpol or any other medicine during the holiday – and there is no evidence the McCanns ever used Calpol or anything else to sedate their children.

He, too, was required to view the videotape of the dogs searching and alerting to the supposed odour of death and to human blood. He had no comment and had no explanation. He did say Madeleine had been prone to nosebleeds, but that he wasn't aware that she had bled during the holiday.

Then the latest inquisition was over – with the prospect, according to the McCanns' lawyer, that Gerry or Kate or both of them might be charged. The possibility that they might be held in custody for many months, separated from their two remaining children, loomed. Then, through British diplomats, the couple learned that although they remained suspects, they would be allowed to leave for the UK as planned.

On legal advice, they chose to pack up and leave immediately in case the situation changed. On the morning of Sunday,

September 9th, the family climbed into the rented Renault to head for Faro Airport and a flight to England. For the best part of an hour, on the 55-mile journey, their car was chased by a posse of reporters and cameramen in cars and on motorbikes. To the effort to get his shots, as they careered along at eighty miles per hour, one cameraman stuck his head and shoulders out of a vehicle's sunroof. A press helicopter hovered overhead.

Hours later, in the sun of an English autumn, they were at East Midlands Airport, climbing down the steps of an EasyJet aircraft – after other passengers had disembarked. Then it was into another car for the twelve-mile journey to their home in Rothley. If less unruly than the mob that had pursued them out of Portugal, the press was still there. In the sky, there were other cameras, peering down at them from other helicopters. Then they were home, welcomed by relatives.

'Kate needed to go into Madeleine's room as soon as she got back,' Gerry's mother Eileen said, 'she wanted time in there alone . . . I can't imagine how she must have felt. Madeleine's clothes and toys were just the way they'd been left. Kate believes Madeleine is still alive, and I imagine said a little prayer for her . . . but she's a strong person.'

After their return to the UK, Kate did not resume practising as a part-time GP but stayed at home with the children. Gerry would soon be back working as a cardiologist at Leicester's Glenfield Hospital. What the couple knew as 'normal life', though, was gone, perhaps never to resume.

In Portugal, the very day after the McCanns had left, the drumbeat of accusation continued. The Polícia Judiciária, quoted by the respected Sky News reporter Martin Brunt, now went public in saying that blood samples analysed by Britain's Forensic Science

Service had given them 'the most damning evidence' to have emerged. 'It shows, as far as [the PJ] are concerned,' Brunt reported, 'the presence of Madeleine's body in the car five weeks after she disappeared . . . The evidence suggests very strongly that it was not that her DNA had been transferred from clothing or a cuddly toy. The allegation is that the DNA shows a full match of 99 per cent.'

Also on September 10th, chief investigator Amaral's senior aide Chief Inspector Tavares de Almeida submitted a nine-page report fleshing out the case. He not only catalogued the physical evidence but, as would his boss Amaral, mentioned the supposedly suspect material found in the villa used by the McCanns after Madeleine's disappearance – including the page found marked in a Bible Kate had used.

Almeida pointed, also, to perceived 'discrepancies' in the testimonies of the friends who had dined with the McCanns on the fateful night. 'From the declarations of the group,' he wrote, 'results a total incoherence, in the context of which it is obvious that everyone is lying.'

The chief inspector did not appear to consider the possibility that there might be entirely innocent reasons for the apparent discrepancies.

From all the evidence, Almeida concluded that Madeleine had died in Apartment 5A, that it had been made to appear there had been an abduction, that the supposed checks on the children during the May 3rd dinner had been concocted, that the child might have died as the result of an accident, and that the McCanns had hidden their daughter's body. They had done so, a police source would suggest to the *Sunday Times* shortly afterwards, by storing it in a refrigerator. That idea was based on no evidence at all – it was plain silly.

The same day, the PJ's Information Analysis Brigade, at its headquarters in Lisbon, produced an eleven-page document drawing on the McCann party's statements and phone traffic. It, too, raised alleged discrepancies and inconsistencies, especially in the McCanns' own statement. Filed with the headquarters document is a British police timeline study that concludes: 'In the confusion following the disappearance of Madeleine McCann, it is conceivable that one of the men or Fiona Payne, "escaped" to join in the searches again later.'

This PJ documentation was prepared, it appears, for submission to the local Public Prosecutor's office. A complex review process then began. It was possible, it emerged, that the McCanns might remain *arguido* for a year without any charges being laid. Portugal's Attorney General Fernando Pinto Monteiro, meanwhile, said the investigation had not ended. The police, for their part, pressed on.

They were reported to want further access to Madeleine's Cuddle Cat and the originals of Kate's diaries, which had been returned to the McCanns before they left. They were interested in a laptop Gerry had been using, and asked for traces on traffic on phones used by the McCanns and all their holiday companions. A report would be made on the number and weight of the suitcases the McCanns and their friends had taken with them on their various return flights to England. In late September, police correspondence would float the notion that agents acting for the couple might arrive to 'sanitise' locations the family had used in Praia da Luz.

There were, though, signs that some of those in authority in Portugal had reservations. National police chief Alipio Ribeiro suggested that, contrary to what the Polícia Judiciária were claiming, the British forensic analysis had not been conclusive.

In mid-September, Attorney General Pinto Monteiro's office said there was no evidence that it was necessary to question the McCanns yet again, as Chief Inspector Almeida had requested.

The PJ's spokesman on the case, Olegário de Sousa, for his part announced that he was no longer prepared to fulfil his current role. Privately, it was reported, he let it be known that he had been 'exasperated' by the cascade of leaks by police colleagues. The leaks, he said, were designed to push Gerry and Kate McCann into admitting that they were responsible for Madeleine's death. In de Sousa's view, the evidence against them was at best flimsy and at worst supposition. He had felt 'caught in the middle of a propaganda war between his police colleagues and the McCanns'.

The conflict had barely started.

14

The discoveries the British sniffer dogs had apparently made had utterly changed the direction of the investigation. Had the dogs not been brought in, it is fair to say, there would have been no Portuguese police decision formally to declare Madeleine's parents suspects.

A careful reading of the case files, however, indicates that the decision that was made was premature and grew out of a perhaps understandable Portuguese misinterpretation of a poorly worded – but key – forensic finding in a preliminary email from the Forensic Science Service. The British liaison officer who passed the email on to the Polícia Judiciária appears to have warned them to wait for the arrival of the formal laboratory report. The PJ team, however, seem not only to have ignored the liaison officer's caution but the caveat in the report of the British specialist who had handled the dogs in Praia da Luz. 'No evidential or intelligence reliability' could be made as the result of a dog having 'alerted', handler Martin Grime had written, 'unless it can be confirmed with corroborating evidence.'

Corroborating forensic evidence that Madeleine had died in the McCanns' Ocean Club apartment, had bled there – indeed had even been there – never would materialise. In his final 2008 deposition on the material recovered from the apartment, the Forensic Science Service's John Lowe reported at length on tests done using both standard DNA and Low Copy profiling, the test developed by the Science Service for use on minimal samples in poor condition. Such samples would include, for example, DNA left on a cup from which liquid has been drunk. Although later resumed, tests using the LCN technique had been suspended for a time during the period of the McCann work, following an IRA trial in Northern Ireland in which its validity had been questioned.

Lowe's final overall conclusion was that 'the laboratory results that were obtained did not help to clarify whether or not the DNA results obtained within the scope of this case were from Madeleine McCann'.

He had again addressed Sample 3A, the specimen lifted from the floor in the lounge of the apartment that he had dealt with in his initial report and that had been interpreted in a Portuguese police summary as being firmly identified with Madeleine (see pp.165). He wrote now that the 'low-level DNA result showed very meagre information indicating more than one person . . . the result could be explained as being DNA originating from Kate [McCann] and Gerald McCann, for example . . . It is not possible to attribute this DNA profile to a particular body fluid.'

In plain English, science was unable even to determine whether the specimen was blood, let alone whether it came from Madeleine.

Of dozens of other samples recovered from Apartment 5A and sent to the UK for analysis, Sample 3A was the only one found to be – possibly – from a member of the McCann family. All the rest were either 'too complex for a meaningful interpretation', 'too meagre', 'incomplete', or (in one case) identifiable with the detective who lifted the sample. In the few instances where Lowe noted a 'mixed' or 'low-level' DNA result, the scientist's view was that there were 'no conclusive indications that justify the theory that any member of the McCann family had contributed DNA to [the] result'.

Though the dog trained to locate human blood had given an alert in the lounge of Apartment 5A, scientist Lowe offered findings only on specimens of DNA from the room, without specifying whether or not the source was blood. Even had he been able to say it was blood, there was no conclusive DNA match between any specimen and Madeleine McCann. There was every reason, meanwhile, to surmise that it may have come from previous occupants of the apartment.

A couple who rented 5A a month before the McCanns, computer technician Simon Fawkes and his teacher wife Claire, would recall that their three-and-a-half-year-old daughter had cut her chin while at the Ocean Club crèche badly enough to need stitches – and may have bled later at the apartment.

The couple who used the accommodation the week immediately preceding the McCanns, moreover, accountant Paul Gordon and his flight-attendant wife Saleigh, had an even more significant memory about bleeding. Gordon had cut himself shaving and had 'walked around the apartment with paper tissues trying to stop the blood' for about forty-five minutes.

Then there was the Renault car the McCanns had hired three weeks after their daughter's disappearance and the sample – numbered 10(2) by the lab – that had been recovered from its boot. As reported earlier (see p.167), Lowe had identified fifteen out of nineteen components of Madeleine's DNA in the sample, but cautioned that components of her DNA profile were not unique to her. A Portuguese police summary, meanwhile, had omitted the cautionary observations.

In his final report, which again addressed Sample 10(2), Lowe found that the sample 'appeared to be from at least three persons . . . In my opinion, that result is too complex for a meaningful interpretation.'

The laboratory findings did not reflect any fluid identifiable as blood having been recovered from the car. As to hair retrieved from the Renault – and compared to hairs removed from Madeleine's hairbrush – Lowe's colleague Andrew Palmer reported that it 'was not possible for me to determine if, or if not, these could have been from Madeleine McCann'. Of the nail fragments found in the car, one turned out to have been Gerry's and another Kate's.

Finally, there was the Budget electronic ignition key and key ring removed from the map pocket on the inside of the driver's door of the rental car. Using the Low Copy Number test, Lowe noted it as having 'an incomplete low-level DNA profile that matched corresponding components in the profile of Gerald McCann'. Not a revelation – since Madeleine's father had driven the car for many weeks.

Forensic study of the samples removed from the Renault, then, produced no evidence that there had been blood in the car, let alone a child's corpse, as the Portuguese police surmised. This in spite of the fact that the British police dogs – both the blood dog and the cadaver-odour dog – had identified the car and responded positively to it. How so?

Much later, the British police would visit and interview other former tourists who had rented the Renault before the McCanns, as well as relatives who had been in it during the McCann rental period. Each solemnly gave assurances that, to their knowledge, no dead person or person who bled had been in the car at those times. Other observations they made, however, may be pertinent.

Amanda Lowes, who had used the Renault in April, said she and her husband 'may have transported raw meat for a barbecue'. Then there was Gerry McCann's brother-in-law, Alexander 'Sandy' Cameron, who with his wife had flown out following Madeleine's disappearance and stayed for twelve weeks, until just days before the dog search of the rental car on August 6th. While staying with the McCanns at the villa they rented, Cameron said, he had driven the car often. He had used it on many occasions to transport the families' rubbish to the local tip. He also recalled an occasion in July when, after shopping at the supermarket, he and his wife Patricia had returned carrying bags containing fresh fish, shrimp and beef home in the Renault's boot.

'When we unloaded the shopping bags,' Cameron said in his police statement, 'we noticed that blood had run out of the bottom of the plastic bag. After this shopping trip . . . I began to notice a strange odour in the car . . . [and] assumed it was likely due to the leakage from the rubbish bags or from the blood which had escaped from the shopping bags. As a result, we removed the carpet from the boot in order to clean it. I beat the carpet of the boot to remove any bits, wiped it with a wet cloth and left it to air out.'

As noted earlier, dog handler Martin Grime had proudly claimed in a brief before the Portugal operation that during work on more than two hundred cases, Eddie, the dog trained to scent dead bodies, had 'never alerted to meat-based foodstuffs'. The following year, after Cameron's and Lowes' accounts of having used the Renault to carry meat and household rubbish – with, in particular, Cameron's specific memory of the 'strange odour' he had noticed – Grime was asked whether the dog could 'mix up traces of human odours with others that are non-human'. His response was to say that the dogs 'appear to be extremely exact. But forensic confirmation is required in all cases to be included as proof.'

Approached in 2014, Grime declined to be interviewed either on the dogs' role in the Madeleine McCann case, because it is still open, or on Eddie's and Keela's abilities in general. The view at the time of the case of another handler, former Scotland Yard specialist John Barrett, was that dogs had been brought in too late – that 'the crucial scent lasts no longer than a month'.

Another key point, the authors were repeatedly told, is that the label 'cadaver dog' is something of a misnomer. Such an animal *can* indicate where a dead body is or has been, but could more precisely be called a 'human remains' dog. It is an important distinction. The dog is trained merely to detect the odour of decomposing human material. This could be only a small decaying piece of human matter, matter that belonged to a human being who is in fact still alive and well.

At almost the same time as the dog searches in Praia da Luz, a court in a murder trial in the USA was told that three sniffer dogs had alerted to the scent of a presumed victim more than twenty *years* after the alleged murder. Told, though, that one of the dog's alerts were mistaken 78 per cent of the time, a second's 71 per cent of the time and a third's 62 per cent of the time – which he deemed no more reliable than 'the flip of a coin' – the judge ruled testimony about the dogs' responses inadmissible. (Ironically, the accused man subsequently confessed to the crime.)

A 2007 Swiss study tested how effectively three animals could pick out, from a line-up of six new squares of carpet, the one that had been exposed for no more than ten minutes to the corpse of a person who had recently died. In hundreds of trials, the dogs selected the correct square with 98 per cent accuracy.

Cadaver dogs can indeed, very evidently, be stunningly accurate. Nevertheless, a 2009 report by Britain's National Policing

Improvement Agency – an officer of which had recommended to the Portuguese that they use the animals in the Madeleine probe – stated that there was 'no consistency in what the dogs can do and how it is done' and they 'had the potential to cause complications in an inquiry'. Canines can be wondrously useful – or misleading and time-consumingly fallible. Without forensic evidence, two veteran dog handlers told the authors, no reliance can be put on the alert indications the dogs made in the Madeleine case.

At the start of October 2007, with the wires still humming with rumour and counter-rumour about the 'discoveries' in the case, there was a new and totally unexpected development. It began with a bizarre report from London that Scotland Yard were investigating an email that had been received on Prince Charles' website. It was from an anonymous sender, the *Daily Telegraph* reported, and suggested that a disgruntled female former employee of the Ocean Club might be behind Madeleine's abduction. Though the woman had worked at the resort, the lead went nowhere – except that, for the oddest reason, it led to the removal from the case of chief investigator Gonçalo Amaral.

According to Amaral, it happened as follows. Late on October 1st, while driving through a rainstorm, he took a call on his mobile phone from a reporter asking for a comment on the email that had been sent to Prince Charles. As he recalled it, he replied, 'off the cuff, that the email was of very little interest, that the British police should concern themselves with following the progress of the Portuguese investigation. Even as I was hanging up, I realised that I had been unfair to the British police . . . a group of competent professional men and women who had helped us a lot.'

As reported next day in the *Diário de Notícias*, Amaral had been rather more voluble. The British police, the paper quoted him as saying, had 'only been working on what the McCann couple want, and suits them'. They had 'been investigating tips and information created and worked on by the McCanns, forgetting that the couple are suspects in the death of their daughter Madeleine'.

Amaral had at a stroke damaged his force's relations with its British counterpart and ensured his own professional disgrace. The very day the *Diário* story was published, the national chief of the Polícia Judiciária, Alipio Ribeiro, removed him from the case and from his position as head of the detective unit in Portimão, and ordered him to regional headquarters in Faro. 'The reasons are obvious,' he told reporters. Amaral would later claim, quoting a source in the British media, that British Prime Minister Gordon Brown personally called a senior British police officer to ask for confirmation that he had been dismissed.

Amaral's career had imploded on his forty-eighth birthday. 'This was not the present I'd wanted,' he was to write, 'but one that I was expecting. Basically, this brought to an end a campaign of defamation and insults conducted against [me], orchestrated and developed by the British media almost from the start of the investigation. The strategy was simple: attack the investigation, blaming those who led it, and at the same time present Portugal as a Third World country with a legal system and police force reminiscent of the Middle Ages.'

Amaral was to leave the force within a year. As reported in Chapter 9, he had since the start of the McCann investigation himself been an *arguido* in a case that cast a quite separate shadow on his career – the allegation made by a convicted murderer that she had been tortured by several of Amaral's detectives. The detectives were eventually to be acquitted on the torture charges. For having made a false statement in connection with the matter, however, Amaral would receive an eighteen-month suspended jail sentence.

In the clamour over the chief investigator's removal in October 2007, there was less coverage of a serious charge against his second in command that became public the very same day. His close friend, Chief Inspector Tavares de Almeida, was accused of the torture under interrogation of another prisoner, a railwayman named Virgolino Borges who had been accused, then acquitted, of involvement in a series of violent robberies. During interrogation by Almeida and two other officers, Borges had alleged, he had been 'handcuffed behind his back and grabbed by an officer in such a way that he couldn't double up, and punched several times in the stomach. Then they took off his shoes and – using a fence post – began beating his feet until the post started to splinter.'

Almeida had reportedly admitted taking part in the interrogation but said he could not remember what occurred or who was in charge. Though the case was to drag on for years, he and one of the other officers would eventually be found guilty of torture – reportedly the first PJ inspectors ever to be convicted on such a charge – given a suspended two-and-a-half-year sentence, and fined. Once formally charged, though, Almeida had taken unpaid leave. From October 2007, neither he nor Gonçalo Amaral played any part in the Madeleine investigation.

The Portuguese police investigation of the Madeleine case, however, would continue for months to come. In overall charge now was Paulo Rebelo, a very senior officer who until now had been deputy director of the PJ at the national level. At the press conference on the day of his appointment, asked about media reports that the McCanns could have been involved in their daughter's disappearance, Rebelo said such talk was 'mere speculation'. He also said, though, that, 'All lines of inquiry are still open, and will remain open until the end of the investigation.'

At that time and for months to come, perhaps due to delays at the British Forensic Science Service over the viability or otherwise of Low Copy Number DNA, the Polícia Judiciária had still received no final results of DNA analysis of the samples taken as a result of the dog searches. A four-man Portuguese team of three scientists and Ricardo Paiva – who had earlier interrogated the McCanns – flew to the UK for a 'DNA summit' and returned with nothing resolved. As a double-check, a part from the boot of the McCanns' hire car was returned for testing at a Portuguese police laboratory.

At Rebelo's direction, the PJ launched a trawl through the telephone records of Praia da Luz residents. The emphasis, logically enough, was on calls that had been made after 9.30 p.m. on May 3rd. Meanwhile, and at the highest level, the Portuguese made it clear that they wanted the McCanns and their holiday companions questioned again. The case records and press reports show that the core team of detectives were at that time focused on the theory that Madeleine had suffered an 'accidental death' on the evening of May 3rd, before the McCanns met their friends for dinner.

A report drawn up shortly before Christmas, seven months after the disappearance, refers to 'disparities', 'some inconsistency', the 'lack of a consistent version', in the statements of the McCann party. This document was composed by Inspector João Carlos, who had worked the case from the start and now – with Almeida gone – took on increasing prominence. Careful reading, however, suggests that nothing in what he wrote about the statements of the McCanns' companions reflects an inconsistency of real evidentiary significance.

Carlos' first concern was to point out that no one except her parents, and briefly David Payne – who dropped in at Apartment 5A at some point in the early evening – had seen Madeleine between 5.35 p.m. and around 10.00 p.m., when she was declared missing. In the absence of an independent sighting during that period, Carlos appears to have thought it possible that 'If her parents actually participated in the disappearance, the minor may have been removed between 5.35 p.m. and 10.05 p.m.'

The inspector's second major query concerned the statements of Jane Tanner – who had reported seeing a man carrying a child near Apartment 5A around 9.15 p.m. – and of Gerry McCann and holiday acquaintance Jeremy 'Jez' Wilkins, who said they had been chatting in the same street at that time. Although Tanner said she remembered having seen Gerry and Wilkins as she passed, neither of them recalled having seen her. The implication, in Carlos' report, seems to be that the anomaly impaired the credibility of what Tanner claimed to have seen.

Considered in context, both these perceived problems become less significant. Certainly there was a gap in time during which Madeleine was not seen by an independent witness. The gap shrinks, however, in the sense that both her parents were highly visible at the dinner table in the Tapas restaurant from about 8.30 p.m. – with the exception of Gerry's departure for a quarter of an hour to go and check on their children. That aside, and unless there was real reason to question the honesty of the McCanns and their friends, there was actually nothing mysterious about the period during which Madeleine was not independently seen. (Inspector Carlos, however, was still confident the dog searches had produced significant forensic information pointing to the McCanns' involvement, and that must have influenced his thinking.)

There is a simple riposte, too, to Carlos' apparent doubt that Jane Tanner really saw a man carrying a child when and where she claimed, and within moments of having seen Wilkins and Gerry McCann chatting with each other. They have both consistently said they *were* chatting in the street outside Apartment 5A at about the same time, so it may seem a little surprising that *they* did not notice *her*. Consider, though, the reality of the situation. It was already fairly dark – Tanner recalled the 'orangey' effect of the street lighting. The trio's memories were fuzzy on precisely where they had been standing or which way they had been facing as they chatted. And why would they not be? This is a question relevant to all the events of that evening.

To plough through the Portuguese police records is to note time and again that detectives ignored the reality of the evening. These were people on holiday, enjoying a relaxed dinner – keeping an eye on time passing, to be sure, so as to make fairly regular checks on their various children – but not at all concerned to keep a precise record of who moved where and precisely when. None of them could have imagined, as they came and went from the dinner table by the pool, that they would ever need to create a precise timeline. The timelines they did produce – on the covers of one of Madeleine's books that night, and the clean-typed one four or five days later (see pp.73–5)– were, without any evidence to suppose they were created with deceit in mind, decent approximations.

To the end, though, at least some Portuguese detectives harboured suspicions that the McCanns' friends had made what the press would repeatedly dub a 'pact of silence' – a conspiracy to keep quiet about something that compromised Gerry and Kate

McCann. That suspicion smouldered on, reportedly fuelled when – six long months after Madeleine vanished – the two doctors and their holiday companions held a meeting at a hotel near the McCanns' home in Leicestershire.

So widespread were the rumours then that Gerry and Kate felt it necessary to have their spokesman say: 'It was really just a get-together to discuss where they are at. Clearly, some might face further questioning at some stage. It was not to change stories or compare notes . . . This was in no way to get their stories straight. This is the age of email and phone. They could have done that a long time ago.'

Before the process ended, the investigation team would press hard for two concessions. They wanted the McCanns' companions re-interviewed, and they wanted the entire party to return to Praia da Luz for a 'reconstruction' of the events of the evening of May 3rd. The group was to comply with only one of those requests.

The friends raised no objection to being questioned again. Indeed, Gerry and Kate had themselves formally asked that their holiday companions, people they had encountered in Praia da Luz and others who knew them, be interviewed or re-interviewed. Portuguese officers could not actually conduct the interviews because only British law enforcement has jurisdiction in the UK. The process took months to complete. Questions were ready and letters prepared by mid-December. There was an unexplained delay, however, in getting the requests to the British police. They did not arrive until late January, after another damaging squabble over who – the Portuguese or the British authorities – was at fault.

Finally, over four days in April 2008, all the McCanns' holiday companions were re-interviewed. British officers posed the multiple questions that had been drawn up by the Portuguese. Interviews were recorded on videotape for monitoring by Polícia Judiciára officers. The transcripts, which the authors have read, provide some fresh detail but contain no surprises.

The belated desire of the Portuguese police to stage a reconstruction in 2008, having failed to do so in the days after Madeleine's disappearance, triggered a protracted bureaucratic tug of war. New chief investigator Rebelo and inspectors Carlos and Paiva, the probe's remaining veterans, made it a priority for discussion during a visit to the UK in mid-April 2008. McCann party members, however, responded to the request with a series of initial questions.

'What were the PJ trying to achieve with the re-enactment? Why not use actors? What protection would there be from the likely media frenzy that would accompany such an exercise?' The Portuguese view, Rebelo replied, was that it would contribute to an accurate record of the events of May 3rd, and that this could only be achieved using the real-life participants. The police would see to it, he said, that the media would be kept at bay.

This did not satisfy the group's concerns, and the toing and froing lasted for the best part of two months. Dr Matt Oldfield and his wife Rachael, for their part, felt they still did not know what the PJ were 'really trying to get out of a reconstruction'. They also raised a telling point:

> Either they [the Portuguese police] believe our version of the events of May 3rd 2007, or they don't. If they do, why the need for a reconstruction? If they don't believe us, do they want a reconstruction so we can convince them otherwise?
>
> If the purpose of a reconstruction is to convince the pros-

ecutor to lift Kate and Gerry's *arguido* status, then we would consider taking part in it. If it is to properly focus the investigation on the person seen [by Jane Tanner] carrying a child away from the apartment, again, we would consider taking part because that would help to find Madeleine.

We just need to be properly convinced.

Jeremy Wilkins, though only an acquaintance with no known motive to protect the McCanns, was also asked to participate. He too, however, expressed doubt as to what purpose a reconstruction would serve. There was a lack of information from the police, Wilkins wrote, 'about anything tangible or constructive that is likely to be achieved by doing this'.

Drs David and Fiona Payne also said they still needed to be persuaded 'that doing this would be wholly beneficial to the investigation . . . and FINDING Madeleine'.

Meanwhile, Dr Russ O'Brien and his partner Jane Tanner said they were 'somewhat reassured' that, according to the Portuguese police, they were not now suspected of 'the commission of criminal acts'. However, they added sceptically, 'we heard something similar in the weeks before Kate and Gerry were made *arguidos*! . . . Furthermore, we cannot help but feel that the re-interviews and re-enactment are all too little and far too late.'

So it went. As the objections continued, the planned date for the reconstruction was put off. When the request changed, as the Paynes put it, 'from informal and friendly to a formal summons', some of those involved sought legal advice. On May 27th, word came that the Portuguese prosecutor's office had given up on the notion of a re-enactment after all.

Inspector Ricardo Paiva had already realised days earlier what the McCann party's obduracy – on top of the lack of other progress in the inquiry – meant. 'Given the tone of the content [of] the witnesses' positions,' he wrote in a short note to his boss Rebelo, 'I shall begin the process of winding up this investigation.' From the Polícia Judiciária's point of view, it was now merely a question of closing up shop.

On June 30th 2008, with the final report from the UK's Forensic Science Service in hand, Inspector João Carlos composed his Final Report. This had been, he wrote, an operation like 'no other investigation in Portugal'. The PJ had spared no effort, provided 'exceptional technical means, manpower, and financing towards the discovery of the child and the determination of the facts'. He bewailed the fact that no re-enactment had taken place 'due to the refusal of some of the necessary members of the holiday group to return to our country'. That, he suggested, might have resolved crucial outstanding issues.

Despite all the force's efforts, the Final Report concluded, it was 'not possible to obtain a solid and objective conclusion as to what really happened that night, and as to the present location of the missing minor'.

Within three weeks, on July 21st 2008, local prosecutors João Melchior Gomes and José de Magalhães e Menezes prepared a fifty-seven-page Summary for the Attorney General and closed the case. They had some criticism of Gerry and Kate McCann. The statement of neighbour Pamela Fenn that she had heard prolonged crying one night suggested, they wrote, that – on one occasion before Madeleine disappeared – they had not done thorough checks on their children.

Articles in the Portuguese press had cited a clause of the Portuguese penal code that referred to the crime of 'abandonment'. The president of Portugal's Missing Children's Association, Patrícia Cipriano, told the authors in 2014 that children should 'not be left alone at home or at any place without an adult who is responsible for their safety . . .'

Prosecutors Gomes and Magalhães e Menezes rejected any notion of bringing a charge as some had suggested possible – the law on abandonment requires that there be evidence of 'intent'. 'The parents,' they wrote, 'could not have foreseen that, in the resort in which they had chosen to spend a brief holiday, they would be placing the lives of any of their children in danger.'

The McCanns, the prosecutors wrote, had 'trusted that everything would go well, as it had on previous evenings . . . it is certain, in any case, that they did watch over [the children] . . . We must also recognise that the parents have already paid a heavy penalty – the disappearance of Madeleine – due to their lack of carefulness in the watching and protection of their children.'

The prosecutors then waxed literary. The Madeleine case, they wrote, was 'not a police novel, a convenient scenario for a crime tailor-made for a successful investigation by a Sherlock Holmes or an Hercule Poirot, driven by the illusion that the forces of law and order always manage to right the order that has been upset and restore peace and tranquillity to society . . . The disappearance of Madeleine McCann is, rather, an implacable and intricate matter of real life . . . Real life, day-to-day life, tends not to follow the rules of logic.'

Nothing remained for the prosecutors but to close down the case. They declared that, because there were 'no indications of having committed any crime' on the parts of Gerry and Kate McCann, their *arguido* status should be lifted. So should that of Robert Murat, who had once – it seemed so long ago – been portrayed as a principal suspect. The case was declared 'archived', the investigation records made available to the public.

This, though, was not necessarily the end of the process. Should new evidence justify it, Gomes and Megalhães e Menezes stated, the case could be reopened.

So far as some were concerned, there was no closure. The McCanns' spokesman, Clarence Mitchell, would say the release of the Portuguese police files held out hope of a breakthrough. There was no evidence that Madeleine had been harmed, he told Sky News. The files might contain 'one little nugget in those tens of thousands of pages . . . that could lead to Madeleine, and that's the priority.'

Meanwhile, the former head of the Portuguese investigation, Gonçalo Amaral, had resurfaced to say that he had written a book and that he expected the case to be reopened 'at any moment'. Gerry and Kate were to sue him for libel over the book – *Maddie: A Verdade da Mentira*, which translates as '*Maddie: The Truth of the Lie*'. As reported earlier, judgement was pending as this edition went to press.

15

There was never the smallest shred of fact or evidence to inculpate Maddie's parents in any way at all. Yet they have faced a host of detractors and critics. 'Disliking the McCanns,' the novelist Anne Enright wrote in the *London Review of Books* a few months after Madeleine's disappearance, 'is an international sport . . . If someone else is found to have taken Madeleine McCann,' the prize-winning author declared, ' . . . it will show that the ordinary life of an ordinary family cannot survive the suspicious scrutiny of millions . . . We dislike them for whatever it is that nags at us. We do not forgive them the stupid stuff, like wearing ribbons, or going jogging . . . or holding hands on the way into Mass.

'I disliked the McCanns earlier than most people (I'm not proud of it). I thought I was angry with them for leaving their children alone. In fact, I was angry at their failure to accept that their daughter was probably dead . . . Guilt and denial are the emotions we smell off Gerry and Kate McCann, and they madden us.'

Enright, a decent person, later apologised for any hurt her article might have caused the McCanns. Writing it, she said, had been for her an 'emotional journey full of nuance and contradiction and self-appraisal'. What she and the *Review of Books* had published, certainly, fades into insignificance beside the many crass, callous articles the tabloid press would run.

Later, in an impassioned statement to the Leveson Inquiry into British press ethics, Gerry McCann would say his family had been 'subject to some of the most sensationalist, untruthful, irresponsible and damaging reporting'. In the eventual Inquiry Report, Lord Leveson would agree. Along with the reporting of the disappearance of schoolgirl Milly Dowler and the arrest for questioning of retired teacher Christopher Jefferies on suspicion of murdering his tenant, Leveson considered that the McCann case coverage exemplified 'the most egregious cases of unethical journalistic conduct'.

The McCanns' police status as *arguidos*, Gerry was to tell the Inquiry, had led the press 'to declare open season' on them. He cited appalling examples. In late 2007, the *Daily Star* had carried a headline reading flatly 'MADDIE MUM "SOLD HER"'. A 'bombshell' police theory, claimed the accompanying article, had been that Madeleine might have been sold to bail the couple out of money trouble. Another *Star* headline, the same month, was 'MADDIE MUM ORGY FURY', coupled to a story about the suggestion – mentioned earlier in these pages – that the McCanns and their party were swingers.

Worse – if worse were possible – because it trod as close as the paper dared to suggesting the couple were involved in their daughter's death – had been a *Daily Express* story headlined: 'MADELEINE: IT WAS HER BLOOD IN PARENTS' HIRE CAR'. Using Carter-Ruck, the London law firm that specialises in libel litigation, the McCanns had sued over this and other coverage. Rather than let the suit go to trial, Express Newspapers, which owns both the *Express* and the *Star*, settled the case and paid £550,000 into the fund established to help find Madeleine. They also printed a front-page apology for articles that had suggested 'that the couple caused the death of their missing daughter Madeleine and then covered it up.' The group also acknowledged that 'there is no evidence whatsoever to support this theory and that Kate and Gerry are completely innocent of any involvement in their daughter's disappearance.'

In Gerry McCann's view, Express Newspapers were 'certainly the worst offenders.' The McCanns also complained about sixty-seven articles published by Associated Newspapers, owners of the *Daily Mail* and at that time of the *Evening Standard*, who agreed to settle out of court for an undisclosed sum and publish an apology in the *Standard*. The *Standard* had run the headline: 'POLICE BELIEVE MOTHER KILLED MADDY'.

The careless, inconsiderate coverage was not confined to the UK and Portugal. In September 2007, the American news channel CNN covered the Madeleine story on a prime-time show named after its presenter, Nancy Grace. Grace had gained notoriety time and again both in her previous incarnation as a lawyer and as a 'legal commentator' on television. The year before the Madeleine segment aired, she and the network had been sued following the suicide of the mother in another missing-child case – the woman's estate claimed that Grace's hectoring interview of the woman had driven her to kill herself. The suit was settled, with no blame accruing to Grace but with CNN creating a trust to assist in finding the missing boy. In that and other cases, a law professor told the *New York Times*, the presenter had demeaned both the legal profession and broadcast journalism with her 'hype, rabid persona, and sensational analysis.'

Grace's anchoring of CNN's coverage of the Madeleine story was an excitable, rapid-fire rant that began with the assertion that 'reportedly' Portuguese police were 'seeking charges of homicide and concealing the baby's body'. She said the McCanns' and their friends' dinner party on the night of May 3rd sounded to her 'like a big drunk'. The notion that traces of fluid supposedly found in the McCann rental car might simply have contained DNA from Madeleine's saliva was 'preposterous'. Gerry and Kate had 'a lot of explaining to do'. She portrayed their entirely legitimate departure from Portugal as 'fleeing the country'.

Another American personality, author and crime specialist Pat Brown, began in 2007 to expound on the Madeleine case – as she would for the next seven years. Brown, who holds an MA in Criminal Justice from Boston University, appeared often not only on Nancy Grace's show but on MSNBC, the Discovery and Court TV channels and Fox. She ran, and still runs, the Pat Brown Criminal Profiling Agency, which – by its own description – 'provides crime scene analysis and behavioral profiling to prosecutors, defense attorneys, media, and international clients'.

Writing in her blog 'The Daily Profiler' five months after Madeleine vanished, Brown stressed the importance of care – in the absence of hard evidence – when analysing whether a person is displaying guilt. Not to be careful, she added, would be to indulge in mere speculation. A paragraph later, she wrote that the presence of Madeleine's DNA in the Renault rental car would mean the McCanns were guilty. (It would not mean that, and the forensic record indicates that Madeleine's DNA was not found in the car.)

In the same blog, Brown objected to a comment by Gerry McCann that they had been 'responsible . . . performing our own baby listening service' when they left the children in Apartment 5A while they went out to eat. Perhaps he had misspoken, Brown said. Perhaps it was similar to a moment, she asserted, when Gerry had pulled his ear while denying publicly that he and Kate had given Madeleine sedatives. Pulling one's ear, it has been suggested by those who study clues to deception, may on occasion indicate that one is not telling the truth. Not a jot of evidence existed, however, at any time, for the theory that the McCanns sedated their daughter, or that they have lied about the circumstances of this case.

Brown was deemed worthy of prominent airtime on American television. By 2010, she would still be expounding her theories on CBS' national, live *Early Show*. The theory that Madeleine died in the apartment, she told viewers, was one the McCanns did not want publicly discussed.

In 2012 Brown flew to Portugal, equipped with metal detector, soil probe and a spade, to conduct what she called a search analysis. First stop on the trip was a meeting with former chief investigator Gonçalo Amaral. She then criss-crossed Praia da Luz, snapping photographs and tramping around the shoreline and nearby gullies. The adventure produced only substantial self-publicity.

In 2014 Pat Brown expressed hope for Amaral's success in defending the long-running libel suit the McCanns had brought against him because of his book. She lamented the fact that, as she saw it, those who struggle to keep the truth alive are labelled conspiracy theorists and nutcases.

Doubts about the McCanns were also raised in Europe. In September 2007, the online edition of the prominent German newspaper *Die Welt* published a long interview about the Madeleine case with Dr Christian Lüdke. Lüdke was described as a criminal psychologist and head of a company that 'supports the victims of robberies, kidnappings, accidents, or disasters'. He had apparently commented on the case before, for the reporter first asked why he had cautioned that 'Gerry and Kate McCann's behaviour indicated that they could have been involved in the crime'. Lüdke began by talking of elements in the couple's behaviour he thought 'questionable', including the fact that as doctors they had left their children alone in the first place, and that they had recently left their twins to travel across Europe. These views were perhaps not outlandish, but by the fourth question he had lurched into outrageous innuendo.

Asked another leading question, about what motive the parents could have had to 'cause their own daughter's disappearance', Lüdke said there existed parents who 'had little or no emotional bond with a child', whose child was a 'burden that had to be disposed of in a brutal or perverse way'. One of the best-known of such situations, he said, was the Munchausen syndrome by proxy – a well-documented condition in which an adult, most often a mother, fabricates symptoms of illness in a child, or causes the child actual harm, to gain attention. There was, of course, no evidence at all that such behaviour applied to either of Madeleine's parents. Lüdke, however, was not done.

Questioned as to whether he thought the McCanns had possibly 'together killed Madeleine and hidden her', the psychologist replied darkly: 'I believe both parents at least have participants' knowledge of what occurred.' Then, asked whether they had planned their own daughter's death, he replied, 'Yes. It is possible they long planned this, had several times played it out – at least in their imaginations – and had talked it through together.'

Lüdke was still not finished. 'It is easier for them to lie than to face up to the truth,' he said of the McCanns. 'Much would point to a psychological disorder. The McCanns' children were so far as I know conceived artificially – that can lead to problems in the relationship. Maybe there were self-esteem issues that were not openly addressed. Perhaps the child had to die because of a problem that had been going on for years.'

Maybe this and maybe that – on the basis of not an iota of evidence. The *Die Welt* interviewer pointed out that people at large thought it impossible that the McCanns could be guilty. Lüdke replied that the media had 'maybe been taken in . . . The parents have been followed around like the Beckhams.'

Then, a final flourish. 'Statistically,' Lüdke noted, '70 per cent of all cases of violence against children are perpetrated by parents, relatives or those they know. That regrettably has remained largely overlooked [in this instance].'

As the interview ended, the psychologist was asked whether he had been criticised for voicing suspicion of Madeleine's mother and father. Yes, he said, there had been an 'enormous' amount of criticism of him. There had been open letters and a 'campaign on the Internet involving professional associations'.

Lüdke's background, *Die Welt* stated, included a decade of working as a criminal psychologist and recent publication of an advice manual dealing with children's fears. His career summary styles him as a Doctor of Philosophy and a Research Fellow of Cologne University, with experience of working with 'difficult children' in New York and with police training in Germany. A greeting on his current website, however, reads: 'Hallelujah, brothers and sisters, dear children, psycho-ramblers and itinerant preachers! . . . Hearty greetings from [computer] screen to screen! Dig in, 'til soon . . . Bye, Christian.'

Another professional, long a bête noire for the McCanns, is the English former solicitor and activist Tony Bennett. Bennett, now sixty-seven, had drawn attention to himself long before he began fulminating about the Madeleine case. A bright man with an excellent academic background, he had worked in local govern-

ment and then as a solicitor until found guilty of 'conduct unbe-
coming' by the Solicitors Disciplinary Tribunal and reprimanded.
Long a Labour Party enthusiast, he had veered right across the
spectrum to become a luminary of the then still nascent UKIP,
the United Kingdom Independence Party.

Bennett, who sees himself as a 'fighter for truth against powerful
people', has gone to extraordinary lengths to pursue his goals.
While a UKIP member, he founded the Active Resistance to
Metrication group, formed to fight the changeover to metric, and
was prosecuted or arrested on several occasions. He ran a campaign
involving the dispatch of purple postcards to the Queen, requesting
that she refuse Royal Assent to any law designed to adopt the EU
constitution. He took steps to bring a private prosecution of the
entertainer Michael Barrymore, in connection with the infamous
night that a man was found dead at Barrymore's house. It was
blocked by a district judge on the grounds of insufficient evidence.

Bennett's harrying of the McCanns began six months after
Madeleine's disappearance, when he asked authorities in
Leicestershire to bring a case against the couple for child neglect.
On the grounds that the case came under Portuguese jurisdiction,
the request was turned down. Then, in January 2008, Bennett
and others agreed to form the Madeleine Foundation, with the
declared aim not only of legislating against ever leaving young
children alone but also of investigating the Madeleine case. It
had, he told the authors, some forty-five members.

Early the following year, the foundation's members made
their presence felt at a London School of Economics debate on
media coverage of the case. They 'showed a lamentable grasp
of debating rules,' the *Guardian*'s Roy Greenslade noted, 'by
interrupting speakers and shouting out a string of offensive
comments about the McCanns and their PRs.' Greenslade, who

noted 'their unconcealed bile, their lack of compassion for the McCanns,' thought them like 'those mobs outside courts in murder trials, deaf to facts, cocooned from reality by their own self-righteous demagoguery'.

In 2009, members circulated leaflets with headings such as: 'The sheer impossibility of the abduction scenario', 'The refusal of the McCanns and their friends to help the police' and 'Changes of story by the McCanns and their friends'. Members caused a stir by distributing the leaflets around the McCanns' home village of Rothley.

Bennett wrote a book, too, entitled *What Really Happened to Madeleine McCann: 60 Reasons which suggest she was not abducted.* He wrote to the General Medical Council questioning whether either Dr Gerald or Dr Kate McCann were 'fit to practise or indeed to remain on the GMC Register'. The McCanns struck back, again using the Carter-Ruck legal firm, and Bennett undertook 'not to repeat allegations that the McCanns are guilty of, or are to be suspected of, causing the death of their daughter Madeleine, and/or of disposing of her body, and/or lying about what happened and/or seeking to cover up what they had done'.

Notwithstanding, Bennett – and a sometime cohort named Deborah Butler – and his foundation persisted in their activities. 'Secrecy surrounds what's billed as the annual conference of the self-appointed Madeleine Foundation,' BBC journalist Simon Hare reported in 2010. 'They've said I can attend, but I have to wait for news of the location. I'm told to make my way to a hotel with conference facilities, but this proved to be just a meeting place. I'm then taken to the real venue, a room in this village hall at Nuthall . . . There were nineteen people at the meeting. I was told that they'd come from all over the country and that one couple had even come from northern France.'

Also in 2010, the foundation declared a Gonçalo Amaral Day, and invited the former investigator to speak at its annual conference. One foundation member characterised Amaral as 'a folk hero, he's sort of a modern day Robin Hood, if you like. It's like a David and Goliath fight.' According to the foundation's website, leaflets were distributed in Birmingham, Borehamwood, Bournemouth, Bristol, Cardiff, Devon, Dover, Elstree, Harlow, Hayes, Hazel Grove, Hull, London, Rhondda Cynon Taff, Southampton, Stockport, Uxbridge, West Cumbria – and the American state of Wyoming.

Bennett again heard from the McCanns' lawyers that year. They told him that his 'misconceived and deeply offensive attacks against them are harming the search for their daughter'. He was, a letter said, repeatedly breaching his court undertakings.

And so it went. More Bennett letters were fired off, calling for a public inquiry into Madeleine's disappearance, to Prime Minister Cameron, Home Secretary Theresa May and then Minister for Justice Kenneth Clarke. In 2011, when a Metropolitan Police review of the case began its work, he wrote saying that his foundation wished to submit a 'dossier of circumstantial evidence' and 'information, of a first-hand nature, received from a female insider within the McCann team whose information strongly tends to suggest that the entire McCann Team private investigation team was exercised in the creation of a huge smokescreen to cover up what really happened'. Bennett was invited to submit his information in writing.

In 2013, the letters Bennett had written to the Prime Minister and the Home Secretary were included in a list of breaches of his earlier undertakings alleged by the McCanns' lawyers. Bennett was convicted and sentenced to three months in prison, suspended for a year. He was sorry for the distress he had caused the

McCanns, he said afterwards, and hoped the case would 'result in both of us drawing a line under the situation'. The Madeleine Foundation website is still on the Web, and a foundation member responds to emails. Bennett himself, he told the authors, still talks about the case with a few people, and conducts research.

'This case has fired literally thousands of people,' he said, 'to delve into the depths of the matter, and many of them who have done most of the delving either do not wish to be named and take credit or are, indeed, fearful of being named publicly because of the potential severe adverse consequences of voicing one's opinions.' There have been and still are, as Bennett told the authors, dozens of McCann-sceptic websites. The sites are the murky substrata of the case, peopled by those who have been dubbed 'the haters'.

16

The hating, in one form or another, began early. Cruel anonymous letters began coming soon after Madeleine went missing. One told the McCanns their daughter was being tortured and that they were responsible, another that she was dead and buried. Back home, at Christmas, they received a card that read, 'You ******* thieving bastards. Your brat is dead because of your drunken arrogance . . . If you have any shame you would accept full responsibility for your daughter's disappearance . . . You are scum.' There was even a death threat.

What caused additional torment was the opportunity to spread poison provided by the Internet, on websites and discussion groups and blogs. In any high-profile case, there will always be people who want to get their personal views across. In the McCann case, the Internet exponentially increased the ability of such individuals to reach a huge audience.

Despite there being no evidence of wrongdoing on the McCanns' part, their critics proliferated – many of them sniping anonymously from cyberspace. The drip feed continues to this day. We report here on some of those whose identities are known or proved traceable.

Tony Bennett of the Madeleine Foundation, who acted openly, was not one of the cowards who hid behind his computer screen. Nor was his enthusiastic supporter Jill Havern, a Birmingham-based driving instructor with a grudge against the National Health Service and Leicester's Glenfield Hospital in particular. By her account, Havern's husband Alan had been misdiagnosed by doctors at Glenfield and later died. Long before he did, she had begun writing a blog entitled 'NHS: Death Row'.

By coincidence, Gerry McCann had worked at Glenfield Hospital – but only from 2005. Kate McCann worked as a part-time GP at a practice near their home in Rothley. Neither of them had had anything whatsoever to do with the care of Jill Havern's husband. Somehow, however, her interest in Madeleine's disappearance – 'due to negligence from 2 NHS doctors' – grew out of that coincidence. 'I can reluctantly kind of understand negligence towards my husband for the sake of saving money,' Havern wrote, 'but negligence towards your own child and then the obvious circus that ensued to make money from her?'

The McCanns have not sought to profit from their situation – and Madeleine's Fund has built-in provisions to ensure this does not occur.

Havern started a new blog, naming it: 'NHS: The McCanns' Abuse of Power'. It had a black background, lurid content and distorted photographs of the McCanns – one of them of Kate, with a voice bubble over her head that read: 'I think we've got away with it.'

Within two weeks of Madeleine's disappearance, a man named John Hirst had posted comments on a blog described as coming from a 'conservative perspective': 'I have not accepted the McCanns' version of events. No sign of a break-in. Only a half-hour window of opportunity . . . I believe the police investigation should centre around Gerry and Kate McCann.' And: 'They were dining out. And this is my point, it was establishing an alibi.'

By his own account, Hirst is a 'law-breaker' turned 'law-maker'. In 1979, having killed his landlady with an axe – he has said he 'snapped' – he was sentenced to life in prison for manslaughter. During the twenty-five years he served, he read voraciously on law and became a perennial litigant. He was the major protago- nist in the campaign to give prisoners in the UK the right to vote.

For several years, Hirst would write a scurrilous blog he named 'Justice for Madeleine' – with the introductory statement that 'The McCanns will not escape justice via the Mainstream Media, this blog seeks to question their version of events.' Kate McCann's new book, he wrote in 2011, 'is obviously a work of fiction'. He imagined a scenario in which the two doctors 'hatch a plot in an attempt to salvage their reputations. The plot involves disposing of Madeleine's body, staging a fake break-in, and inventing an abductor.'

There is, too, the 2010 book *Faked Abduction,* by an author who styled himself 'Brian Johnson'. He has given interviewers, however, as Steve Marsden – and goes by the name 'Stevo' on his website truthformadeleine.com, which he started in the late autumn of the year Madeleine disappeared. The blurb for *Faked Abduction* states that the book exposes 'the Madeleine McCann Cover-up'.

His charges, made in the book and online, include the notions that: the Madeleine investigation 'was controlled and steered in one direction from Day 1 by the British Establishment'; MI6 was involved; Gerry McCann is privy to information implicating the Royal Family in the murder of Princess Diana (the inquest into the Princess' death was soon to start 'and the Royals could not have Gerry McCann upset the applecart'); the founding of the Madeleine Fund involved a 'large network of Freemasons'; and the death years later of Colin Sahlke, a former British soldier who had helped in searches around Praia da Luz, is 'a mystery'.

The ramblings and loaded innuendo of some McCann-case sceptics is ostensibly buttressed by a mass of information. One of the principal gatherers of data is a retiree named Pam Watson who uses the pseudonym 'Pamalam'. Early on, she began posting screenshots of Gerry McCann's blog entries – copied from the McCanns' website – on to a site of her own.

Though at first sight innocuous enough, Watson had created an illusion – for newcomers – that the site was Gerry's. She soon added further pages. Alongside links to analysis of the Madeleine Fund's yearly accounts, the site today displays both Kate McCann's diary entries as leaked to the press in 2008 and former investigation head Gonçalo Amaral's book – in the original Portuguese and in an English translation – in spite of the fact that both had been the subject of legal action by the McCanns when initially published elsewhere. Although the McCanns' legal firm Carter-Ruck sent Watson's web host a stern letter, both the diary entries and the Amaral book were still to be found on the site when this book went to press.

Although she herself appears to be a sceptic, another of Watson's sites includes an extensive, efficiently mounted archive of the available Portuguese police records. With the help of a team of anonymous translators – 'Ines', 'Albym', 'Luz' – some thousands of pages of files are available both in the Portuguese original and in quite accurate English translation.

Watson did not respond, however, to a request by the authors to discuss her work. Nor did Nigel Moore, the registered owner of another of the sites for 'serious' researchers. Moore's site, like

Watson's, was up and running within five months of the disappearance and, according to press reports, he was giving the work his 'virtual full-time attention, seven days a week'. The site is a vast compendium of McCann-related press reports and video material – and Moore's own take on the case.

The stated purpose of the Moore site is 'to find out what really happened to Madeleine and bring her home'. The caption beneath a photograph of Gerry McCann, however, speaks volumes. It is the warning of Disney's Blue Fairy to Pinocchio that: 'A lie keeps growing and growing until it's as plain as the nose on your face.' The site's contacts pages and index, meanwhile, refer to the 'claim' that the McCanns and their friends 'checked regularly on their children' and to their 'carefully orchestrated use of the media'. It prominently quotes Gonçalo Amaral as saying of the McCanns, 'They know that Madeleine is dead and that there were no abductors' and 'They are drowning in the lies they have been saying.'

On Twitter, Moore has cited a critical analysis of the Madeleine Fund's most recent – 2013 – accounts. He himself, meanwhile, has long included a 'donate' button on his own website. 'To enable me to continue to maintain and develop the site, I need support. Yours!' he wrote in 2008. Then, with a nudge and a wink to those who knew funding for the search for Madeleine had come in from wealthy individuals: 'I do not have the luxury of rich benefactors behind me.' That line has since been removed, but the donate button was still there in 2014.

Portugal also has a prominent online dissenter to what one might call the conventional version of the McCann saga. This is Joana Morais, filmmaker and blogger – she is the daughter of Graça Morais, a prominent artist. The website she runs offers a chronological database of Madeleine-case related newspaper and television stories, English translations of the released police files and more. A scan of Morais' Twitter profile indicates that a large number of her seventeen thousand tweets to some four thousand followers have been about Madeleine.

Then there is Morais' personal blog, which makes clear that she supports former Polícia Judiciária chief investigator Amaral. The blog is pointedly dedicated to the clause in the Portuguese constitution that relates to free speech and requires that there not be 'any type or form of censorship'.

Morais is another of those who did not reply to the authors' correspondence. She articulated early on, though, a key element of her motivation. In September 2007, in the first of what would be her more than two thousand posts, she ran a story from Spain's *El Pais* newspaper on how the McCann case had 'opened a gap between two historic allies, the United Kingdom and Portugal'.

'I felt desperate at times,' Morais wrote in 2008, '[in] not understanding the support given to the McCanns by the British press and the British authorities. I even felt disgusted and embarrassed with [PJ national director] Alipio Ribeiro's attack, in the media, on the PJ officers handling the case . . . Sometimes I felt like dropping everything and closing my eyes to all the injustice, racism and media attacks – but then I found that I'm very proud of my small and beautiful country, and even prouder of our people and history, and – though by writing my blog and using my real name I'm running a risk – I'll keep on defending my country.'

Of those who long treated the McCanns as targets, to be lambasted with criticism and worse, one has admitted publicly that she rues what she has done. This is Bren Ryan, an Englishwoman in her mid-fifties. She founded one of the largest anti-McCann websites – at one point it had some seven thousand members on its forum.

She called it 'The3Arguidos', a reference, of course, to Gerry, Kate and Robert Murat – the man who had first been allotted suspect status. For two years, she has recalled, she genuinely 'thought the McCann family did have something to hide and like others classed them as being guilty . . . I allowed people to post the most horrendous allegations possible.'

In 2009, however, following squabbles amongst leading members, 'The3Arguidos' site was taken down. Bren Ryan, for her part, had begun to have a change of heart. By the following year, when she had finally done something she had never previously done – taken time to read the police files carefully – she had completely reversed her position. 'I started,' she wrote, 'to think that Kate and Gerry McCann and their friends are innocent in this.' She had come to feel that a forum like 'The3Arguidos' 'should never in this world have been given an inch of cyberspace . . . There was no evidence to support the many allegations pertaining to the theory that Kate and Gerry McCann were involved in their daughter's disappearance.'

In 2014, in a letter to the authors, Ryan said the realisation of what she did has made it hard to live with herself at times. She had done 'something that was morally wrong'. So, she said, 'I did the only thing I could do, apologise to the family in an open letter, and put the true facts to the many myths, rumours and speculation that surround this case.'

17

All along, while the McCanns' haters were propagating their poison, Madeleine's father and mother never ceased doing what they could to move the investigation – what they saw as a stalled investigation – forward.

They held to the belief, a belief that on occasion faltered, that their daughter could still be alive. Their return to the UK, Gerry had said immediately after disembarking from the aircraft that carried the family back from Portugal, 'does not mean we are giving up our search for her. As parents we cannot give up on our daughter until we know what has happened.'

Three days later, on September 12th, a man who was to be of great and lasting assistance got in touch with the McCanns. Forty-seven-year-old Brian Kennedy, an immensely wealthy businessman, had been following their story as it unwound in Portugal and wanted to do something to help. 'I was incredulous,' he told the authors in 2014. 'I'd been losing all hope and faith in human nature. I had been asking myself, "How is this possible?" This woman is grieving. My instincts were telling me there was a great injustice being done. I called my in-house lawyer at the Latium Group and said, "I want you to reach out to these poor folks and see if we can help them."'

Kennedy, the son of a window cleaner, had amassed a fortune by 2007 – his net worth as head of Latium was said to be £250 million – by leapfrogging from trainee accountant to a management role in a kitchen-equipment company, then to the mobile-phone business, double-glazing and plastics – and the purchase of a rugby team. An experiment with retirement having driven him 'nuts', he was now back in the business fray. A philanthropist, he had a reputation for doing the unexpected.

When he began talking about trying to help the McCanns, friends and colleagues told him not to get involved, that his intervention would end in tears. '"What," he recalled someone saying, "if the parents turn out to be guilty?" I remember saying, "What happens if they're innocent?" Can you imagine the horror of losing your daughter . . . and then the world turning against you and accusing you of being responsible for her murder? Is it not bad enough, the terror, the agony they are going through. I could understand it – I've got five kids. I told my lawyer, "If you feel they're innocent, then we'll get behind them and help them."'

The lawyer made contact with the McCanns and they were whisked to a meeting with Kennedy in London. 'Within fifteen seconds of listening to Kate,' he said, 'I made a decision, using all the emotional intelligence one builds up over many years. I was a hundred per cent convinced of their total innocence. I told them that, one, we would find a top Portuguese lawyer to defend them, and get them off as *arguidos*. Two, we'd do everything in our power to influence the public's perspective and views. And three, we'd support them in setting up some private investigators . . . The Portuguese police had stopped investigating. It was urgent to get some other guys on to it.'

Top-level legal help was found in Portugal. At Kennedy's bidding and at his expense, the British government adviser who had acted as the McCanns' spokesman in Praia da Luz, Clarence Mitchell, promptly quit his job and came back on-board. As another insider put it, he was to work steadfastly with the couple 'almost in the way in the way a minder would look after a celebrity'.

Kennedy has preferred not to reveal how much he spent on helping the McCanns, beyond saying that there were 'substantial' outgoings – principally the legal and media-related costs. Spa owner Stephen Winyard and Sir Richard Branson also contributed. The Madeleine Fund would in time deal with the cost of private investigators, once that effort went into high gear.

Present at Kennedy's first meeting with the McCanns, in London, were representatives of Control Risks, a long-established firm specialising in security and crisis management that had sent detectives to Portugal to see the couple right after Madeleine's disappearance. They had been there on that occasion, the first time the use of private detectives had been discussed, at the expense of an anonymous donor whose identity has never been revealed.

Kate McCann had not enjoyed that first encounter. One of the men Control Risks had sent to Praia da Luz was a somewhat mysterious figure who introduced himself only as 'Hugh'. He was one of the many former intelligence officers the company employed, and a main part of his role now was as a potential kidnap negotiator. Kate, already distraught, had not liked the James Bond atmosphere he brought with him. Besides, and in a sense tragically, there never would be anybody other than hoaxers with whom to negotiate.

In the UK, with the McCanns at home again, Control Risks checked the house in Rothley and the couples' telephones for possible bugs. The company also arranged for forensic analysis of samples of the twins' hair – in case it might be possible to find evidence that an abductor had sedated them on May 3rd. (Kate's hair was also tested, because of rumours that she had been on medication at the time. The results of the tests were negative.)

As the McCanns' use of Control Risks began to be mentioned in the press, noises of disapproval came from Portugal. 'You cannot have private detectives intervening in criminal cases,' sniffed Carlos Anjos, head of the Polícia Judiciária's union. The McCanns planned to go ahead anyway, confirmed in their resolve by advice Gerry had noted during his research trip to the USA back in the summer.

A document issued by the US Justice Department for use by parents of missing children, *The Family Survival Guide*, recommended considering using private detectives if it was believed they could 'do something better or different than what is being done by law enforcement'. Given what they saw as the fiasco of the Portuguese police probe, the McCanns did nurture that hope.

'I had no experience at all with private detectives,' their benefactor Kennedy remembered. 'But the way you run a business is all about surrounding yourself with people who understand industries that you don't understand.' He initially hired two former Metropolitan Police detectives, and in late September decided to follow up a tantalising rumour that Madeleine might have been sighted in Morocco (see pp.119–20).

Kennedy and the detectives, who flew out aboard his private jet, hired a Moroccan tourist guide to accompany them to the mountain village where it had been said the missing girl might be. She was not, of course, but the guide – promised a reward – subsequently spoke of having travelled vast distances circulating Madeleine's picture. 'If I find her,' he said, 'I will be rich. I have been promised I will never have to work again – maybe a million pounds.'

'I suppose,' Kennedy said in 2014, 'we had been looking for low-hanging fruit. After a few weeks, though, we decided we needed to go about it in a very professional way.' Enthusiasm and energy aside, Kennedy had set a potentially really useful process in motion. Months earlier, the Portuguese police had produced an entirely useless drawing of the man the McCanns' friend Jane Tanner had seen carrying a child near Apartment 5A the night Madeleine vanished. A featureless image the police showed around Praia da Luz – based on their questioning of Tanner – was remembered by her as having resembled nothing so much as 'an egg with hair'. It contained no useful information.

Now, in England, a British forensic sketch artist took on the job of extracting more and relevant information from Tanner. This was Melissa Little, whose background included a training course at the FBI Academy in the United States. The result, a profile image in both black and white and colour versions, offered at least a notion – albeit without facial details – of how she remembered the man, his hairstyle and his clothing (see photo 26, left). Released in late October, it received major media coverage – giving the case the oxygen of publicity and raising the possibility of generating new leads.

Later, working with information supplied by one of the Praia da Luz witnesses who had been approached by a man collecting for a non-existent orphanage – which put him among the suspects – forensic artist Little produced another image. Her work became a permanent part of the dossier and – what we have of British police files shows – sparked work on new, computer-generated images. Attention was given, for the first time, to other men seen near Apartment 5A before Madeleine went missing.

Brian Kennedy, meanwhile, cast around for suitable private

investigators to hire and picked Método 3, a Spanish company. One of the agency's claims included having located twenty-three missing children and teenagers and reunited them with their parents. Given that it was not legitimate for investigators to work for the McCanns in Portugal while the police probe was still under way, moreover, Método – with its knowledge of the region and its connections in Spain's police force – might prove effective.

It seemed, briefly, that the detectives might be able to rebuild bridges to the Portuguese Polícia Judiciária. At the request of the head of Spain's anti-kidnapping unit, two PJ officers sat down with two Método 3 operatives. The points the detectives raised, two of which related to long since discarded investigative leads relating to Robert Murat, did not interest the Portuguese.

The Spanish detectives followed up on a vast number of potential openings in the hunt for Madeleine. Nothing tangible resulted, but they made some startling statements that kept the case in the public eye. 'We are 100 per cent sure,' their boss Francisco Marco told the American network CBS, 'that she is alive. We know the kidnapper. We know who he is and how he has done it.' On the BBC's *Panorama* programme, he said: 'We are very close. I am not saying maybe, no, no, no . . . We are very close to finding the kidnappers.' Then, in early December: 'We know who kidnapped her. We believe she is in an area not very far from the Iberian peninsula and North Africa. And we have a fairly certain idea who she is with.'

No facts would ever emerge, however, to back up Marco's claims. According to the *Daily Telegraph*, a source close to the McCanns had already said the couple had started to think 'they might have been sold a pup'. A veteran Spanish police detective was derisive. Método 3 would solve the case, he said, '*cuando las ranas crecen los pelos*' – 'when frogs grow hair'.

Three days before Christmas 2007, in a special television broad-cast, Madeleine was seen opening a present she had been given the previous year – the pink suitcase she had a few months later taken with her to Portugal. Together, Gerry and Kate McCann made a direct appeal to their daughter's presumed kidnapper. 'Clearly for us and the rest of our family,' Gerry said, 'it's going to be the hardest Christmas imaginable without Madeleine here.' Kate said: 'You must understand that you hold the key to ending all this despair and anguish . . . At this time of year, when so many families are coming together, we beg you to help us be reunited with Madeleine. Please do the right thing and come forward.'

Kate then addressed Madeleine herself, saying that, though it seemed unlikely she was really seeing the programme: 'It's Mummy and Daddy here . . . Just know how much we love you, Madeleine. We all miss you so much. We're doing everything we can, Madeleine, to find you.'

The couple ended the broadcast by appealing to anyone who might have information to call a confidential hotline manned by Método 3. Almost 350 people did phone in, and the couple's spokesman said the content of their calls would be gone through 'with a fine-tooth comb'. For now, whatever their doubts, the McCanns were keeping the faith, hopeful that Método 3 might turn up something significant.

There was a flurry of activity at the turn of the year when a five-year-old named Mari Luz – out on a hundred-yard walk to buy pastries from a kiosk – went missing in the city of Huelva, across the border in Spain. Because Huelva and Praia da Luz lie on the same arterial road, it was thought for a while that her disappear-ance might be linked to Madeleine's. Método 3 took a keen interest. After Mari Luz's body was discovered and a convicted paedophile found guilty of her murder, though, police concluded the cases were unrelated.

In early 2008, serious investigation was obscured by a bizarre episode. A lawyer named Marcos Aragão Correia began telling a story that – if accurate – was the worst news possible for the McCanns.

Underworld criminals, he claimed, had told him days after Madeleine went missing that she had been raped and murdered, then dumped in a reservoir. Aragão Correia said that, though he had passed this information to the Polícia Judiciária, they had failed to act on it. The Método 3 team were now briefed, he said, and deemed the lead significant.

Presenting himself as a man of initiative, Aragão Correia hired a sub-aqua team to dive in the reservoir at a point near the Arade dam – some twenty-five miles from Praia da Luz. On the face of it, the reservoir was a rational enough place for such a search. After prolonged efforts in muddy water with poor visibility, the divers eventually brought up lengths of rope, a child's sock and a bag containing bones. The bag, Aragão Correia said, was large enough to have contained a child. Though the bones were small, he thought 'they look like they come from a child's fingers'. The finds would be handed to Método 3 for analysis.

The results of the dive received major international coverage – brutal reading for Madeleine's parents. As rapidly became clear, however, the episode amounted to nothing at all. The bones in the bag, the Polícia Judiciária let it be known, were not of human origin. Somebody, apparently, had been drowning kittens.

Three years later, Aragão Correia would publish a book entitled *The Love Spirits: The Little Girls Who Came from the Stars*, a 'fantastic adventure book that includes real facts'. It combined, he wrote, his 'knowledge from more than a decade studying the parapsy-chology and the paranormal, along with important information' gleaned during investigation of the Madeleine McCann and Joana Cipriano abductions. Joana was the eight-year-old who had vanished, presumed murdered, three years before Madeleine (see p.110).

His information about Madeleine, he now said, had come to him not from underworld figures but in a vision he had following a spiritualist meeting two days after the little girl went missing. To this he added little details like the McCanns' supposed 'influ-ential connections in the government of the UK', the 'enigmatic code messages' Gerry had received on his mobile phone, 'major international terrorist [President] George W. Bush' and 'perverted secret societies'.

Laughable stuff, perhaps. Not, however, for the McCanns, as the media churned out its coverage of the dives in the reservoir, the child's sock and the discovery of the bag of little bones.

The authors learned, though, that Método 3's investigators knew all along that Aragão Correia's claim to have received an underworld tip was only a cover story. The lawyer had made it clear in his early contacts with the detectives that his information had come from a vision.

'Even so,' Método 3's then Barcelona chief Elisenda Villena told the authors, 'leads we had suggested Madeleine's body had been thrown into a lake . . . But I also wanted Correia to get me other information.' Their clients, Villena told the authors, were not told of Método 3's involvement with the dive.

Villena also wanted to explore the possibility that Madeleine's disappearance might be linked with that of little Joana Cipriano, only a short distance away. In that case, as in Madeleine's, she noted, 'the police did not find a body.' In the hope of getting closer to the truth, the detective got Aragão Correia, in his capacity as a lawyer, to conduct a prison interview with Joana's uncle, by then serving time for his niece's presumed murder. The interview was conducted, but did not result in a breakthrough. It marked the beginning of a long and tangled involvement between lawyer Correia and the Cipriano case – an involvement too complex to be described in detail here. Detective Villena believes to this day that the possibility that the two cases may have been connected should be further investigated.

'My feeling is that Método 3 spent too much time on that,' Brian Kennedy said years later. Even as the macabre circus at the dam was under way, he was beginning a four-month exchange of correspondence with an individual in Africa. Salisu Suleiman, then a Nigerian government information officer, had for weeks been sending emails to addressees in the UK – including the Child Exploitation and Online Protection Centre, Sky News and the *News of the World* – to say he had 'information that may lead to finding Madeleine McCann'. Madeleine was alive, he wrote, being looked after by a woman in the Portuguese capital Lisbon. He forwarded a map, with an area circled in red, asking that the McCanns' detectives be informed. The *News of the World*'s then news editor, Ian Edmondson, responded by forwarding the messages to Kennedy. On February 15th 2008, Kennedy wrote to Suleiman:

> Thanks for your input. Can you tell me the substance behind your knowledge? The PIs have many leads to follow and we need clarification of the resource before we use valuable time and manpower in searching . . .
> Kind regards,
> Brian Kennedy

The email toing and froing that followed was to last till late spring. Suleiman promised:

I would love to provide you with the substance behind the information and the map, and will do so with time. All I need for now is somebody to believe me, and work with the information I sent . . . I don't want to be told that the search team was given this information a long time ago and failed to act.

Kennedy was back to him within hours with a sensible question:

I appreciate your honesty. Is your intuition based on a psychic? If so, that is fine, as sometimes it is effective, but we need to know.

Suleiman fended off the question, responding that his information was 'reliable', not based on intuition. The exchanges continued until, on February 20th, Kennedy emailed:

We have agents in the area. Can you give me more information?

Kennedy's son Patrick and a Método 3 detective travelled to Lisbon, and Suleiman then sent detailed information as to Madeleine's whereabouts:

Please, the team should focus their attention on the roughly triangular block starting from Travessa das Monicas, right to R. de Sao Vicente, right to R. de Santa Marinha, right to

Calçada da Graça, and right again to Travessa das Monicas.
That is where Maddie is. Focus the surveillance on this
roughly square area.

Then, on the heels of these details, Suleiman sent an email
that described the nature of his purported source for the first
time. His source on where Madeleine was being held, he claimed,
was 'an illegal African immigrant . . . on the run from the authorities' who 'dare not walk up to the police with his information
and has decided to use a third party' – hence his, Suleiman's,
involvement.

The Suleiman tip-off led nowhere, however and – though
exchanges continued intermittently until late spring – the
Kennedys finally ceased to respond.

Suleiman, by then a director at Nigeria's Civic Media Institute,
told the story in the book *Madeleine and the Seventh Mystic*,
published in the United States in 2011. His interest in the case
had started, he at last revealed, when – as he followed the news
on Madeleine from far-off Nigeria – he learned the investigation
was going nowhere. There was, too, the huge reward that had
been offered for information leading to Madeleine's safe return.
For him, it represented unimaginable riches.

Nigeria's 2007 election campaign, when 'prayer warriors' and
'shamans' – or witch doctors, as they have been termed in the
West – flourished, had inspired what Suleiman did next. Though
he considered himself 'modern, open-minded, rational', he wrote,
it was easier in Africa 'to believe in the existence of alternative
realities'. He had set out to 'see if we could use the powers of
extrasensory perception some people possessed to find Madeleine.
Could we find her using purely psychic mediums?'

He was persuaded that it was possible – by one of the mystics he consulted (the seventh contacted, hence the title of his book), a callow youth who performed his marvels by sprinkling fine sand in a tray. This youth was to tell him that Madeleine McCann was in Lisbon and – eventually – where to find her.

Suleiman's book is an odd mix of scepticism and suggestibility. His account reads as though, in the end, he came to believe that the information he offered Brian Kennedy had not necessarily been bogus.

The fact that Kennedy responded as he did to Suleiman's emails does not reflect gullibility on his part. 'When you're desperate,' Kennedy told the authors, 'when you've nowhere to go and your enquiries are going nowhere, when you can't find the haystack – let alone the needle – you tend to follow every lead that comes in. I think we suspected the psychic nature of this lead, but Suleiman was very persistent, as I recall. You never know – and we were all passionate about finding Madeleine.'

The Suleiman story is a parable for a case in which fragile hope vied with sad probability.

18

May 3rd 2008, the first anniversary of Madeleine's disappearance, came and went. In Praia da Luz, a church service was held to mark the day. By now, though, the church was almost the only place to find a poster appealing for help in the hunt for Madeleine. Most of the posters that had once been ubiquitous in the village had been taken down months earlier. Then Mayor Domingues Borba, a former policeman, had declared earlier that he thought the McCanns – as parents – 'guilty of negligence, at the very least'.

There had also been a special church service in the McCanns' home village of Rothley. Though parish council chairman Percy Hartshorn grumbled that the media was a nuisance, local vicar Rob Gladstone said people remained 'strongly supportive'. Two thousand cuddly toys that had long dotted the ground around the war memorial had been washed, then sent to children in areas of Belarus contaminated by the Chernobyl disaster. Now, a single candle burned in front of the memorial.

Gerry and Kate McCann made several television appearances. Days later, when Madeleine should have been at home celebrating her fifth birthday, they had a tea party for family and close friends – and would continue to do so year after year.

In one of the couple's broadcasts, Gerry had reminded viewers that they were 'not characters in a soap opera or fiction. This is about a real child and a real family who have been traumatised.' 'The focus,' Kate said, had to be on the fact that a 'hideous crime' against a child had been committed, and that the perpetrator was still at large.

She emphasised, too, that there was reason to think Madeleine could be alive. 'There's no evidence, absolutely no evidence, that any harm has come to her. And if you look at the United States, where they have a lot of statistics relating to this kind of crime, children are recovered. A lot of children are recovered, and the younger the child the better the chance of that.' The McCanns sought to fill what they saw as 'huge gaps' in the jigsaw of the case.

From Portugal, with the lifting of their *arguido* status and the release of police files, came the opportunity – as they had put it in the latest television appeal – to 'know exactly what has been done and what hasn't been done. Who's been eliminated and on what grounds, and what leads are still actively being followed . . . and that information has not been forthcoming to us.' In the UK, the McCanns went to the High Court to ask that they have access to files accumulated by police in their home county of Leicestershire, the force that handled liaison with the Portuguese. A small amount of that material was eventually released to them, though access remained closed to the public at large.

Meanwhile, the couple moved on in the way they used private detectives. The team currently employed, Método 3, had early in 2008 – while hunting for Madeleine – uncovered a network generating images of child sex abuse in Spain. Passed the information, the police had duly made a number of arrests. Madeleine, however, was not among the wretched child victims featured in the footage. Método 3, though doggedly committed, did not make the breakthrough her parents craved. Then, as the months slipped by, the McCanns made a move they were to regret.

A contract was agreed with a US-based company named Oakley International, described by a source close to the McCanns as being apparently 'the big boys . . . absolutely the best, but they are extremely secretive'. The company was said to employ former FBI, CIA and US Special Forces personnel. 'But I am unable to say anything at all about them,' the McCanns' spokesman said in August 2008, 'because of the covert nature of their work and the need for secrecy, not only in looking for Madeleine but also in relation to previous operations.' It was reportedly agreed that the Madeleine Fund would pay Oakley £500,000 under a three-stage contract – with more to come should Madeleine be found alive.

At least one leading operative for Oakley, Henri Exton, was indeed a veteran of British government service, a distinguished sometime head of a police undercover unit. He was the genuine article, an honourable professional who had been awarded the OBE and the Queen's Service Medal. Much less was known about the man heading the company, an Irishman named Kevin Halligen.

The McCanns and Kennedy at first got the impression that Oakley was doing its job. Its investigators appeared to be collating and following up information that came in as a response to the parents' appeals, and were conducting covert interviews in Portugal. They worked with Martin Smith and his family – who, like Jane Tanner, had encountered a man carrying a child on the night Madeleine vanished – to generate computer e-fits for identification purposes (see two photos to right at 26).

As would emerge much later, however, hundreds of calls to a

dedicated hotline thought to have been operated independently were never checked by Oakley. Tapes of interviews conducted in Portugal were said to be useless, conducted with people irrelevant to the case. Specialists used by Oakley, including Henri Exton, began to find that their bills went unpaid. An undertaking to deliver satellite images of Praia da Luz on the night of May 3rd 2007 resulted only in pictures grabbed from Google Earth. With little or no real progress, and as funds continued to haemorrhage, Brian Kennedy called time.

Oakley's boss Kevin Halligen, it turned out, was a fraud. While playing a dubious role in efforts to free two businessmen held hostage in Africa, he had conned a commodities trading company out of $2.1 million. And he had contracted a phoney wedding in Washington – the 'minister' had been an actor, and Halligen already had a wife – attended by guests drawn from the capital's elite.

After his involvement in the Madeleine case, Halligen was arrested in the UK in connection with charges relating to the trading company fraud, and extradited to the United States. He was convicted on the fraud matter, then deported.

'The Oakley episode went sort of sweet and sour,' Brian Kennedy told the authors. 'There were genuine guys breaking their back, trying to make a breakthrough. The lion's share was spent on the investigation, despite what the newspapers say . . . [But] it all ended in tears.' The McCanns and their advisers moved on, placing their trust in investigators who were to serve them for years to come.

David Edgar, a former detective inspector in Cheshire and Northern Ireland with thirty years' experience behind him, was hired on the recommendation of the head of Manchester's Serious

Crime Squad. 'Dave is a top guy, the professional,' Kennedy said. 'I let him get on with it, and he worked fervently, meticulously.' Edgar and a senior colleague, former Detective Sergeant Arthur Cowley, began the assignment by trawling through the voluminous available police files. They worked slowly, made no unjustifiable claims of progress, and remained barely visible for months.

When the detectives surfaced, it was to do interviews with a major newspaper and for a ninety-minute documentary aired to coincide with two years having passed since Madeleine's disappearance. In the documentary, they were shown overseeing filming of a reconstruction of significant events as described by witnesses. They also released an artist's impression of one of the men seen apparently watching Apartment 5A before Madeleine vanished – an ugly, pockmarked individual, as one witness remembered him (see p.63 and photo 25, at centre).

The detectives had tried to build bridges to the Portuguese authorities, Edgar said, but with 'no response'. The considerable time he had spent in and around Praia da Luz, however, had led him to form quite firm theories.

Edgar and Cowley did not subscribe to the notion that Madeleine had been taken by child traffickers. They surmised, rather, that just one person was involved, 'someone with knowledge of the area', the sparsely populated, impoverished region near to, but beyond, the tourist strip. Their special focus was information they had gleaned on a number of men believed to be paedophiles and on the sex assaults committed on the children of tourists in the period before Madeleine vanished – reported elsewhere in this book.

'Is it possible,' Edgar asked rhetorically, 'that Madeleine is alive and living in the Algarve despite all the publicity? The answer is yes. There is a very strong possibility that she is within that area.'

Three months later, in August 2009, the detectives' work was in the news again. With McCann spokesman Clarence Mitchell at his side, Edgar appeared at a press conference to announce what he described as 'a very strong lead'. A man had come forward, he said, to report a brief encounter he had had two years earlier, some seventy-two hours after Madeleine was first missed, in the Spanish port city of Barcelona.

The man, apparently a British executive, had been in Barcelona for his younger brother's stag party. In order to keep an eye on his brother, it may be important to add, he maintained that he himself had not been drinking. It had been around 2 a.m. on May 7th, he said, as he and the brother sat in a bar in the Port Olímpic marina, when they had noticed a woman walking up and down outside. She appeared 'agitated' and – when the witness approached her – appeared to think he might be the person for whom she was waiting.

For what he termed 'operational reasons', former Detective Inspector Edgar did not reveal at the press conference what the woman had supposedly said when approached. It was her words, though – as the witness remembered them – that had grabbed the detectives' attention. According to subsequent reports, she had said something to the effect of 'Are you here to deliver my new daughter?' or 'Have you got her? Have you got the child?' She asked three times before realising the witness was not the man she was expecting. Eventually, after spending 'a lot of time' with the witness, she walked away.

In the context of the Madeleine case, the possible implications are obvious, perhaps – one should say sceptically – too glaringly obvious. Questions abound:

If the unknown woman really was waiting for a live, kidnapped

Madeleine, would her first words to the man who approached her – who could have been anyone – have been so idiotically transparent?

Would criminals arranging such a meeting have selected such a very public place for it?

If the unknown woman really was expecting Madeleine, how had the child been transported there? Possibly by road – the distance from Praia da Luz to Barcelona is eight hundred miles. There are, too, train and bus connections from Faro, only fifty-seven miles from Luz. Expert advice to the authors is that it would have been possible to make the journey by sea – with stops for refuelling, a mid-sized powerboat could have made the voyage in the available time – though any handover would presumably not have been made at a busy Barcelona marina. There is no ferry service between the Algarve and Barcelona – travel by ferry, in any case, would have exposed a perpetrator to unacceptable risk.

Last but certainly not least, one must also ask why the unnamed executive did not come forward two years earlier, when the media was first buzzing with the Madeleine mystery. The man had apparently claimed that he remained silent in 2007 for 'personal reasons', seemingly – a press report later suggested – because he did not want his wife to know he had been approaching a strange woman. Detective Edgar, who accepted that, judged him to be a 'very credible witness'.

For all these questions and doubts, Edgar said he deemed the unknown woman a 'very significant individual'. The witness described her as having been thirty to thirty-five, about 5 foot 2 inches tall, slim and with short or 'spiky' brown hair. She was well dressed and – the witness heard her addressing someone else – fluent in Spanish, perhaps as spoken in the country's north-east. When speaking English, he thought she sounded somewhat Australian.

'Please, please contact us if you know this woman,' Edgar pleaded at the press conference. 'We need to speak with her urgently.' A thousand people called or sent emails in response. There was short-lived excitement that the woman might have been found – in Australia – but that turned out to be a case of mistaken identity. The woman who asked that strange question in Barcelona remains unidentified.

She is still thought potentially significant today. An e-fit of her, generated following interviews with the unnamed male witness, remains on the McCann website (see photo 19). She is a 'Person of Interest to the Inquiry'.

Gerry and Kate McCann, their spokesman Clarence Mitchell told the 2009 press conference, had obviously been 'hoping this will prove as significant as Dave [Edgar] believes it might be'. As Kate had said earlier, 'there's always that little bit of hope'. One day, a new lead could turn out to be 'the real thing'.

Since her daughter's disappearance, Kate had sometimes been at a very low ebb indeed. One such period had been in the summer of 2008, when Gonçalo Amaral launched his book about the case. *Maddie: The Truth of the Lie* was shot through with the imputation that the McCanns had had something to do with their own daughter's death. The book became a bestseller in Portugal, and would soon be available in translation in six European countries.

On top of all the other pressures on her – she was wading through the Portuguese police files at the time – the news about Amaral's book drove Kate to despair. Not for the first time, but perhaps more than at any other time since her daughter's disappearance, Kate's faith faltered. 'I'm not embarrassed to say I felt angry with God,' she told Piers Morgan on CNN's *Tonight*. 'We just felt so many challenges, particularly in Portugal.'

A year later, in spring 2009, when a television documentary based on the book was aired, Kate became – according to crisis counsellor Alan Pike – 'even more devastated'. Pike, who had continued to advise the family long after Madeleine's disappearance, recalled that she was 'in such a bad state that Gerald had to quit his job for some time to care for her'. She was, he said, 'not well at all . . . helpless; she said she'd prefer not to be there.' Patricia Cameron, Kate's sister-in-law, said she became 'very low . . . wasn't able to face daily life'. Michael Wright, who had known Kate since childhood, said 'anger and anxiety' overwhelmed both her and Gerry.

The McCanns moved to bring an injunction to stop further distribution of the Amaral book and the documentary based on it, and issued a writ for alleged libel. An extended legal wrangle began. They were to get an injunction, only to see it overturned later. The suit dragged on in the courts.

In November that year came a moving official exhortation, an online viral message from Britain's CEOP, a sixty-second video entitled 'A Minute for Madeleine'. Over an artist's age-progression image, the voice-over ran:

Madeleine is now six years old. This is how she might look today. We know that there's someone out there who knows who's involved in her disappearance. They may be keeping this secret out of fear, misplaced loyalty – or even love. Keeping this information secret only increases the anguish of Madeleine's family and friends, and increases the risk to other children. If you know who is involved, and you're keeping the secret, remember that it's never too late to do the right thing . . . give that information to their local police.

The appeal to the conscience of someone who might have guilty knowledge went unfulfilled. As 2010 began, the couple marked yet another melancholy date. 'Today,' the McCanns said on January 27th, 'marks 1,000 days since Madeleine was taken from us. It's hard even to say the number . . . Nothing has changed since that terrifying first night. Madeleine is *still* missing. Sometimes it even feels "wrong" to be coping. And yet if we weren't, there would be no search and no campaign to find Madeleine and that just doesn't bear thinking about.'

On the evening of the 27th itself, a £150-a-head dinner was held to raise money for the fund to find Madeleine. In spite of the generosity of many people, money was now much tighter.

Earlier that day a sonnet for Madeleine, penned by the award-winning poet Simon Armitage, had been published in *The Times* – its lines inspired by the lone candle, enclosed in a lantern, that still burned beside the memorial in the McCanns' home village:

> Dusk, doubt, the growing depth of an evening sky,
> dark setting in as it did that night,
> the forever vastness of outer space
> reflecting the emptiness here inside,
> shadowing, colouring, clouding the mind.
>
> But somewhere out there there has to be life,
> the distance only a matter of time,
> a world like our own, its marking and shades
> as uniquely formed as a daughter's eye,

> distinctly flecked, undeniably hers,
> looking back this way through the miles and years
>
> to a lantern cupping a golden blaze,
> its candle alive with a fierce blonde flame
> for the thousandth time, for as long as it takes.

As the months had passed, with no significant development, Gerry and Kate had conferred with CEOP chief Jim Gamble. 'I had a meeting with them as to how it was best to go forward,' Gamble recalled. 'They had a number of ideas. And I said, "It would be best if you wrote to me in my role as ACPO [Association of Chiefs of Police] lead for child protection and head of CEOP, asking what could be done." They did send me a letter, and I copied it to the Home Office.

'It took a while for things to happen. First, officials at the Home Office had a meeting with the McCanns. And then the Home Secretary of the day, Alan Johnson, met personally with them. His officials' view, as expressed to me, was that there were potentially insurmountable problems – like diplomacy with the Portuguese, and cost issues. Cost was very much part of it. They questioned whether anything could actually be achieved.

'But Johnson is perhaps the most humane of the all the politicians I've engaged with. He called me in for a meeting, and said, "I understand the issues. But I've met these parents. What can we do for them?" His officials tried to dampen his enthusiasm. But he just cut them off and said, "I want to do something. Can we have a review?"'

The best course, Gamble suggested, would be for him to carry out a 'scoping exercise' to determine whether there had been 'missed opportunities, whether there were lines of investigation that could be pursued – and whether we could reconfigure the system to ensure that some of the mistakes that had been made in the McCann case wouldn't be made in the future. Johnson agreed immediately, and I put together a team and set about it.'

Then, months later, shortly before the review was delivered, Gerry and Kate lost patience – very publicly.

19

On the last day of April 2010, on the eve of what should have been Madeleine's seventh birthday, the McCanns gave interviews to the BBC World Service, the Portuguese weekly *Expresso*, Portugal's public broadcasting corporation RTP and Cuatro, a leading Spanish channel.

'If this was a murder enquiry,' Kate said, 'there'd be an active investigation – because they'd want to find the perpetrator. But as it stands we have a perpetrator who's still at large and therefore puts – potentially puts – other children at risk. And we have a missing child.'

Gerry banged home the point. 'Officially, for eighteen months, law enforcement are not proactively doing anything to find Madeleine and who took her. And I just think that is fundamentally unacceptable.' There was a new and specific reason for their frustration. During their legal action against former senior PJ officer Amaral, he said, documentation had emerged showing that 'almost every single piece of information . . . has been treated in exactly the same manner . . . being declared "not relevant".'

Madeleine's father was referring to two thousand pages of Portuguese documents recording how reported sightings of the little girl had been handled since suspension of the police probe. Some had been merely outlandish or mischievous: an email from the 'Madeira Liberation Army' claiming to be holding Madeleine hostage; a report that she was in Germany in the hands of secret service agents; an Australian tip that she was a slave, being kept in a cellar. Other reports, however, had been more plausible.

In November 2008, there had been reports about a girl resembling Madeleine from three different cities in Belgium. There was CCTV footage, taken in a supermarket in New Zealand, of a girl who looked like Madeleine accompanied by a man. A security guard had thought it so possible that this was the missing girl that he had contacted the authorities. A French detective monitoring sex images on the Internet had seen pictures of a young girl being sexually abused who might, the detective thought, have been Madeleine. And so on – there were many, many reports.

While these could well have been false leads – and probably were – the impression the McCanns had from the files was that there had been little or no competent police follow-up. Kate labelled the Portuguese probe 'a farce'. 'The key test,' Gerry said, 'is: "Has everything that could reasonably have been done, been done?" And the answer to that is "No." There's no law enforcement [agency] that's been proactively doing anything for eighteen months.'

Twice in early 2010, the couple called on Portuguese law enforcement to carry out a thorough review of the case. At home, there had been their meeting with Home Secretary Alan Johnson – and his decision to get CEOP chief Jim Gamble to conduct a 'scoping exercise'. The activity at government level in Britain was out of the public eye until, on March 6th, the *Daily Telegraph* reported that the Home Office was 'secretly' conducting a review that could lead to a fresh probe by the police.

Eight weeks later, in a much reported interview with GMTV, Gerry upped the ante. 'It's not right,' Gerry said, 'that an innocent British citizen is essentially given up on. And I don't think it's right that, as parents, we have to drive the search . . . I think it's pretty cruel. We need to have a proper review.' The review headed by CEOP's Jim Gamble was, of course, in the works, soon to be delivered. Gamble recalled what he learned from interviews with participants in the British side of the initial probe – interaction with the Portuguese had been considered too sensitive. His team had tough things to say, though, about the performance of law enforcement in both nations.

The Portuguese police, Gamble remembered reporting, had appeared 'incompetent, haphazard' at the very start, during what police call 'the golden hours', the minutes and hours immediately after it was realised that Madeleine was missing. 'The golden hours aren't called that for nothing,' Gamble said in 2014. 'You can't go back and recover them. They hadn't secured the scene right away – there were people coming and going. There was contamination of the scene. They didn't have structured house-to-house or apartment-to-apartment searches.

'They told British officers that everyone in the resort's apartments had been interviewed. But it became apparent that wasn't so. Holidaymakers who had been at the Club got in touch with British police and said they hadn't been interviewed. Not all the staff at the resort had been fully eliminated from the investigation, either.

'Statistics tell us that there is often parental or family involvement. The Portuguese hadn't begun with the parents as suspects. They hadn't cleared the ground in front of them. Then they went down the [Robert] Murat route, were totally focused in that direction, and when that hit a dead end they went off in another direction. Later, when the dogs went in, they seemed to think they had the silver bullet. But the forensics tell you that they had not.

'I remember in the interviews [with British officers who had been involved], that nobody could talk coherently about the forensics because it had become such a bugger's muddle. People were afraid to talk about it in case they would be misquoted . . . There was at first a beauty contest among the British agencies about who could or would help and how. That created a bunfight. There was an unhealthy competitive element at the beginning along the lines of "Me, me, me, we'll help."

'From the Prime Minister of the day [initially Tony Blair, then Gordon Brown], to all the ministers, to senior police officers, they were well intentioned. But I believe they congested the environment, confused others about priorities and agendas . . . CEOP was no different. We all rushed to the door. Leicestershire, who had the lead, understandably became extremely territorial, would say, "You must come through us." They were a small force focused on local policing, not necessarily with the capacity to upscale.'

Gamble recommended that there should be renewed and stronger engagement between British and Portuguese law enforcement, an exchange of all information on the case – and action to pursue all outstanding leads, including those developed by the McCanns' private investigators.

'When you looked at the volume of information passed by the UK to the Portuguese in 2007,' Gamble said, 'only ten per cent had been actioned.' High on the review's priority list for renewed effort was: further work on analysing phone calls on the night Madeleine vanished, a reassessment of the forensic investigation – and other crimes committed in the Algarve in the relevant period – and information on known sexual offenders.

The one UK force with the capacity to handle the fresh work, Gamble thought, was the Metropolitan Police, and Portuguese cooperation would be essential. In contacts with the Met, senior officers indicated willingness to come in 'if there was a likelihood of it being successful, of bringing someone to justice and if funding requirements could be met'.

The CEOP review landed on Home Secretary Johnson's desk in early May 2010, just days before the Labour government was thrown out in the general election. Abruptly, it ceased to matter whether Alan Johnson supported a review of the Madeleine McCann case or not.

The McCanns, however, had hedged their bets by meeting with Conservative Party leader David Cameron well ahead of the election. This had perhaps not been difficult to arrange, for their spokesman Clarence Mitchell – a future Conservative candidate – worked for the Conservative election campaign. Cameron, who had himself tragically lost his eldest child to illness the previous year, might be expected to sympathise.

With the new Conservative–Liberal Democrat coalition now in power and Cameron installed in Downing Street, the McCanns kept up the pressure and met with the new Home Secretary, Theresa May. CEOP's Gamble met with her, too, but differed with her about his agency's future independence – he was to resign by the autumn. She 'hemmed and hawed' on the matter of the Madeleine case, according to Gamble.

For many months, nothing happened – it looked as though the couple would not get the action they wanted. Yet again, though, they continued to drum up publicity for their cause: Gerry – the cardiologist and fitness enthusiast – cycling through Scotland's Highlands to raise money for Madeleine's Fund; the McCanns speaking out on International Missing Children's Day;

organising Madeleine T-shirts and luggage tags to be used by people going on holiday.

By late 2010 they were pushing openly and loudly, online and publicly, for action by the British and Portuguese authorities. 'We need action,' Kate told one interviewer. 'I don't need fluffy, worthless words. We need somebody to do something.' Nothing was done, and more months passed.

Meanwhile, Madeleine's mother was taking action herself – and writing a book. When she was done, she recalled, she went into Madeleine's bedroom – still as it was before the holiday in Portugal – and read to her from the manuscript. 'It's for her,' Kate said. 'Sometimes I feel that girl in the red dress in that famous photo of her has become almost a fictitious character. But Madeleine is our daughter, a real little girl.'

Publication of *Madeleine: Our Daughter's Disappearance and the Continuing Search for Her* came on the fourth anniversary of Madeleine's disappearance. The book ended with 'A Call to Action', asking readers to write to the Prime Minister and the Home Secretary pressing for a binational, 'joint, independent and comprehensive review of Madeleine's case'.

Initially, Kate has maintained, she had insisted that, in light of the repellent earlier coverage of the case by some newspapers, she did not want the book serialised. She was swayed, though, by the argument that newspapers would not only run extracts but also support the fight to get a government review of the case. Serial rights were sold to the *Sun* and the *Sunday Times*.

Published in May 2011 amidst massive publicity, the book became a runaway bestseller. In the first week, 72,500 copies were sold – a record. It was to sell more than two hundred and fifty thousand copies in hardback and, the following year, seventy thousand in paperback. It was published in eight other European countries.

Income related to the book would bring in more than £700,000 to boost the now depleted fund to finance the search for Madeleine.

On May 11th, as the book was launched, Sky News crime correspondent Martin Brunt wrote that he had been told that, while the Home Secretary 'continues to waver over calls for a joint UK–Portugal review of all evidence, her boss David Cameron may shake things up. A study last year, by former Child Exploitation and Online Protection Centre chief Jim Gamble, backed such a review. He's supported, I'm told, by the Association of Chief Police Officers, but Mrs May is still not convinced . . . Stand by for Cameron to take a personal interest.'

The following day, May 12th, the *Sun* ran an open letter from the McCanns to the Prime Minister. It read:

Dear Prime Minister,

As a devoted father and family man, you know the importance of children. Our beloved eldest child, Madeleine, was abducted from Praia da Luz, Portugal, four years ago. Since then, we have devoted all our energies to ensuring her safe return.

Today we are asking you – and the British and Portuguese governments – to help find Madeleine and bring her back to her loving family.

We live in hope that Madeleine will be found alive and returned to us. One call might be all that is needed to lead to Madeleine and her abductor.

To this end, we are seeking a joint INDEPENDENT, TRANSPARENT and COMPREHENSIVE review of ALL information held in relation to Madeleine's disappearance. Thus far, there has been NO formal review of the material held by the police authorities – which is routine practice in most major unsolved crimes.

It is not right that a young, vulnerable British citizen has essentially been given up on. This remains an unsolved case of a missing child. Children are our most precious gift.

Please don't give up on Madeleine.

Kate & Gerry McCann

The previous night, the *News at Ten* blog had carried a longer version of the letter, including wording that was testier, more confrontational. In an interview with the *Sun*, which ran with the edited version of the letter on the 12th, the couple said they 'didn't seem to be making any progress with the Government' in getting a formal inquiry.

The *Sun*'s headline above the McCann letter shouted 'OPEN THE MADDIE CASE FILES' and an article urged readers to sign a petition calling on British and Portuguese authorities to review the case. Twenty thousand people had signed the petition by that evening. Now, the McCanns made instant progress.

The Prime Minister's reply, also dated the 12th and starting with the handwritten salutation 'Dear Kate and Gerry,' read in part:

Thank you for your heartfelt and moving letter. Your ordeal is every parent's worst nightmare and my heart goes out to you both. I simply cannot imagine the pain you must have experienced . . . We discussed this when we met, but I realise that a full eighteen months have gone by since then . . . I have asked the Home Secretary to look into what the Government can do to help find Madeleine. She will be writing to you today, setting out new action involving the Metropolitan Police service . . . We will, of course, stay in close touch with you throughout.

Yours,

David

Also that same day, Home Secretary May wrote to Metropolitan Police Commissioner Sir Paul Stephenson saying that – following a diplomatic initiative – the Portuguese government had offered to cooperate with the British police. She asked that the offer be taken up, noting that this request had Cameron's backing. May's spokesman announced that the Metropolitan Police 'agreed to bring its particular expertise to the Madeleine McCann case'. The Home Office would fund the review.

Voices were raised in objection. 'I can imagine,' blogged Lord Harris, a member of the Metropolitan Police Authority, 'that the senior leadership of the Metropolitan Police are not exactly happy about this. It again embroils their officers in a high-profile investigation, where the chances of success are unclear, and which will divert limited investigative resources.' The government-driven intervention would have a negative impact on the force's operational independence. Another member of the Metropolitan Police Authority, Jenny Jones, said the move smacked of 'preferential treatment'. A Liberal Democrat peer Lord Bradshaw dismissed the project as a PR exercise and declared himself 'mightily worried about the politicisation of the police force'.

Lord Harris also wrote that the decision on the review was 'entirely predictable in terms of the "pulling power' of News International [owners of the *Sun* and the *Sunday Times*] on government policy".'

Later, on the BBC's *Panorama*, reporter Richard Bilton would say the programme had 'been told by the highest government sources that enormous pressure was being exerted on David Cameron by News International and by the *Sun* newspaper in particular, as well as by the McCanns . . . a source at Number 10 said David Cameron acted as a sympathetic parent.'

The former chief executive of News International, Rebekah Brooks

– a Cameron friend – had personally negotiated the serial deal with the McCanns and authorised the *Sun*'s campaign to support a review of the Madeleine case. Two weeks after the *Panorama* broadcast, testifying about the matter to the Leveson Inquiry into press ethics, she denied having told the Prime Minister's office or the Home Secretary that the *Sun* was going to demand a review and that Cameron 'should agree to the request because the *Sun* had supported him at the last election'. She said, though, that she knew one or other of her senior editors would have 'spoken to them'.

Not satisfied with Brooks' initial response, Inquiry counsel Robert Jay QC asked her whether she recalled if the Home Secretary had been told that, were she to agree to a review of the Madeleine case, the McCanns' open letter to the Prime Minister would not run. She said she did not recall that.

Still not satisfied, Jay said he was informed that Brooks had 'told Number 10 that unless the Prime Minister ordered the review by the Metropolitan Police, the *Sun* would put the Home Secretary, Theresa May, on the front page every day until the *Sun*'s demands were met.' Brooks said this was untrue.

Jay pressed again, this time saying it was alleged she had 'directly intervened' and issued the same warning to the Prime Minister. At that point, Lord Justice Leveson himself asked Brooks whether she had been part of a strategy that had involved 'putting pressure on the government with this sort of implied or express threat'.

BROOKS: . . . I think the word 'threat', sir, is – is too strong.
LORD LEVESON: Well, give me another word then for 'threat', could you?
BROOKS: 'Persuade' them?
LORD LEVESON: Persuasion. All right.

The Prime Minister himself and Home Secretary Theresa May both told the Inquiry they had not felt pressured by Rebekah Brooks. Cameron said he had been advised that there was a special Home Office procedure for helping with investigations and that the Madeleine matter had been dealt with 'properly and effectively'.

'As government,' the Prime Minister testified, 'you have to think: "Are we helping with this because there's media pressure, or is it genuine public pressure? Is there a genuine case?" And I did ask those questions of the Permanent Secretary at Number 10, and so I think we made an appropriate response . . . I don't remember any sort of specific pressure being put on me.'

The grateful McCanns expressed renewed optimism. 'We are very pleased, and we would like to thank David Cameron for his intervention,' Gerry said. Kate said she really believed the review could take them 'one step closer' to finding Madeleine.

20

Within days of the Home Secretary's May 12th announcement that there was to be a review of the Madeleine case, Police Commissioner Sir Paul Stephenson let it be known that the matter would be taken 'very seriously'. An early figure given for the project's expected cost was £3.5 million. Operating costs would include a great deal of translation work on the thousands of documents generated and held by the Polícia Judiciária, as well as travel to and from Portugal.

For all the initial publicity about its inception, information about the project was to be closely held and issued very selectively – essentially only to elicit potentially useful help from the public. The final report on the review, Commissioner Stephenson said, would not be published. A source predicted – correctly, as it would turn out – that the work could take years.

Senior Scotland Yard officers' initial irritation over the assignment, one crime reporter was told, would be replaced by the urge to do the best possible job. The decision might have been political, a Yard source said, 'but at the end of the day a child is missing'. And there was, as Madeleine's parents had always insisted – and as the Commissioner also now maintained – 'always a chance' that the little girl would be found alive.

Some thirty detectives would be assigned to the project, reporters were told, and it would be called Operation Grange. Leading it would be Detective Chief Inspector Andy Redwood of the Homicide and Serious Crime Command. A twenty-seven-year veteran, he had been a driving force on a fresh investigation, leading to a conviction, of a twelve-year-old London double murder. He had led the 'cold case' probe that brought to book a Portuguese murderer who had long vanished abroad – using false identities.

Gerry and Kate McCann met Redwood and senior colleagues at Scotland Yard within a week of the decision to conduct the review of their daughter's case. They had welcomed the announcement of the review as a 'step in the right direction' towards, they had indicated in their letter to the Prime Minister, a *joint* review by British and Portuguese law enforcement.

How to engage and keep the confidence and cooperation of their counterparts in Portugal was a challenge for British officers. 'The Portuguese authorities retain the lead,' a Yard spokesman said at the very start, 'and we are not prepared to discuss it at this time.' The Madeleine McCann case was strictly within Portugal's jurisdiction and – for all the concept of a Europe with open borders and the existence of Europol, which is there to support and liaise with national police forces – in that country's jurisdiction it remained.

Normal collegiate collaboration had long since been compromised by British press references to Portuguese police 'blundering' and 'bullying', even 'lies'. There had indeed been omissions and failures, but every country – Britain included – has its police failures and scandals. In Portugal, the insults rankled. Establishing

15. Kate and Gerry McCann, the day they were questioned again about the disappearance and declared 'arguidos' – suspects in their own daughter's disappearance.

16. There were Madeleine 'sightings' all over the world, from Albufeira, in Portugal...

...to New Zealand (right). Excitement about a little blonde girl photographed on a woman's back in Morocco (below left) and as recreated by a British newspaper (below right) proved unfounded.

SITE : 100-001
TIME : 2007/12/05-21:08:37- 1

17. Brian Kennedy, the double-glazing magnate who saw 'a grave injustice', helped the McCanns, and recruited private detectives.

18. Divers searched a reservoir not far from where Madeleine disappeared, in vain. Detectives thought the Madeleine case might be linked to that of another missing child.

19. In 2009, a 'very strong lead'. A McCann investigator appealed to the public to identify a woman who – a witness said – had asked, 'Are you here to deliver my new daughter?'

The energy behind The FA Cup

20. The search for Madeleine had massive public support. The McCanns wore themselves out travelling, generated huge publicity, and persisted (below) later, when no one else was doing anything.

CORRIE BETTY'S HOSPITAL DASH

EXCLUSIVE by COLIN ROBERTSON, TV Editor

CORRIE legend Betty Driver has been rushed to hospital — just days before her 91st birthday. The actress, telly barmaid Betty Williams, is believed to have pneumonia.

Betty . . . in hospital   *Full Story — Page Three*

McCANNS' LETTER TO CAMERON

OPEN UP THE MADDIE FILES

Plea . . . letter from parents of Madeleine to the Prime Minister

DEAR PRIME MINISTER,

As a devoted father and family man, you know the importance of children. Our beloved eldest child, Madeleine, was abducted from Praia da Luz, Portugal, four years ago. Since then, we have devoted all our energies to ensuring her safe return.

Today we are asking you – and the British and Portuguese governments – to help find Madeleine and bring her back to her loving family.

We live in hope that Madeleine will be found alive and returned to us. One call might be all that is needed to lead to Madeleine and her abductor.

To this end, we are seeking a joint INDEPENDENT, TRANSPARENT and COMPREHENSIVE review of ALL information held in relation to Madeleine's disappearance. Thus far, there has been NO formal review of the material held by the police authorities – which is routine practice in most major unsolved crimes.

It is not right that a young vulnerable British citizen has essentially been given up on. This remains an unsolved case of a missing child. Children are our most precious gift.

Please don't give up on Madeleine.

KATE & GERRY McCANN

SEE PAGES 4, 5, 6 & 7

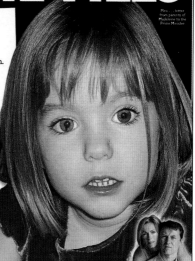

21. The breakthrough. The parents' 2011 appeal to the British Prime Minister led to action at last.

22. Detective Chief Superintendent Andy Redwood
headed a new Scotland Yard probe – and the
Portuguese eventually reopened the case.

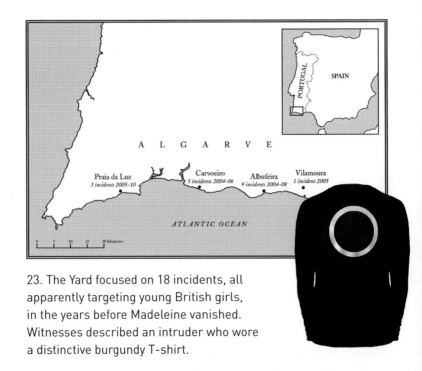

23. The Yard focused on 18 incidents, all
apparently targeting young British girls,
in the years before Madeleine vanished.
Witnesses described an intruder who wore
a distinctive burgundy T-shirt.

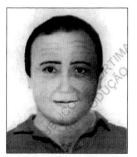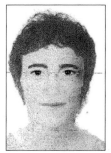

24. **THE 'CHARITY COLLECTORS'**. An e-fit (left) of a man who visited Apartment 5A before the McCanns arrived. And (right) a 'collector' who told the same story the day Madeleine disappeared, as described by another witness.

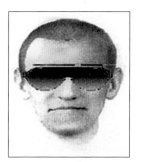

25. **THE WATCHERS**. An 'ugly' man (left) twice seen 'staring' at Apartment 5A during the McCanns' stay. A seemingly different 'ugly' man (centre) seen watching the apartment the same week. A third witness described a man (right) acting 'stealthily' outside just hours before Madeleine went missing.

26. A man carrying a child. An artist's impression (left) of a man Jane Tanner claimed she saw carrying a child near the apartment, some forty-five minutes before Madeleine was missed. And e-fits (right), drawing on differing descriptions by members of the Smith family, who later saw a man carrying a child elsewhere in the village.

27. Pursuing the worst possibility. In June 2014, a Scotland Yard team searched wasteland and a drainage system in Praia da Luz.

28. A sliver of hope. Statistics indicate that, of children abducted by strangers, most survive. In 2012, Scotland Yard released an image suggesting how Madeleine might look as she approached her ninth birthday. Today, she would be eleven.

© Teri Blythe

real cooperation was essential and was going to be a challenge.

For all Home Secretary Theresa May's earlier statement that the Portuguese government had offered to cooperate with the review, some officials in Portugal made different noises. The office of Portugal's Attorney General said neither it nor 'the magistrates that are responsible for the case have received any request or application, neither for cooperation, nor for the reopening of the process'. The deputy director of the Polícia Judiciária, Pedro do Carmo, however, did eventually acknowledge that there had been contacts between his staff, the British Embassy and Scotland Yard. The Yard, he said, 'will have our full support'.

Information on the review's progress was rare and minimal. The mere fact that there had been first, formal meetings between British officers and Portuguese authorities – two months into the operation – made news. Seven months in, word came that there had been talks with colleagues in Spain. Also in Spain, officers liaised with Método 3, the private investigation company long used by the McCanns, and left with box-loads of files.

In March 2012, almost a year after the announcement of the review, PJ deputy chief do Carmo let it be known that there had by now been four visits by British representatives, and that a police team in Oporto – Portugal's second city, almost three hundred miles from Praia da Luz – had themselves for some time been conducting a new analysis of the case 'with a fine-tooth comb'. Heading the Oporto unit was Helena Monteiro, who had led a difficult investigation of another missing-person case, and the detectives working with her were – in do Carmo's words – 'fresh eyes' who had had nothing to do with the initial probe.

'We want a more distanced look,' do Carmo said. 'Even if the [case] was shelved, there is still an unexplained disappearance.

That does not mean that there is less interest in searching for answers.'

There could be no reopening of the case, he added, however, without new evidence, and as yet there was none. There were signs, moreover, of continuing discord within Portugal. The Oporto prosecutor suggested the new police team's activity had no legitimacy because the Attorney General's office had not authorised it.

In the UK the following month, Operation Grange chief Andy Redwood radiated efficiency and cautious optimism – and revealed precious little. Interviewed on *Panorama*, he said three detective inspectors, five detective sergeants, and nineteen detective constables, plus civilian support staff, were still busy assimilating forty thousand pieces of information drawn from the files accumulated in Portugal, during the initial police work in the McCanns' home county of Leicestershire, and by private detectives. 'Ultimately,' he said, the job demanded the unexciting process of 'us turning every single piece of paper over and interpreting and analysing what is contained within them'.

The team had identified one hundred and ninety-five fresh leads, it was revealed – without saying what they were. The probe was 'gathering momentum' and the case was 'solvable'. 'We genuinely believe there is a possibility that she is alive,' Redwood said of Madeleine.

By now as much diplomat as detective, Redwood spoke very carefully of the Portuguese side of the operation. He had an 'excellent' working relationship with Helena Monteiro, his opposite number on the new PJ team in Oporto. 'It would be wholly inappropriate,' though, for him to comment on 'how the Polícia Judiciária feel.' Any decision about moving from a review to reopening the case was a decision not for him but for the Portuguese.

To the press, the detective chief inspector was that most frustrating – but respected – of policemen: courteous, but silent as a clam. Not so, presumably, in conversations with his superiors that required him to justify pressing on with the investigation.

Later in 2012, when it became clear that Operation Grange had already cost £2.5 million – a figure that was rising – a new Metropolitan Police Commissioner, Sir Bernard Hogan-Howe, would express concern. Hogan-Howe consulted with the government, however, and funding was found. It would continue to be found – even as the cost inexorably increased. A Freedom of Information request established that, as of November 30th 2013, outgoings amounted to almost £6.5 million.

When Redwood did speak out, it was because he wanted something. He well understood the extraordinary, durable public interest in the Madeleine story, and knew how to pull the levers of publicity. The 2012 appearance on *Panorama*, on which he revealed nothing of substance, was geared to a broader statement timed to coincide with the approach of Madeleine's ninth birthday.

The statement opened poignantly with an 'age-progression' image of Madeleine as she might look five years after her disappearance. Missing persons' organisations in both Britain and the United States favour the use of such images, which are generated using not only out-of-date photographs and pictures of other family members, but computer software and sometimes advice from forensic anthropologists. As on previous occasions, Gerry and Kate McCann had also had input into the latest image (see photo 28).

DCI Redwood asked that people who had been in Praia da Luz during the week Madeleine disappeared – and who might never have been interviewed – get in touch with Scotland Yard. A simple request but one that repaired an omission. In the five years that had passed, no police force had used the power of the media to reach such potentially vital witnesses before. The response to this and later appeals helped the investigation.

Redwood also made the very general, time-honoured request that anyone with information contact the police. He qualified it by saying he needed 'new, direct information', because there was still a steady drip feed of claims from all over the world – some more impetuous than careful – from people who thought they had 'seen' Madeleine.

Right after the start of Operation Grange, a British tourist had been sure she had spotted her in India. Madeleine had and would be 'seen' – again – several times, in New Zealand. A photograph would surface, apparently taken in Brazil, showing a girl somewhat like Madeleine walking hand in hand with a 'foreign-looking' man. An old sighting, resurrected, had her doppelgänger seen in the USA, in Maryland. A witness in Cyprus thought she might have been with a British family who had been renting a house he owned but had suddenly left the country. A British barrister would report an encounter with a man who claimed – he thought credibly – that he had seen Madeleine on an unnamed Mediterranean island. The Scotland Yard team had to give their attention to almost all such tips.

They also had to deal with the findings of self-appointed sleuths. A South African property developer named Stephen Birch – no connection to Danie Krügel, also a South African, and his 'matter orientation' gadget for finding missing people (see page 137-) claimed in 2012 to have discovered the location of Madeleine's body. Using a ground-penetrating radar device, he said, he had 'established that the infant was buried approximately 500 mm below the surface' of the driveway of the home of Robert Murat, the earliest person to be formally declared a suspect in the case.

According to Birch, he had spent £40,000 achieving this. As of the date this book went to press, he was still running an online petition – it bore the extraordinarily insensitive heading 'Digging 4 Madeleine' – asking that the driveway be excavated.

Murat, long since cleared of any involvement in the Madeleine case, has said he would sue the South African for his admitted nocturnal trespassing on the Murat property to obtain his radar scans. Birch, for his part, said he had sent copies of the scans – his 'overwhelming proof' – to Scotland Yard. According to Sky News, a Yard spokesman responded that 'it would always consider any new potential evidence and pass it on to the Portuguese'.

The Operation Grange team were as polite as they could muster with purveyors of the weird and unsolicited, and slogged on.

In the spring of 2013, Scotland Yard broke silence again. Hamish Campbell, head of the Homicide Command, summoned reporters to tell them the Grange team had been making 'fantastic' progress, sufficient for him to recommend that the Portuguese authorities reopen the investigation. He said, without explaining, that detectives had developed 'forensic opportunities'. They had also 'identified a number of Persons of Interest'. That was all, but it made headlines.

In July, at another media briefing, team chief Redwood said the Yard's reading of the evidence had made it possible to shift 'from review to investigation'. He flatly exonerated Gerry and Kate McCann and their holiday companions from any involvement in Madeleine's disappearance. 'Neither her parents nor any members of the group that were with her,' he said, 'are either Persons of Interest or suspects.' Thirty-eight other individuals, however, were 'Persons of Interest'. They included British citizens and known child offenders who had been in the Algarve in spring 2007.

Behind the scenes, the Crown Prosecution Service had sent two senior officials to discuss developments with their Portuguese counterparts. Shortly afterwards, an International Letter of Request was sent to the Portuguese Attorney General. Its contents were secret, but a Freedom of Information request extracted the information that there were 'several suspects at large'.

In October 2013, Detective Chief Inspector Redwood turned up the volume. At a media briefing, an assistant commissioner at his side, he said Portuguese officers in the Algarve were now making inquiries on his team's behalf. There were forty-one 'Persons of Interest', of whom fifteen were British. Thirty-one foreign countries, meanwhile, had been sent Letters of Request asking for information related to phones used in Praia da Luz in May 2007. The BBC's *Crimewatch* programme, and broadcasters in Holland, Germany and Ireland, would carry further information, and a police appeal, in a week's time.

The hour-long *Crimewatch*, featuring Gerry and Kate McCann as well as Redwood, averaged an audience of almost seven million – the largest the programme had ever had. Introduced as the 'truest' account there had ever been of the events of May 3rd 2007, it put forward the new police theory as to the timeline of that night.

A revelatory moment, Redwood said, had been his team's interviews with a father who had picked up his daughter from the Ocean Club crèche shortly before the McCanns' friend Jane Tanner had seen a man carrying a child near Apartment 5A at about 9.15 p.m. The man said *he* had walked near Apartment 5A – which might mean there had all along been an innocent explanation for Jane Tanner's sighting of a possible abductor.

Instead, Redwood said, the investigation was now focusing on the only other known sighting of a man carrying a pyjama-clad child that night, by Irishman Martin Smith and his family – about forty-five minutes after the Tanner sighting, at around 10.00 p.m. If the man the Smiths encountered just four minutes' walk away from Apartment 5A had in fact been the abductor, that meant not only changing the timeline but looking for a man answering the Smiths' description. For the first time, the programme showed e-fits of the man, remembered by the Smiths as having been in his mid-thirties, with short brown hair (see photos to the right at 26).

The Operation Grange chief discussed, too, men who had been seen apparently 'lurking' near the McCann apartment at various times, and the supposed 'charity collector' visits to apartments close by. Police thought that one of them, it was reported after the programme, might have had a Dutch or German accent – hence the subsequent broadcasts in Holland and Germany.

In the early months of the year Madeleine vanished, Andy Redwood noted finally, there had been a 'four-fold increase in the number of burglaries that were taking place in the vicinity . . . There is a scenario where Madeleine could possibly have disturbed somebody trying to commit a burglary.'

Following analysis of mobile-phone traffic in Praia da Luz on the night the little girl went missing, a 'needle in haystack' task never previously done thoroughly, Redwood thought the team might have found 'part of the needle'.

The task had involved enlisting the cooperation not only of Portuguese colleagues but of authorities in thirty nations. The potentially significant result, however, was in Portugal itself. The phones of three known thieves, it turned out, had been so busy late on the evening of May 3rd 2007 – and in the vicinity of the Ocean Club – that the traffic between them was characterised as 'red-hot'.

Did it mean anything in the context of the Madeleine case? The Operation Grange team sought to glean detailed information about the three burglars, who had reportedly been opportunistic operators – employees of the Ocean Club preying on tourists. British detectives asked the Portuguese authorities to arrange for the men to be thoroughly investigated.

The review by Portuguese detectives in Oporto, meanwhile, had itself been edging forwards. It had been able, the PJ said in a statement, to 'identify new evidence requiring further research [that] meets the requirements . . . for the reopening of the investigation'. Not long afterwards, it would be reported that the Oporto team had 'uncovered shortcomings in the initial investigation conducted by their counterparts in the Algarve and were now actively pursuing the theory that Madeleine was abducted'.

The British and Portuguese teams, however, reportedly differed on what the focus of this part of the inquiry should be. The Portuguese were said to be concentrating on a former Ocean Club waiter, Euclides Monteiro, who had died in an accident in 2009. Monteiro, who had worked in one of the club's restaurants, had been fired for stealing from the till the year before Madeleine disappeared. He had previously served time for burglary and – according to his widow – had been questioned by police about break-ins that involved sexual assaults on children. He had been cleared, the wife said, following DNA tests.

Monteiro had no record of sexual offences. He was, moreover, a very dark-skinned black man, a fact that runs contrary both to witness testimony about suspicious men seen near the McCanns' apartment – and indeed to testimony about sexual assaults in the area.

On *Crimewatch* in 2013, Redwood's emphasis was not on a burglary gone wrong as an explanation for Madeleine's disappear-

ance so much as on 'a pre-planned abduction. That would undoubt-
edly have involved reconnaissance.' He appealed to viewers for
any information that might help identify the various e-fits shown
on the programme – of the man the Smith family had seen carrying
a sleeping child, as well as of the men witnesses said they had
seen behaving suspiciously near Apartment 5A.

The broadcast elicited a huge response: three thousand five
hundred calls, texts and emails, by the BBC count, contacts that
ranged from the significant to the mischievous.

The Smith family's description of the man now fingered as
having been a possible abductor, the *Sunday Telegraph*'s Colin
Freeman thought, 'could arguably apply to a large section of the
male population in Praia da Luz that night, and indeed much of
the rest of Europe'.

The e-fit of the man the Smiths saw, Freeman wrote, 'looked
like a Wanted poster for Mr Ordinary'.

21

Time now to reconsider all the possibilities as to what might have happened on May 3rd 2007.

The notion that Gerry and Kate McCann have some guilty secret to hide has persisted. It was pushed by the first Portuguese chief investigator, Gonçalo Amaral, and is still propagated by the online community of 'haters'. So successful has the deluge of black propaganda been over the years that the authors regularly encountered people, otherwise sensible individuals, who wondered aloud: 'I can't help feeling the McCanns had *something* to do with it.'

In Portugal, the suspicion is apparently even more common. Isabel Duarte, the lawyer acting for the McCanns in the libel suit arising from Amaral's book, has said that pleading their case makes her feel isolated. 'I don't feel support,' she has said, 'not in public opinion ... Because everyone believes in Gonçalo Amaral. Everyone believes that I am defending a father and a mother who have killed the daughter and got rid of the corpse.'

There is not a jot of evidence to support such an idea. Police always allow for the possibility because – as discussed later in this book – available statistics indicate that the person most often responsible in killings of children is a parent or relative. For an investigation to lean towards such a suspicion, let alone prove it, however, there must be evidence or initial grounds for suspicion. In the McCann case, there is no such evidence and there are no such grounds.

There is nothing in the background of the McCanns, in their family history or what is known of their personalities, to suggest that either of them might harm their child – rather the contrary. Those who cast aspersions on the McCanns, or suggest their holiday companions conspired with them to conceal the truth, propose that one of the parents may have been responsible for Madeleine's supposed accidental death – and then, because they might have feared for their reputation as doctors, striven to cover up the truth. The idea is a huge stretch, and always was a stretch, totally unsupported by any facts.

Those hostile to the McCanns point to supposed improbabilities or inconsistencies in their testimony and that of their friends – particularly with regard to the timeline of the evening of May 3rd. This book is written with the advantage of access not only to the bulk of the Portuguese police files but also to the lengthy transcripts of the formal 'rogatories', the questioning by British police of the seven McCann friends at the request of the Portuguese.

The authors see no significant inconsistencies in the testimonies of the McCanns or their companions. Anyone with experience of testimony – be they policemen or lawyers, reporters or insurance investigators – well knows that individuals' memories of detail, and specific times, are notoriously fallible.

The McCanns, meanwhile, have all along behaved in two distinctive ways: at first, how parents at their wits' end might well behave on losing a much-loved child; later, the way determined, resolutely activist parents can in this century – empowered by the Internet – campaign for the truth as to what happened to their daughter. Except in very rare instances – the murder of celebrity aviator Charles Lindbergh's infant son in the United States in the early 1930s was one such exception – attracting such global attention would once have been unlikely or impossible.

The facts, and common sense, demand that suspicion of the McCanns be left to those who have not, for whatever reason, taken note of the hard evidence. That canard once rejected, there is another possible explanation of Madeleine's disappearance that would – almost certainly – have involved no malfeasance.

It is that Madeleine – just short of her fourth birthday – conceivably woke, got out of bed and wandered out into the night of her own volition. This was the possibility first considered by the patrol car officers who responded to the emergency, and suggested to Kate the following day by regional police chief Guilhermino Encarnação. The British priest Paul Seddon, whom Kate called in the early hours, recalled trying to calm her by saying 'that Madeleine could have had a bout of sleepwalking and that she would be all right. I remember that Kate was worried by the fact that Madeleine was wearing short-sleeved pyjamas and could catch a cold.' Father Seddon, who knew the McCanns well – he had baptised Madeleine and often played golf with Gerry – continued to hope the child 'could have left alone, as she was a very adventurous girl'. Even the next day, a spokesman for the tour operator that ran the Ocean Club expressed the hope 'that she is sleeping under a bush somewhere'.

Though both Kate and Gerry rejected the possibility that their daughter had wandered off, the notion was not preposterous. Children can and do sometimes wander. Two years later, in New Zealand, a two-year-old did indeed stray in broad daylight and apparently crawled or fell into a nearby manhole with a faulty cover. She was found dead, after a week's intensive searching.

There were, as reported earlier, such hazards in Praia da Luz in 2007. A police report in the files records the fact that 'open trenches' in two streets, Rua Direita and Rua Helena do Nascimiento Batista, had been left open on the evening of May 3rd. For an adult, at any rate, both streets are only a few minutes' walk from Apartment 5A. When the trenches were checked, though, on the morning of May 4th, as word spread that a child was missing, nothing was found.

An adventure resulting in a fatal accident, while not impossible, is less than probable. Had Madeleine wandered out of the apartment, she would almost certainly have made her exit by the patio doors – left unlocked to make checking on the children easier – that led to the terrace and the steps down to the street. Her most likely route then would have been to walk the few yards downhill to the entrance that led to the swimming pool and the Tapas restaurant. It was a route with which she was familiar, and her parents were eating in the Tapas.

It is Kate McCann, though, who articulated the best reason to dismiss the notion that Madeleine left the apartment of her own volition, and by the patio doors. One would have to accept, Kate has reasoned, that on leaving Madeleine would have: opened the curtains on the patio doors and closed them behind her; opened a patio door and closed it behind her; and opened and closed both a child safety gate and the gate to the street. Would such a little girl really have done that?

All the accumulated evidence indicates, rather, that Madeleine was abducted. As Operation Grange chief Andy Redwood has said, the probability is that 'This is a criminal act [by] a stranger who has taken Madeleine McCann.'

Kate, of course, has never thought otherwise. A couple of times a year, she has flown to Portugal, slipped quietly into Praia da Luz, walked the streets near the Ocean Club, and tried to think the way an abductor may have thought, to imagine his movements on the night of May 3rd 2007. 'I look at the apartment,' she has said, 'I kind of step into that person's shoes. And I think, "Where did you go?"'

What sort of stranger would enter an apartment in a holiday resort and make off with a little blonde girl almost four years old, the daughter of tourists? The knee-jerk response may be to think only of the male paedophile, the 'evil beast', the 'monster' of tabloid newspaper imagery. In Madeleine's case, the former head of one of Scotland Yard's kidnap teams believed that may not necessarily have been the case.

Former Detective Inspector Ian Horrocks, who was with the Metropolitan Police for thirty years, studied the case over many months, visited Praia da Luz and produced a lengthy summary of his views. While acknowledging that the motive for snatching Madeleine may have been sexual, he thought it 'most likely' that she was 'taken by a person or couple with the intention of keeping her'. He theorised, drawing on his experience of kidnapping cases, that the abduction may have been done by 'someone who wanted her as part of his or their family'. His hunch – going on the fragmentary evidence of what is known of the circumstances, and the possibility that an abductor may have had an accomplice in a car waiting – suggested to him that two people may have been involved.

Thefts of babies, often by women who have miscarried or are infertile, do occur. Typically, an infant is taken within days of his or her birth, often from hospitals. Not for nothing have hospitals installed especially strong security systems in maternity wards.

A typical such abductor, studies by the US National Center for Missing and Exploited Children (NCMEC) suggest, may be a previously pregnant woman who has miscarried, or one who finds herself infertile, or one who has a male partner but is not living with him and wants to get him back.

In the UK, there was for a time a charity that – among its other causes – supported women who had kidnapped children, the Portia Trust. The trust's founder, Ken Norman, claimed most such women are not mentally ill but simply 'cannot accept that their child is dead or have an unbearable desire for a baby of their own. They may have spent months, even years, looking for a child that resembles the one they have lost and is of the same age.' Though such thefts invariably make headlines, they are extremely rare.

The positive factor in almost all such cases – if it is possible to speak of a positive factor – is that the very purpose of such child thefts is to nurture the child, to raise it to adulthood as if it were the woman's own. 'The babies are very rarely harmed,' a NCMEC spokesman has said. 'The recovery rate is very good.' In one case in the United States, a woman aged twenty-three contacted NCMEC on realising she had no birth certificate or Social Security card. Her case was investigated and her true biological parents identified.

The parents had never given up hope that they would find their missing daughter, as the McCanns have said they will never give up hope of finding Madeleine.

'It's upsetting to think she might be living a different life, and calling someone else "Mummy" . . . ' Kate has said, 'but bring it on! We'll deal with anything.' For Kate, of course, the worst vision by far – a key focus of her prolonged anguish – has been the possibility that her daughter was abducted by a sex offender.

It was something she has never been able to block out of her mind. 'The idea that my Madeleine was taken by a paedophile is my worst fear,' she has said. 'I became consumed by it. It was torture for me. Horrible. So vivid.'

The ancient Greeks coined the word 'paedophilia' – 'paedo' from *pais* or *paid-*, meaning 'child', and *philia*, meaning 'fondness'. The child in question was generally a boy, and sex between child and adult was seen as educative for the child. In Europe four centuries ago, for adults to meddle sexually with children was still fairly common.

By 1886, however, the psychiatrist Richard von Krafft-Ebing was describing paedophilia as 'violation'. In 1953, on the other hand, the sex researcher Alfred Kinsey wrote that it was 'difficult to understand' why a child should be troubled by being touched sexually. 'People expect paedophiles to be recognisable, to have horns and a tail,' the late British sex-crime consultant Ray Wyre said, 'but they are just ordinary men who are able to hide their sexual attraction to young children. In fact, some hide it so well that they get jobs working with children. To be honest, as a society, we haven't yet begun to understand paedophilia.'

For the psychiatrists who authored the 2013 edition of America's authoritative *Diagnostic and Statistical Manual of Mental Disorders*, 'paedophilia' refers to: 'recurrent, intense sexually arousing fantasies, sexual urges, or behaviors involving sexual activity with a prepubescent child or children.' The *Manual* defines an individual with such a disorder as one 'who has acted on these sexual urges . . . at least age 16 years and at least 5 years older than the child.'

The mother and father of an abducted child, however, would surely relate more to the phrase used in an earlier American study, that a paedophile's actions cross the 'last frontier of child abuse'.

Statistics on the prevalence of paedophilia are elusive. America's *Manual of Mental Disorders* suggests that paedophilic disorders affect 3–5 per cent, at most, of males in the US population. The figure for females is much lower. A tentative figure offered for Britain is that 'one in five of all adult men are to some degree capable of being sexually aroused by children'. The year Madeleine vanished, Britain was reportedly the only country in Europe keeping a register of sexual offenders and maintaining intelligence on their movements, as required by a law passed four years earlier. Only three additional European nations keep such registers now.

In Portugal, there have been several major paedophile cases in recent years. Most notoriously, there gradually emerged a horrendous scandal involving prominent public figures and culminating in convictions in 2010. From the 1970s, according to the victims, a paedophile ring had used state-run orphanages to procure scores of teenage boys – and reportedly some girls – to be sexually abused. This became known as the Casa Pia – 'House of the Pious' – case after the name of the orphanages, which were originally religious institutions.

Those finally convicted included a former diplomat, a celebrated television presenter, a prominent doctor, a deputy principal at an orphanage, a solicitor and a driver who ferried children to encounters with the abusers. Of the many disturbing details, one that stood out was that the doctor convicted often selected children who were deaf and dumb – probably to ensure the filthy secret remained secret – and that he checked them for sexually transmitted diseases before delivering them to clients.

However, it is by no means only Portuguese citizens who have committed paedophile offences in Portugal. In 2000, according to the English-language weekly *Portugal News*, several men 'aged fifty and over and all foreigners (predominantly British), were arrested for holding up to fifty twelve-year-old boys at a villa in Sintra [a town near Lisbon] for their pleasure. The boys were often taken to the Algarve for holidays.' For all its significance, the paper noted, few other papers carried the story.

In 2006, in Lisbon itself, Sintra and other towns in the Lisbon region, forty-six men were arrested on suspicion of paedophilia. 'The majority of the victims,' reported the *Algarve Resident*, another English-language paper, 'were girls between the ages of five and thirteen.' Later, a further eight men were arrested on suspicion of being members of a paedophile ring.

Soon after Madeleine McCann's disappearance, a Portuguese child psychologist who runs a refuge for abused children, Dr Luís Vilas-Boas, asserted that: 'There is no paedophile problem in Portugal.' By contrast, lawyer Pedro Namora – himself a former child victim working on the Casa Pia case – said: 'Portugal is a paedophiles' paradise.'

Long before the Madeleine case a spokeswoman for Innocence in Danger, a charity working to protect children from sexual abuse, had criticised the Portuguese police for their reluctance to investigate child sex abuse. 'Time and again,' she said, 'complaint files are lost, witnesses are seldom interviewed, and suspects let off the hook, by totally inept search methods and investigative procedures.'

Sexual-crime consultant Ray Wyre, who had been to the country several times investigating paedophile rings, said Portugal attracted large numbers of paedophiles. 'British paedophiles have always operated there,' he told the *Daily Telegraph* soon after Madeleine went missing. 'If a child was being snatched on behalf of a barren couple, they would probably have taken one of the twins. The sad thing is that paedophiles are attracted to beautiful little girls, like Madeleine.'

Paedophiles have long craved not only the reality of sex with children, but images of it. The distribution of sexual images, some of them involving children, has flourished in Europe since the invention of photography. Fans of the writings of Lewis Carroll, creator of *Alice in Wonderland*, perhaps do not know that he had a penchant for photographing little girls naked or semi-naked – and several of his biographers have speculated without proof that he was a paedophile. The many sex shops of late-nineteenth-century London featured lewd pictures of naked girls.

The availability and nature of sexually explicit images of children, and of adult pornography, ebbed and flowed down the years before starting to burgeon during the so-called sexual revolution of the 1960s. Polaroid and movie cameras, then video, helped the industry. In the 1980s, the advent of computers meant a great leap forward for pornography of all sorts. The nineties brought the Internet, tailor-made for distribution purposes, a vast increase in worldwide demand – and corresponding calamity for little children.

The western world woke up to this on the eve of the Millennium, when a joint US–EU international conference in Vienna acknowledged that child pornography 'does not know or respect borders'. Across Europe, men were browsing so-called newsgroups with blatant labels such as 'Alt Sex Paedophile', even 'sex.babies'. They watched and listened as young children were abused live on the Internet. 'We're talking,' the head of the Internet Watch Foundation has said, 'about prepubescent children being raped.'

The investigative journalist Julian Sher, who has made a study of online predators, has observed that the Internet 'doesn't create paedophilia but it certainly does fuel it . . . Offender after offender will tell you about their "Eureka!" moment, when they first went online and saw not only the images – the live images – available, but immersed themselves in the acceptance, the assurance they were among like-minded people.'

In 2001, *Panorama* reported in depth on the 'Wonderland Club', an international ring of paedophiles who had been electronically sharing and boasting about their exploits with children. Police investigation of it had begun with the discovery that a man in California had been flaunting himself abusing a ten-year-old girl on camera, and broadcasting the acts to others watching in countries as far away as Australia, Canada and Finland. 'Wonderland' membership, it emerged, involved a formal club structure complete with committee and rules. To enter, a new member had to submit no less than ten thousand original images of child sex abuse. The probe identified more than a hundred potential members in twelve counties – including the UK. The seven men convicted in Britain had traded some seven hundred and fifty thousand images of children on the Internet.

The other European nations in which there were arrests were Austria, Belgium, France, Germany, Italy – and Portugal. Reports over fifteen years indicate that paedophiles active in Portugal, including British citizens, at first shipped film of their activity to other countries. Then, once the Internet was fully functional, they shared it online. Distribution of sex images of minors was not illegal in Portugal until 2001, while possession of such material was not outlawed until September 2007.

By that year, the year Madeleine vanished, it was calculated that worldwide child abuse activity on the Internet had quadrupled over the previous four years. Like the criminals involved, investigators struggling to identify the victims today use computers

– facial recognition software that searches through hundreds of thousands of images to get a match, sometimes successfully. During the 'Wonderland' probe, police believed they had identified some images as being of Rui Pedro, an eleven-year-old boy who vanished in northern Portugal in 1998.

During the early phase of the McCann investigation, and after Operation Predator, a Portuguese police operation targeting child sex abuse, investigators would sift through seized material focusing on images of blonde girls who in some way resembled Madeleine. None was of her. Kate McCann, though, learned more than she had ever wanted to know about the subject, and felt sick.

There were, too, scare stories in the press suggesting that Madeleine might have been taken by 'child traffickers'. A notion that has cropped up time and again is that 'Gypsies' were responsible and reports came in of: 'three Gypsies . . . in a cart accompanied by a young blonde girl'; a 'Gypsy couple with a pram carrying a child that did not look like their daughter'; a woman with a girl who 'looked like Madeleine' in a group of Gypsies who ran off when some police officers appeared; and two 'fat Gypsy women' leading a 'gaunt' child 'wearing what was clearly a black wig'.

As do all European countries, Portugal has its Romanies – the Portuguese call them *ciganos* – some forty thousand to fifty thousand of them according to a European Commission study. There was a group of them foraging for scrap on the outskirts of Praia da Luz, according to a report in police files, and word locally was that they were responsible for a number of robberies. A police check turned up nothing. Romanies are the perennial butt of allegations, real and misplaced. Professor Thomas Acton, Professor Emeritus of Romani Studies at the University of Greenwich, has said he knows of no documented case of Gypsies stealing non-Gypsy children anywhere. There is no evidence to link them to the Madeleine McCann case.

There were dark suggestions, too, that sex traffickers had seized Madeleine and moved her out of Portugal. An email from British police to Portugal some ten months after the disappearance read:

> Intelligence suggests that a paedophile ring in Belgium made an order for a young girl 3 days before Madeleine MCCANN was taken.
> Somebody connected to this group saw Maddie took a photograph of her and sent it to Belgium. The purchaser agreed that the girl was suitable and Maddie was taken.

The Polícia Judiciária forwarded the information to Interpol with a request for a follow-up. The lead came to nothing.

Given that it is fairly easy to travel from Portugal to Morocco, there was speculation that was where traffickers might have transported Madeleine. Briefing information published by the US Department of State a month after her disappearance did say Morocco was a nation where children were trafficked. The emphasis, however, the Portuguese Association for Victim Support said that year, was 'usually from Africa to Europe, not the other way around'.

Child trafficking for one purpose or another does occur on an appalling scale – there are almost 1.2 million cases each year, United Nations figures suggest. Such statistics as there are, though, indicate that victims of international trafficking are overwhelmingly from Latin America and the Caribbean, Asia and Africa. Western European children barely figure in available surveys.

'The talk of Madeleine being kidnapped by a paedophile ring, for a client in some distant place,' veteran Metropolitan Police kidnap specialist Ian Horrocks has written, is 'not credible . . . Sadly, there are many places throughout the world where this is a far simpler task than in a busy holiday resort in Portugal.'

Without any evidence, to have flailed around looking for some sinister paedophile ring never was, and never would be, a rational way for investigators to tackle the Madeleine mystery.

From the start, in the absence of other clues, a priority was to look for known sexual predators who might be at large in the Algarve.

22

Within days of Madeleine's disappearance, Gerry and Kate McCann had found themselves poring, hour after hour, over photographs of known offenders. Pictures of local men aside, they included those of British citizens – either residents of Portugal or individuals known to have visited the country in the days and weeks leading up to May 3rd.

The information on offenders' movements was culled from the UK's Sex Offender Register – all individuals on it have since 1997 been required to provide police with details of their foreign travel before leaving the country. The list, a lengthy one, had been provided to the Polícia Judiciária by specialists in abduction and paedophile behaviour from the Child Exploitation and Online Protection Centre. CEOP is staffed by police officers and child-protection specialists and has police powers.

At the request of the Portuguese government, two CEOP consultants had flown to assist on the Madeleine case. Detective Superintendent Graham Hill was a veteran of missing-children cases, including the then ongoing Milly Dowler murder investigation. With him on the assignment was Joe Sullivan, a forensic psychologist who had studied child abductions and child murders across Europe.

During the early phase of the investigation, Sullivan outlined what he had learned was the key to hunting down sex offenders. 'We don't have the luxury of allowing ourselves to see them as monsters,' he told an interviewer. 'That may be a comfortable place to be, but it's dangerous. Seeing someone as a monster dehumanises him, makes him so different from us that we cannot really begin to understand him.' In appearance and ordinary behaviour, a paedophile is likely to resemble any ordinary citizen.

In the Portuguese files now available – some were briefly released but then withdrawn to protect individuals' privacy – there is scant specific information to show which paedophile suspects were investigated in the McCann case. British suspects aside, they also included Portuguese citizens and individuals from several other nations.

A 2008 police summary does include a few paragraphs on local men initially considered potential suspects. An individual identified only as 'A.K.B.' was located, compared with an e-fit image based on witness information on one of the men suspected to have behaved suspiciously before Madeleine disappeared, then cleared. He bore only a partial resemblance to the man described by the witness, and his mobile-phone history indicated he had not been in Praia da Luz on the night of May 3rd. Another man, 'M.R.A.', attracted police attention because he was 'suspected of crimes of a sexual nature in an ongoing investigation'. His home was searched, but 'nothing relating to the disappearance of Madeleine was found'.

The police summary noted, too, that the strange behaviour of a British man aged between forty and fifty had 'raised suspicions of possibly practising acts of paedophilia and exhibitionism . . . This individual would walk around with a long lens camera and appeared to have a special fixation on children. Nothing of relevance was found.' By the end of 2007, presumably with input from CEOP, no less than fifty-two potential British suspects had reportedly been cleared.

Much later, after perusing material not now available to the general public, Kate McCann was not impressed by what she had learned from the files of the Portuguese conduct of the investigation. They were replete, she said, with reports of the crimes of Portuguese and British paedophiles, and paedophiles of many other nations. The police, though, seemed to her to have done little more than catalogue the criminals' existence, and not enough to establish whether they had anything to do with the Madeleine case.

A number of men at one point or another considered possible suspects have been named publicly. Three months after the disappearance, in Switzerland, a five-year-old named Ylenia Lenhard – blonde and cute like Madeleine – vanished after visiting a swimming pool. Her decomposing body was found the following month, and forensic evidence showed that she had died as the result of poisoning with toluene, a solvent used in paint thinners. As reported earlier in these pages, toluene has been used to render victims unconscious during sexual assault.

Also discovered not far away was the corpse of a sixty-seven-year-old man named Urs Hans von Aesch, an apparent suicide. Forensic evidence would establish that he had indeed had little Ylenia in his white Renault Trafic van, and that – a few weeks earlier – he had purchased a bottle of paint thinner. The precise circumstances remain unclear, but everything indicates he was responsible for the child's death.

It looked at first as though there might be a connection to the Madeleine case in Portugal. Von Aesch had long been resident in neighbouring Spain, and he had been living there at the time

Madeleine vanished. He had had psychological problems, and had once threatened to hold a child to ransom. Though he had no history of paedophile offences, questions were raised when videotapes were found at his home featuring photographs of children in bathing suits. A man in a white van, moreover, had been seen parked near the McCanns' apartment in Praia da Luz.

The Swiss police saw to it that the Portuguese were alerted early on about von Aesch, and Scotland Yard detectives would travel to Switzerland in 2012 to confer with their counterparts there. The elements that made von Aesch seem suspicious, however, appear not to add up. The white van seen parked in Praia da Luz had been not a Renault but a Mercedes, and seemingly had no connection to the Madeleine case. Von Aesch, moreover, was much older than any of the men potentially linked to the case by testimony, and there is no known evidence that he had been in the Algarve in May 2007. Statements by his widow, and his diaries, moreover, indicate that he had not visited the Algarve since 1994.

The Swiss police, nevertheless, reached no hard and fast conclusion. They could 'neither make any connection of von Aesch to the disappearance of Madeleine McCann nor exclude a connection with absolute certainty,' the police chief who ran the original investigation, Bruno Fehr, told the authors in 2014. Scotland Yard detectives, he added, were trying to resolve definitively whether or not von Aesch had been in Portugal at the time of Madeleine's disappearance.

A more promising lead, one that interested the McCanns' private detectives, concerned an Englishman who indeed had a record as a paedophile. This was former soldier and sometime fairground worker Raymond Hewlett, who had repeatedly been jailed for sexual assault and attempted rape of minors in Britain in the

1970s and 1980s and had been suspected of other similar crimes. In one attack, on a twelve-year-old girl, he placed a rag soaked in paint thinner on his victim's face to render her unconscious.

A judge at one of Hewlett's trials had described him as 'most dangerous'. Long wanted for questioning about another attack, he had been listed on a Crimestoppers' list of Most Wanted Paedophiles. In May 2007, he had been living with his wife and a brood of children – their home was a large blue van – at a campsite some seventy miles from Praia da Luz.

The suggestion that Hewlett might have abducted Madeleine became public in May 2009, when a couple who had met him in Portugal – but not at the time known about his past – reported that he had chattered about 'Gypsies' having offered him money for one of his own daughters. Another couple, who encountered him in Morocco, said he had talked about the McCann case a lot, saying he knew Praia da Luz and the Ocean Club and had often parked his van near Apartment 5A. A hue and cry began when this information emerged, and Hewlett – by then seriously ill with throat cancer – was tracked down to a hospital in Germany.

Approached by the McCanns' private detectives for interview, Hewlett demanded 'thousands of pounds' in payment. The McCanns sensibly declined, but the dying man did make some statements. He reportedly told police that he had been to Praia da Luz and twice seen Madeleine before she died – at such close quarters that he remembered the coloboma, the distinctive mark in her right eye.

Subsequently, however, in an interview with the *Sunday Mirror*, he came up with a quite different story. Gasping for breath because of his illness, he insisted that he 'didn't kill the McCann girl . . . I'd take a lie-detector test . . . The only time I've seen Madeleine McCann is on missing posters. And I saw her on TV in a bar once. But I've never seen her in real life. Yes, I've been to Praia da Luz, but not since 2002.' He claimed he had been in Vila Real de Santo António on May 3rd 2007 when Madeleine vanished.

After Hewlett's death at the age of sixty-four, his estranged son Wayne claimed he had received a deathbed letter from him. In an interview with the *Sun*, Wayne Hewlett quoted his father as having written that: 'He didn't want to go to his grave with us thinking he had done such a horrible thing. He said he had nothing to do with taking Maddie but did know who had. He said a very good Gypsy friend he knew in Portugal had got drunk and "let it out" that he had stolen Maddie to order as part of a gang. My dad said this gang had been operating for a long time and had snatched children before for couples who couldn't have children of their own. Maddie had been targeted. They took photos of children and sent them to the people they were acting for. And they said yes or no . . . Dad said there were huge sums of money involved. And he totally believed what the man was saying.'

The claims were dramatic, and made a good story for the *Sun*. Whether Hewlett really wrote the letter, however – and whether his son ever received it – remains unknown and unknowable. Improbably, not least because of its potential monetary value, the son claimed he had burned the letter because it 'unnerved' him so much. Even if such a letter did exist, there is reason to doubt its veracity.

In his lengthy interview with the *Sunday Mirror*, Hewlett had said nothing of his supposed knowledge of a 'Gypsy gang' that had abducted Madeleine. Moreover, press stories about what he had told acquaintances in the past suggest he was an unreliable, marijuana-smoking gossip. At one point before Hewlett died, the McCanns' spokesman said carefully that it was hoped he would share any 'credible' information he might have about the case with investigators. Hewlett apparently had a long history of lying.

Reportedly, and by his own account, Hewlett had been questioned by Portuguese police shortly after Madeleine's disappearance – presumably because he was one of the men on the British Sex Offender Register known to be in Portugal. He ceased to be a suspect, apparently, when it was found that his bank card had been used in Lisbon at the time Madeleine went missing. British police took an interest in the Hewlett matter in 2012 early in the Operation Grange probe, but his name has not come up since. Though Hewlett was a known child molester, there is no substantive evidence that he had anything to do with the Madeleine case.

Three other British citizens are known to have attracted investigators' interest since the disappearance. Charles O'Neill and William Lauchlan, who committed multiple child sex assaults over a long period, are today serving life sentences for the murder of a woman they feared would expose them. The pair twice spent extended periods in Spain – first on the Costa Blanca and later, from 2006, in the Canary Islands. The notion that they might have been in the Algarve when Madeleine vanished, however, seems to be unsupported by any evidence. It seems, moreover, that O'Neill and Lauchlan preyed only on boys, not girls.

There have, too, been speculative press stories on David Reid, from Northern Ireland, who had been jailed for three years for the indecent assault of his four daughters. Because he had been released from prison before the Sex Offender Register was established, Reid had been able to travel outside the UK without informing the authorities. He had indeed moved – to Portugal. A guitarist, he had worked for years entertaining customers in bars around the small tourist town of Carvoeiro, in the Algarve. This fact was seized on by the *News of the World*, which ran an article exposing Reid the year before Madeleine vanished. Confronted by the paper's reporters, he had insisted, 'I did wrong at home [in Northern Ireland], very wrong . . . and I paid the consequences. I did my time. I am very sorry and I have lived with the guilt every day for twenty-two years . . . I am not a paedophile.' Despite his protest that his crimes were long behind him, and despite his previous popularity locally, the *News of the World* exposé wrecked Reid's hitherto peaceful existence in the Algarve. He was ostracised, beaten up and lost his job as a singer. Reid died in his early sixties, still in Portugal, in 2013.

The media dug up Reid's story again, months after his death, with headlines like: 'Missing Madeleine McCann – British Paedophile Was Living Next to Resort Where Three-Year-Old Was Snatched' and 'Was Madeleine McCann Snatched by British Paedophile David Reid?' Though by no means necessarily accurate, the speculation was natural enough.

If, as it appears, David Reid was still in Carvoeiro in May 2007 when Madeleine vanished, that fact deserved investigation – whatever his claims to be a changed man. For, depending on the route you take, the resort is either twenty-three or twenty-eight miles from Praia da Luz. Carvoeiro, moreover, has been of special interest to investigators for years – and still was, as this book went to press, to detectives running the Metropolitan Police investigation.

As early as 2009, working from police records released to the McCanns and other material, private detectives working for Gerry and Kate McCann had identified four villages and towns – all within forty miles of Praia da Luz – where intruders had in the period before Madeleine's disappearance assaulted, tried to assault and in one case tried to abduct, young girls.

Two incidents had occurred in Carvoeiro, three in or near the town of Albufeira and one in the town of Silves. Most had occurred at night and had involved an intruder entering an apartment. Five of six attacks had targeted British children. The victims had all been young girls, most of them around nine or ten years old. One, the child in Silves, whom the intruder appeared to have tried to abduct, had been a girl only three years old – almost the same age as Madeleine.

One of the incidents in the Carvoeiro area was described to the authors by a British resident of Portugal, a well-known face on British television who prefers not to be named here. It occurred some three years before Madeleine vanished, and the target was the then eight-year-old daughter of an English couple – friends of the resident – who were renting a villa nearby. 'The parents called me right afterwards,' the resident said, 'and described what had happened during the night. They had been asleep in their room with the door closed, and their two children – girls aged eleven and eight – were in their beds in another room. It was only when the girls woke them that they learned there had been an intruder.

'From what the children told their parents, it seemed the man had come in and got into bed with their younger daughter. He hadn't actually done anything to her. And she said, "Is that you, Daddy?" And he said, "Yes." She knew it wasn't her daddy, perhaps because he talked differently or was the wrong size or something. They'd got some other people staying in the villa, so she asked, "Is that you, Uncle?" and again he said, "Yes." But that was it.

'The older girl woke up at that point and saw what was happening. The man got up and walked out of the room into the kitchen. And I gathered the older girl told her sister something like, "Keep quiet. Just keep quiet." But then, when the man had gone, the kids got up and went and woke up their parents.'

It had been, as the authors' source said, 'very strange, bizarre'. The intruder had apparently worn a surgical mask and – to avoid leaving footprints, they speculated – had taken some laundry and wrapped it round his feet. The parents concluded that it had been the same man who, the previous day, had tampered with the mechanism of the glass sliding doors. Once that was done, getting into the villa had been easy.

Years later, after study by the Metropolitan Police of the various attacks – and as the public responded to appeals broadcast on *Crimewatch* – Operation Grange chief Andy Redwood would update the information on potentially relevant incidents before and after Madeleine's disappearance. There had in fact been eighteen break-ins that involved children, he said, in properties where British families had been staying between 2004 and 2010. Five had occurred in Carvoeiro, nine at locations near either Carvoeiro or Albufeira, one in the village of Vilamoura and three in Praia da Luz itself (see map at photo 23).

In most of the incidents, there had been no forced entry and nothing had been stolen. In one chilling incident in 2006 in Praia da Luz, at the Ocean Club itself, children in a ground-floor apartment had seen a man break in through a patio door. He had taken nothing, but merely stood staring into a child's travel cot.

The previous year in Praia da Luz, however, a ten-year-old girl had been sexually assaulted. Nine children had been sexually assaulted in all. There had been three 'near misses' – where the offender was in close proximity to the potential victim – and six other occasions in which an intruder had been interrupted before he could carry out an attack.

The authors learned from a British source of what may have been one of the 'near misses' and may give real significance to the 'orphanage' soliciting described earlier in the book.* As the authors have reported, between April 20th, 2007 and the day Madeleine disappeared May 3rd, one man – and on occasion two men – came to the doors of British residents and tourists claiming to be collecting for an orphanage. There was no such orphanage in the location they described, and it is a reasonable speculation that the men were in fact casing the premises with intent to commit a crime. One account given to the authors, however, suggests there was a sexual motive behind the 'orphanage' visits.

A British citizen long resident in the Algarve has described the chilling episode when a man claiming to represent an orphanage came to the door of her friend, also English. 'There was a knock at the door,' she recalled, 'and the man standing there said he was collecting for some orphanage. He looked rather unkempt, scruffy. But what made her very uncomfortable was that, all the time he was stood there, he wasn't looking at her but past her – at her three-year-old daughter.'

A couple of hours after the doorstep encounter, when the British woman went to pick up an older child from school, she spotted him again. 'He was still there, waiting at the end of the road,' her friend told the authors. 'Her sense of uneasiness increased. And the following day, she left her three-year-old daughter downstairs for a minute or two while she went upstairs to fetch some laundry. Then, when she was coming back down the stairs, she caught a glimpse of a man – really only his legs – in the living room with her child. He left rapidly as she came down the stairs, obviously.

'My friend thought it was the same man who had come to the door the previous day collecting for an orphanage. She thought

---

* See pp.57–60.

he had got in through the sliding patio doors and believed – even then – that he had meant to take her daughter.'

The man who made this woman fear for her child had come to her door very shortly before Madeleine disappeared. The family's rented villa was, moreover, in Praia da Luz, where all six other 'orphanage' incidents had been reported – one of them, the week before Madeleine went missing, at the Ocean Club's Apartment 5A, where the McCanns were to stay.

In April 2014, Operation Grange's Chief Inspector Redwood made public a description of the intruder. 'The offender, we know,' he revealed, 'is described as being a male, with dark hair, who has got dark brown tanned skin. He often speaks to the victims in a foreign accent, in English, with his voice being rather slow or possibly slurred.'

The man had had unkempt hair, and had been unshaven. Some witnesses had described him as having a pot belly, and three of the children said he had – in Redwood's words – 'a noticeable odour'. One of the victims suggested that he had smelled of tobacco, another that he smelled of aftershave. A third spoke merely of 'a funny smell'.

He had on occasion been bare-chested. On two occasions, though, the man had worn a distinctive long-sleeved burgundy-coloured top. Witnesses in one family, who had seen the individual from the rear, have described the garment as having a white circle on the back (see photo 23). Some have said it sounds from the description like the logo on shirts once worn by the Arsenal football team. One former police detective, meanwhile, has suggested it might have been a promotional T-shirt for Super Bock, a brand of beer. The shirts were of a type some bars in Portugal give free to regular customers. Just possibly, checks could trace at least some of the people who received the shirt in the relevant area of the Algarve.

It is DNA or fingerprint evidence, of course, that could identify the child molester and perhaps lead to a breakthrough in the Madeleine case. Operation Grange chief Redwood alluded to this during media briefings in the spring of 2014, and there was press speculation that his team might have obtained some relevant forensic material.

If the Operation Grange team have obtained such material, and if further forensic evidence were to turn up in Portuguese police records, there might be an important development. Many if not all of the child sex assault cases were handled only by the GNR – the Guarda Nacional Republicana – and never passed to the Polícia Judiciária, the detection arm of the Portuguese police force. Relevant material, Redwood thought, might be lying forgotten 'in police exhibit stores somewhere in the Algarve'.

If such evidence does exist, could be retrieved and if – the big 'if' – it led to identification of an individual, the investigation might take a great leap forward.

23

Kate McCann had got wind of the fact that there had been previous assaults on little girls the very morning after her daughter's disappearance. The then British consul in the Algarve, Bill Henderson, told her about them as she waited to tell the Portuguese police about the previous night's events. Months later, when Henderson had retired and she got in touch with him again, he shared further details.

Eventually, Kate learned that word of the incidents reached British police from parents who came forward on learning what had happened to Madeleine. According to the parents' reports, Portuguese police had not taken the parents' complaints seriously. There had been no adequate follow-up, they said, no statements taken, no search for DNA or fingerprint evidence. It was hard to understand, then, one mother had written in a letter to the police, how a profile of the man could be developed. What might he do, she asked, if he was not stopped?

Some British tour operators, former consul Henderson had told Kate, had been concerned that information about such sex assaults should remain confidential. In 2014, the authors wrote to Mark Warner, the company through which the McCanns booked their 2007 holiday, to ask whether it had known before Madeleine's disappearance of previous child assaults or recent break-ins to premises in the area – including the Ocean Club – and whether tourists had been alerted to the danger on arrival at the resort. Warner's head of customer services replied that the company's policy was not to comment.

The authors also asked the Foreign Office whether it had been aware, before Madeleine vanished, of the recent break-ins and child assaults in the Algarve, and whether steps had been taken to alert incoming British tourists or residents to the danger. The Foreign Office replied that it was 'currently unable to provide [the authors] with the information' requested.

In early 2007, in connection with robberies in the area, the British consulate in the Algarve told the local press that it did not 'undertake to issue advice on crime prevention measures to residents . . .'

Had Gerry and Kate McCann known of the history of sexual assaults on tourists' children in Praia da Luz and the surrounding area, they would surely not have left their patio doors unlocked to make dinner-time checks on their children easier. Had they known about the sex attacks in advance of the holiday, indeed, they might well not have chosen to travel to the Algarve.

Had the couple known that several witnesses saw an individual or individuals who appeared to be watching their apartment that week, they would surely have been alert to possible peril.

Had they known that there had recently been a series of break-ins at the Ocean Club, they would surely have taken more precautions. One of those break-ins occurred only the week before they arrived, when Pamela Fenn, the elderly woman who lived directly above their apartment, had disturbed an intruder and sent him packing.

Had they known that, after 10 p.m. one night that week – on the Tuesday, Mrs Fenn said she thought it had been – the old lady had heard a small child crying and crying for an hour or more and calling 'Daddy! Daddy!', they might have worried.

Mrs Fenn had 'no doubt', she would later tell police, that the crying had come from directly below her, the McCanns' apartment. She might have been mistaken as to the source of the crying. Nineteen-month-old Grace, daughter of the McCanns' friends the Oldfields, was in Apartment 5B, right next to the McCann family. Two-year-old Evie, daughter of the McCanns' friends Russ O'Brien and his partner Jane Tanner, who were staying a couple of doors away, had been ill on the Tuesday. Perhaps there had been an innocent explanation for the crying. Or perhaps not.

Had the McCanns known, though, about the history of sex assaults on children and break-ins when – on the Thursday morning – Madeleine asked why their mother had not come when they cried the night before, they might have been more than merely momentarily perplexed. They might have pressed her to explain when and why she and her brother had cried. Just conceivably, she might have told them something that would have led them to suspect something troubling had occurred the previous night. Perhaps a marauder had been interrupted as he began to make his entry, possibly by one of the checks they made on the children as they lingered longer than usual over dinner at the restaurant sixty yards away across the pool.

Had they known what had happened later that fateful Thursday, while they and the children were enjoying themselves, they would certainly have been alarmed. It was late that afternoon that Mrs Fenn's niece Carole – sitting on her aunt's terrace directly above the McCann apartment – had seen a man acting furtively in the lane below. He had appeared to come out of a ground-floor apartment, had looked to one side then the other, had shut the gate very carefully as though ensuring it did not make a noise, had done so several times, moving stealthily as though not to be seen. It had looked, Mrs Fenn's niece had thought, 'very strange'.

Had Gerry and Kate McCann but known . . .

24

On May 3rd 2014, the McCann family – Gerry and Kate and twins Sean and Amelie, now nine years old – again marked the anniversary of Madeleine's disappearance.

It was seven years since Kate had tucked Madeleine into bed in Apartment 5A at the Ocean Club in Praia da Luz; since a sleepy elder daughter had asked to try on Kate's engagement ring, as sometimes she did. There had been the last story of the day, the one that went:

> If you're happy and you know it,
> And you really want to show it,
> If you're happy and you know it,
> Shout!

When the song called for everyone to shout 'WE ARE!', Madeleine's eyes had already been drooping. After last kisses goodnight, all had been quiet.

Seven years since Gerry had returned from dinner to check on the children, had looked at the sleeping Madeleine in her Eeyore pyjamas, thought how beautiful she was, how much he loved her.

And seven years since Kate in turn had checked on the children and found Madeleine 'not there'. The moment of terror when she 'literally flew around the apartment . . . realised the window was open and the shutter was up,' when she had run out towards where her husband and their friends were sitting at dinner and 'just screamed'.

Now, the best part of a decade on, laden with fame they had not wanted, their names familiar worldwide, the McCanns stood under the lime trees with relatives, friends and people from their home village. There were prayers for all missing children. Behind the couple as they spoke of Madeleine was the village war memorial, now known to most as much for its use as a shrine to their daughter as for honouring local men who died in the twentieth century's conflicts. There were photographs of Madeleine, yellow 'awareness' ribbons, yellow spring tulips, a 'Have You Seen Her?' poster of Madeleine as she might look after the passing of the years, and a candle in a lantern.

In an interview two days earlier, Gerry and Kate had talked of their frustrations about the status of the current investigation. They reflected, with passion, what necessarily diplomatic Metropolitan Police statements only hinted at. Why, when the investigation seemed to be making progress, did the Portuguese seem loath to give full cooperation?

Wires seemed to be crossed. Portugal's Attorney General had in autumn 2013 said new leads justified pressing forward with the investigation. Within a month, Metropolitan Police Commissioner Sir Bernard Hogan-Howe had called for a joint investigation team – as prescribed under EU law. He had observed, though, that, 'We've got one particular set of lines of inquiry and they have a different one.' So far did things deteriorate that four months later, in March 2014, Prime Minister David Cameron had said publicly that he might 'make further representations' to the Portuguese government in the hope of giving the investigation traction.

'As a parent,' Kate McCann told the BBC, 'I find the slowness of action in Portugal really hard to take . . . quite distressing . . . I suppose I struggle with the fact, you know, "Would you please work together?"' So far as he could gather from his contacts at the top of the Scotland Yard investigation, Gerry said, the Polícia Judiciária team now at work did want to solve the case. Yet still progress was blocked.

Public opinion in Portugal, once sympathetic to the McCanns, had long since hardened. The editor of the local English-language newspaper the *Algarve Resident*, Inez Lopez, had said in 2011 that: 'People want to move on, not be forever attached to or identified with Madeleine. Of course we still feel for the McCanns but we want to be associated with a happier place. Frankly, it was an isolated incident that could have happened anywhere in the world. In Praia da Luz the feeling is that it has hurt our local economy.'

'The shock factor,' Paul Luckman, editor of the national English-language paper the *Portugal News*, said the following year, 'has been replaced by apathy. Nobody is interested. The attitude is, "It's gone, it's over. Can we please get on with our lives?"' Where 'Missing' posters about Madeleine had once proliferated, it was reported in 2013, there was now only an appeal for information about who might have vandalised the bowls club lawn.

That same year, the deputy editor of Portugal's second most popular daily, *Jornal de Notícias*, let loose with a rant about the case – and the British police investigation. 'The disappearance of Maddie,' wrote Jorge Fiel, 'not four years old when imprudently left alone at home with her younger siblings, received the greatest media coverage of all time – everyone had an opinion on the matter – and ousted the Lindbergh baby's abduction from the *Guinness Book of Records* . . . I suggest that Scotland Yard hire Sherlock Holmes, who is second to none at solving mysteries . . . And I advise Kate and Gerry to kick the habit of drinking their grief through a straw – and realise that it is right to mourn the dead, but that one also has to let them go.'

This was a cruel jab. Others with relevant experience, though, have long echoed the suggestion that Madeleine is likely dead. British sex-crimes expert Ray Wyre said within days of the disappearance that, 'Children abducted by paedophiles have often been killed a few hours later, or – at most – within the day. A child stolen for sex is often dead before anyone even reports they have gone.'

Mark Harrison, of the UK's own National Policing Improvement Agency, had that same summer told the Portuguese police that they needed to consider 'the possibility that she has been killed and her body hidden'.

By July 2008, in their summary of the case for Portugal's Attorney General, local prosecutors Melchior Gomes and Magalhães e Menezes had stated that it was 'more likely' that Madeleine was dead.

After two years' work on the case, however, Scotland Yard's Detective Chief Inspector Andy Redwood held out hope. 'There is no clear, definitive proof that Madeleine McCann is dead,' he said in 2013. 'On that basis I believe there is a possibility she is still alive . . . I would like to ask the public to continue to look for her.' He held to that position in early 2014.

The missing girl's father and mother, of course, have never given up on the possibility that she might be alive. 'We won't accept Madeleine is dead,' Gerry said in late 2013, 'until we see evidence, *clear* evidence, that that is the case . . . We've always had hope. And there've been a number of cases over the last few years of children and young women being found after having been taken and held for *very* long periods of time.'

This was true. There had been: Stephen Stayner, abducted in 1972 at the age of seven in California, later joined in his confinement by a five-year-old – also abducted – escaped seven years later; Dimitri Thevenin, abducted in 1986 in France aged three, recovered after seven months; Carlina White, abducted as a baby in 1987 in New York City by a woman, brought up not knowing she had been stolen, discovered her true parentage after twenty-three years; Jaycee Dugard, abducted in 1991 in California by a sexual predator at age eleven, recovered eighteen years later; Sabine Dardenne, aged twelve, and Laetitia Delhez, fourteen, abducted in Belgium in 1996, recovered three months later; Natascha Kampusch, abducted in 1998 aged ten in Austria, escaped in 2006; Shawn Hornbeck, abducted in 2002 in Missouri, recovered five years later; and – also in 2002 – Elizabeth Smart, abducted at fourteen in Utah, recovered nine months later.

Gerry and Kate McCann had early on acknowledged that Madeleine might be dead. 'We are not naïve,' Gerry told an interviewer in 2010, 'and there is a probability that she is dead. However, she is a small child, and in abduction cases the younger you are the greater the possibility of adapting and surviving.

'That isn't some kind of dream,' Gerry insisted. 'The National Center for Missing and Exploited Children in the United States – with the most experience in child abduction cases – [say] that the younger the child, the more likely they have been taken to be kept.' More than half the children abducted by strangers in the USA are recovered alive – but usually not long after having been abducted.

Early on, Gerry had visited the Center and consulted its then CEO, Ernie Allen. In the US, NCMEC has stated, 'One in seven missing children is found as a direct result of somebody simply recognising their face on a poster or flyer and notifying law enforcement. Ninety-seven percent are located using a variety of efforts in addition to photograph distribution.'

NCMEC's published recommendation to parents whose child goes missing is: 'Make every effort to obtain local and national media attention regarding your missing child. Conduct television, radio and newspaper interviews to discuss and direct attention to your child.' The McCanns have followed this advice to the letter.

Some Portuguese law-enforcement officials took the view, to the contrary, that publicity imperilled Madeleine. 'Intelligent people,' Chief Inspector Tavares de Almeida wrote in an early report on the investigation, 'should know that publicity is detrimental to the investigation of the crime of kidnapping and, above all, to the safety of the victim.'

'With the whole world having Madeleine's photo,' *Vanity Fair* quoted then Attorney General Fernando Pinto Monteiro as saying, an abductor would have felt so pressured that 'there's a greater probability of the little girl being dead than alive.' He repeated that view in an interview with the authors in 2014.

If Madeleine was abducted – and the sensible consensus is that she was – there is of course one person who knows well what has become of her: the abductor, and perhaps someone close to the abductor. By now, he or they have surely seen and heard the publicity, have become aware of the hue and cry.

Four days after the disappearance, in Praia da Luz, Gerry's arm around her, Kate had tremulously made a televised appeal to the abductor. She said:

Madeleine is a beautiful, bright, funny and caring little girl. She is so special.

Please, please, do not hurt her. Please don't scare her. Please tell us where to find her or put her in a place of safety and let somebody know where she is.

We beg you to let Madeleine come home. We need our Madeleine . . . and Madeleine needs us. Please give our little girl back.

Then, haltingly, she repeated that final sentence in Portuguese:

Por favor, devolva a nossa menina.

The following year, when the McCanns had applied to the High Court in London for assistance in pursuing their hunt for the truth, the judge made a similar formal appeal to the presumed abductor – the more moving for its formality. Mrs Justice Hogg said:

I ponder about that person: whether that person has a heart and can understand what it must be like for Madeleine to have been torn and secreted from her parents and siblings whom she loves and felt secure with, and whom she no doubt misses and grieves for. Whether that person has a conscience or any feeling of guilt, remorse, or even cares about the hurt which has been caused to an innocent little girl; whether that person has a faith or belief, and what explanation or justification that person will give to God.

I entreat that person whoever and wherever you may be to show mercy and compassion, and come forward to tell us where Madeleine is to be found.

CEOP's former head Jim Gamble said in 2014 that he believed the remorseless continuing hunt for Madeleine and the massive publicity will have frightened the individual or individuals who took her. 'They need to recognise that we are closing in on them. They should be constantly looking over their shoulder, waiting for the knock on the door . . .

'Some people have no conscience, don't worry about what they did. But somebody likely knows them, knows something and may suspect them, worries about the guilty knowledge they are carrying. They may have a conscience and may come forward. I think the person responsible will be caught in the end.'

Gerry's and Kate's anguish aside, there is another pressing reason to track down the presumed abductor – if the person is a sexual predator. Paedophilia is a permanent condition and sex offenders strike again and again. 'The person responsible for the disappearance of Madeleine McCann is a significant risk to children,' said CEOP's Dr Joe Sullivan. 'This person is very likely to behave in the same way again. It's critically important that we identify that person.'

'This much I know,' said former director of NCMEC's international division Elizabeth Yore. 'Someone knows who took Madeleine. If you know, tell Scotland Yard. Break free of your fear. Madeleine's abductor will strike again. Some innocent little girl is asleep in her bed blissfully unaware of the monster that roams free . . . You know his name.'

In 2014, with the seventh anniversary of Madeleine's disappearance approaching, Kate McCann sought to explain how she felt after so much time, so many hopes, so many disappointments. 'Obviously our ultimate hope is that we find Madeleine, and we re-establish her into our family and spend the next few years of her life getting it all as good as it can be,' she said. 'We obviously want Madeleine back . . . But we do want an answer, whatever.'

Kate did not underestimate the pain she and the family would suffer if they were to learn her daughter had been killed. 'But,' she said, 'we do want an answer, whatever . . . Regardless, we need to know.'

Yet again, as they have countless times, Kate and Gerry sat for television interviews. On a BBC programme, they talked of Madeleine's upcoming birthday. 'It's hard. It's really hard,' Gerry said. 'She's not there and you should be celebrating, and it's by far the toughest day of the year.'

Kate said: 'You think, "eleven . . ." She's due to start secondary school in September. It's been, you know, a long time.'

She was visibly fighting back tears. Then, asked what she would say to Madeleine if she could, she said: 'We love you, Madeleine. We miss you every day, as we did that first day. And we're waiting for you. We're never going to give up. We'll do whatever we can to find you.'

On the day of the anniversary itself, May 3rd, when she and her husband addressed the little gathering for prayers under the lime trees in front of the village war memorial with its flickering candle in a lantern for Madeleine and all the world's missing children, Kate read the words of the old song 'I'll Be Seeing You':

> I'll find you in the morning sun
> And when the night is new
> I'll be looking at the moon
> But I'll be seeing you.

25

The months that followed brought new headlines. Scotland Yard announced 'operational activity on the ground in Portugal', digging in and around Praia da Luz. Though the police did not say as much, this was evidently a search for possible human remains. Nothing of relevance was found. In a new development weeks later, a number of witnesses were questioned. To comply with national law, Portuguese detectives posed the questions with British officers sitting in as observers.

Though press reports had suggested otherwise, Assistant Commissioner Mark Rowley emphasised that the new work 'should not be seen as a sign that the investigation is nearing a conclusion'. It was, he said, 'part of the routine slog'. Operation Grange chief Andy Redwood had earlier noted that his team had worked through more than 2000 'actions', or tasks – with more than that number still to be done.

Autumn 2014 brought headlines of a very different sort, news that coincided with publication of the first edition of this book. It shone harsh light on the machinations of some McCann 'haters', people who had for years used the Web to pump out vicious bile. As reported in earlier chapters,* the Web has harboured not only the moderate observers and enthusiastic supporters of Kate and Gerry McCann, but also many out-and-out foes.

Such individuals have poured out their poison on platforms like Facebook and Twitter, the rise and rise of which have coincided with the years since Madeleine's disappearance. Constantly evolving, this explosion of social media has enabled users to connect with like-minded individuals instantaneously, often anonymously – and outpaced law enforcement's ability to police it. It was a raw example of this phenomenon of our time, in the context of the Madeleine case, that attracted attention in late 2014.

To many of the online 'antis', it has seemed not to matter that Gerry and Kate McCann are the distressed parents of a missing child, a couple not known to have committed any wrongdoing. Their friends and acquaintances, including those who accompanied them on the ill-fated holiday in 2007, Gerry's sister Philomena – and CEOP's former chief Jim Gamble – have also suffered abuse. Publication of this book made the authors targets too.

In September 2014, the day before *Looking for Madeleine* went on sale, a colleague let us know that members of anti-McCann Facebook groups were already labelling the book pro-McCann 'propaganda' and urging a 'fightback'. On Twitter, two female anti-McCann zealots, one using the username @sweepyface – later to be identified as Brenda Leyland – the other using @portugalonline, an American named Isabelle McFadden, discussed the notion of flooding Amazon with bad reviews. 'We need a concerted effort on Amazon,' Leyland tweeted, 'it is really effective.'

Customer reviews on Amazon's website, which rate books by

---

* See Chapters 15 and 16.

allocating stars, can have a powerful effect. Potential buyers are encouraged to say whether a customer review of a book was helpful – or not. The more people mark a review as helpful, the more prominently that review is displayed. 'The effect of a bad review,' author Robert Groese has explained, 'goes far beyond the impact it has on the author's ego . . . The prominence of a book on Amazon.com is dictated by two factors: how well the book has sold and how positive the reviews are. More highly rated books are displayed more prominently, which leads to more sales.'

Brenda Leyland's and Isabelle McFadden's negative reviews, which both gave *Looking for Madeleine* just one star – the lowest rating – appeared rapidly on the book's Amazon sales page. Leyland also posted negative comments on some of the good reviews that had begun to appear. McFadden, who by her own admission did not have the book, based her 'review' on fifty pages she said had been emailed to her. 'I urge anyone in a position to do so,' Leyland tweeted, 'to comment on Amazon in response to the S&S [Summers and Swan] book . . . the star ratings are going down!'

Within forty-eight hours, more than a dozen further one-star reviews would pop up on the page. One that appeared was purportedly posted by Jim Gamble – the real Gamble liked the book and had already tweeted *positively* about it. While such manipulation of Amazon reviews may not be illegal, it clearly distorts the very purpose of reviewing. Our publisher accordingly raised the issue with Amazon. We for our part contacted the Society of Authors, which advised us to 'encourage – as far as is appropriate – the positive reviews . . . ' We suggested to several associates of our own that in light of the Internet attacks – and when they had read the book – they might wish to post authentic reviews on Amazon.

Whatever the attacks on *Looking for Madeleine*, of course, the real victims of the hate campaign were, as they have long been and as documented earlier in these pages, Gerry and Kate McCann. About two weeks before our book came out, a group of ten concerned citizens had written to the Commissioner of the Metropolitan Police, Sir Bernard Hogan-Howe, alerting him to 'an appalling campaign of abuse directed at the parents and wider family of Madeleine McCann'.

The abuses, the citizens' letter said, had 'raged for over seven years now, but have lately become worse. We are very concerned that it is now getting out of hand'. In support of their complaint, the group submitted an eighty-page report and a DVD that included screenshots of the most egregious posts on social media. As a courtesy, they copied the letter to the McCanns, who – according to the group – had not until then been told of its work. The full submission – the letter (with names of signatories redacted) and the report – was later seen by us and, separately, made available to Sky News' crime correspondent Martin Brunt. Sky News began an investigation of the group's allegations.

The concerned citizens had gone public, we learned, because they feared the Metropolitan Police might do little or nothing in response to their initiative. No action appeared to have been taken yet, according to a group member, on a previous complaint on the same subject lodged by an unrelated individual.

The abusive behaviour, moreover, was going from bad to worse. In July a photograph of the McCanns' by then nine-year-old twins, Sean and Amelie – as they attended the Commonwealth Games in Glasgow – was posted on an anti-McCann Facebook page.

None of the authors of the letter of complaint to the Metropolitan Police, we were told, were related to or even knew the McCanns. It was, rather, the haters' behaviour in recent months that had decided them to turn to law enforcement. 'It will only take one mentally unstable person,' a group member said, 'to act out on the fantasies of assaulting the McCanns or contacting their twins, or one pathetic soul seeking praise and affirmation. I personally cannot have it on my conscience that I didn't at least try to bring these activities to the attention of the police . . . No family should live in permanent fear.'

The concerned citizens' report was a sickening compendium of scatological, violent, or defamatory insinuations against Madeleine's parents that had all been posted on the Internet. The report did not dwell overly on the juvenile sexual filth. Its main focus was on the truly sinister utterances of those the citizens' group characterised as 'the most persistent and prolific anti-McCann activists'.

Some members of the Facebook hate groups – their numbers had grown in recent months, according to the report – claimed to see the McCanns quite often. Some published the couple's home address online. Most disturbing were the posts that spoke of violence against the couple. 'Friends' in one Facebook exchange 'jokingly' suggested the fate they wished upon the McCanns. Friend 1 suggested someone should 'shoot the fuckers'. Friend 2, a female, declared that 'these 2 should burn in hell'. Friend 3 said he would 'supply the petrol . . .' Friend 4, who claimed elsewhere that he attended gym classes with Kate and Gerry, babbled about being able to dig out 'a box of Swan Vesta' matches.

Twitter posts cited in the submission to the Metropolitan Police also came from people who said they lived near the McCanns. One suggested she would 'nip round' to the home of Madeleine's parents with 'handcuffs . . . pass the twins to a loving family and then lynch 'em!!' Another tweet asked: 'Is there Any Terrorists [sic] want to murder the #McCann parents id support it is gone on too long #goforit.' (Hashtags on Twitter denote key words or themes to make items easier to locate.) There was also: 'I'm in the mood for some waterboarding, who's first K or G? #McCann lets sort this shit out.' Other tweets – some libellous, many merely grossly offensive – cannot be published here. Further instances of abuse, on Instagram and YouTube, featured in the citizens' complaint.

A month after the complaint had been submitted to the Met, Sky News covered the subject in a lengthy report. In the course of the item, correspondent Martin Brunt conducted interviews with the authors and Jim Gamble, who now heads INEQE, a security consultancy that promotes safety on the Internet. Also interviewed – disguised and in silhouette because of concerns for her safety – was one of the signatories of the recent complaint to the police. The segment included a Met statement that the Commissioner had received the complaint and that it would 'be assessed and a decision made as to what further action if any should be undertaken'.

The pivotal element in Sky's coverage, however, was a doorstep interview Brunt had conducted with the woman who – under the username @sweepyface – had authored 'dozens' of the anti-McCann postings on Twitter. Approached by Brunt outside her home in Leicestershire, only some 15 miles from the McCanns' home in Rothley, the woman had initially declined to be interviewed. She acknowledged having posted the messages, however, insisting that she was 'entitled' to do so. Later, having admitted Brunt to her house to talk – though not on film – she said she hoped she had not broken the law.

Before airing the Sky report, Brunt and his editor decided not to identify the woman by her real name nor state where she lived. Brunt emphasised in the broadcast that the @sweepyface tweets were not among the most offensive of those he had seen. His report got worldwide attention, sparking intense debate on Internet 'trolling'. Asked about @sweepyface by BBC News during an otherwise unrelated interview the following day, Gerry McCann said he had not seen the woman's tweets – he and Kate, he said, did not habitually use social media. He expressed concern, however, as to what the couple's twins would read when they began using the Internet without supervision. 'It's not just us,' he said, 'I do think we need to make examples of people who are causing damage.'

Following the Sky report, the press quickly identified the person behind @sweepyface as sixty-three-year-old Brenda Leyland, a divorced mother of two sons. Some newspapers ran grabbed photographs of her getting into her car, looking harried. Since 2010, it was reported, she had sent more than 4000 tweets, almost all of them about the McCanns.

On Saturday, October 4th, two days after the item featuring her had run on Sky News, Leyland was found dead in a room at a hotel on the outskirts of Leicester. At the inquest, one of her sons said his mother had a background of mental illness and had 'always struggled with depression'. In a statement, Sky News offered condolences to the family. Correspondent Martin Brunt, who testified at the inquest, told of having called Leyland the day after his interview with her, because he had undertaken to keep her fully informed. She had asked whether she would be identified in the broadcast, and he told her that – though her face would be shown – he would not name her or say where she lived. Asked how she was feeling, Leyland replied that she 'had thought about ending it all, but I am feeling better – I have had a drink and spoken to my son.' Brunt recalled thinking the reference to 'ending it all' was a mere 'throwaway comment'. Sky's correspondent had had no knowledge of Leyland's background history which, as revealed at the inquest, included a previous attempt to kill herself. He had been 'devastated' by news that Leyland had been found dead, and said 'the enormity of what happened' would always be with him. The coroner, who declared herself satisfied that no one could have known what Leyland was going to do, recorded a verdict of suicide. Leyland's Twitter record for the final weeks of her life indicates that she had sent some 600 tweets, most of them barbs aimed at the McCanns and their defenders, whom she characterised as 'shills' – stooges – or 'fuck-tards'. She aimed similar remarks at the authors of this book.

By contrast, the record also showed that on occasion Leyland had expressed herself more moderately. Her involvement in the McCann case, she maintained, was 'to find justice for Madeleine'. She had written, too, of her sympathy for the family of Reeva Steenkamp, killed by Paralympic sprinter Oscar Pistorius in South Africa, and for the parents of the critically ill child Ashya King – they were in the news at the time for having taken their son from a British hospital. 'If my child was so ill,' Leyland had written, 'I would drive to the North Pole if it offered hope, with or without permission.'

Leyland's tweets that same month, however, had also labelled two former prime ministers – Tony Blair and Gordon Brown – as sex offenders. She was amused, too, by the fantasy that people who supported the McCanns might 'do a Jonestown' and commit mass suicide. Nine days before her death, she tweeted on #McCann: 'I "hate" cruelty, liars, those who profit from an others [sic] tragedy, ergo my "hate for Kate and Gerry" is justified . . . "hate" [is] a powerful emotion, it is a compliment to Maddie that we "hate" her parents who betrayed her.'

On September 25th, on Twitter, #McCann had come alive with chatter that Sky's Martin Brunt was looking for 'anti-McCanns' to interview. (Brunt was doing just that as he prepared for Sky's report on Internet abuse of the McCanns.) According to one of those approached, a man who calls himself @veniviedivici – a mangling of Caesar's famous phrase with a crude sexual meaning – the planned interviews would address the subject of 'cops clamping down on #McCann #sceptics'. The Twitter handle @veniviedivici had been one of those included in the report sent to the Metropolitan Commissioner of Police.

Brenda Leyland had participated in this Twitter exchange, suggesting that Sky's purpose might be to 'set up faux sceptic who is weak and inarticulate'. When @veniviedivici wrote that he had turned down Sky's interview request, she wrote: 'Good move, it wd be edited to Buggery, pointless.' She directed these tweets not only to her fellow anti-McCann contacts but to Brunt himself.

A week before her death, during Twitter exchanges in which threats were made to expose a former Ocean Club nanny – a young woman the 'antis' deemed to be a McCann supporter – Leyland tweeted: 'She'll be bloody scared now that everyone knows where she works, haha . . . I would not agree to naming unless the perp [perpetrator] was actually a danger, **** has proved to b so.'

That conversation drew criticism from veteran Portuguese anti-McCann blogger Joanna Morais. At 'a time that we are under scrutiny,' Morais tweeted, 'you gave ammunition to Team #McCann, S&S and any UK hack to call us "haters" & stalkers'. Leyland riposted with: ' . . . we have always been under scrutiny'. That night, September 29th, Leyland noticed that Brunt had become one of her Twitter followers. She tried to engage him in conversation and then – twenty minutes later – tweeted for what would be the last time. The next day, the 30th, following her encounter with Brunt, she seems to have closed her Twitter account.

The day after Sky aired its report, a Twitter poster using the name 'Rainne' addressed a series of tweets to Leyland at the @sweepyface account. The tweets were threats, savage threats. One read: 'Hoping you get beaten so bad you beg for mercy, only to have gasoline thrown on you and set ablaze.' Another: 'You have reached the end of your torturing campaign against the McCann family, understand.'

Given that Leyland had by then seemingly closed her @sweepyface account, it is not clear whether she ever saw these tweets. A newspaper would characterise the sender, Rainne, as a person who had 'aggressively defended the McCanns on the Internet'. The person had, in fact, mentioned the McCanns only once in two years, and had heaped similar violent threats on all manner of other people.

Brenda Leyland's death further fuelled public debate on Internet abuse. Some sought to dismiss the malicious babble as mere name-calling. Could people not simply ignore or block abusive messages? Were there McCann supporters who were just as bad as the Internet haters? And what, exactly, constituted 'trolling', as opposed to other forms of online abuse or harassment?

Had the McCanns really been the victims of trolling, given that they themselves did not use Twitter? That being the case, some quibbled with calling the late Brenda Leyland a 'troll'. There have, however, been successful prosecutions of individuals – also characterised in press reports as trolls – who had not targeted specific living individuals. Matthew Woods, who posted sick comments about the murdered Welsh five-year-old April Jones on his Facebook page – 'despicable' comments, the sentencing magistrate called them – was jailed for three months. Robert Riley, who tweeted offensive remarks about Ann Maguire, the teacher murdered by a pupil in her classroom, was sent to prison for two months.

Some insist anonymity is not merely an electronic rampart behind which cowards can hide. It is a necessary tool, they say, to protect freedom of expression. The right to freedom of speech is, of course, a cornerstone of democracy. With it, however, come responsibilities and limits. There are laws to protect us from 'threatening, abusive, or insulting' language, from verbal and physical harassment and from stalking. There are laws limiting how matters can be reported in the press, on television and radio, and what may be printed in books. Such laws may on occasion seem restrictive. The right to free speech, however, must be balanced against a citizen's right to be free from unproven allegations and slurs – racial, religious, sexual or otherwise.

The law does in principle offer protection from the sort of abusive and threatening messages that have been posted online about Madeleine McCann's parents – and for that matter about Brenda Leyland. The UK's Malicious Communications Act of 1988 makes it a criminal offence 'to send an electronic communication in any form that is indecent or grossly offensive, or which conveys a threat, or which is false, provided that there is intent to cause distress or anxiety to the recipient.' The Communications Act of 2003 outlaws the sending of such messages via public networks like Twitter and Facebook. Some online abuse may be an offence under the 1997 Protection from Harassment Act, covering any 'course of conduct which causes alarm and distress, which includes the publication of words provided there have been at least two communications.'

Legal tools aside, do overworked police forces have the capacity – or the will – to follow up such cases? Facebook, Twitter and other social media sites must share responsibility for what users publish. 'I'm frankly ashamed of how poorly we've dealt with this issue,' Twitter CEO Dick Costolo told staff in February 2015.

'We're going to start kicking these people off right and left and making sure that when they issue their ridiculous attacks, nobody hears them.'

Ultimately, of course, responsibility must lie with the man or woman at the computer keyboard. Even were the McCanns' critics to any extent justified in their multiple suspicions, their online attacks would still amount to vigilantism. Both British and Portuguese police have stated, however, that such suspicions are entirely unjustified – and the intensive research for this book indicates that they are right. Those who hurl online abuse at the McCanns – or other victims – are cyberspace hooligans who should not be allowed to continue their rants. At the time of writing, though, there was still no word as to whether the Metropolitan Police intend to take action against the McCanns' abusers. The abuse continues, day after day.

The uproar about Internet trolls in late 2014 diverted attention from what for the McCanns was the only reason to cultivate a public profile in the first place – the search for their daughter.

26

By early 2015, as we prepared this new edition of *Looking for Madeleine*, what was once a constant stream of news stories had slowed to an occasional trickle. There were rumours that the British police investigation might soon end. People supposedly in the know were saying the case had dragged on too long – almost four years – had become too expensive. The cost of the probe, funded by the Home Office, was £10 million and rising. Working with the Portuguese authorities, always frustrating, supposedly remained nigh on impossible. Political backing, it was said, was ebbing.

Detective Chief Inspector Andy Redwood, who had headed Operation Grange since its inception, had recently retired and been replaced by an officer of the same rank named Nicola Wall. Some saw Redwood's departure as 'sending a message' that the case would soon be wound down. More speculation followed when, months later, a Metropolitan Police union spokesman talked of 'resentment' about the diversion of scarce personnel and funds to a case outside the UK.

The authors' conversations with sources over several months, however, suggest a different reality. A senior source told the authors it was still 'business as usual. We're just working through the jobs, one by one. Nicola Wall is an experienced veteran of homicide cases who has brought a fresh eye to the case. We report to the Home Office every quarter – that's routine – but there's no money problem. And no sense that there's a political wind blowing against continuing the investigation, no hint that we might be closed down.'

In one significant area, moreover, there has been a development. While the Met had earlier said it was studying eighteen incidents in which an intruder had broken into properties housing British families between 2002 and 2010 – well after Madeleine's disappearance – the figure had now risen. Police were now analysing as many as twenty-eight episodes over a period starting as early as 2002. 'The offences are not all the same,' a source said. 'Some involve not little children but teenagers or young women . . . But there are similarities. We're seeing a sort of consistent theme.

'Perhaps there is a burglar, a thief, who's also got a weakness for this sort of thing. We don't know. We're not saying all these offences are definitely linked, but there's potential here. It's not the only line of enquiry we're following, not at all, but we're looking at it broadly – a lengthy job. If we dig down into those incidents and find out who's responsible, if we find that a single person is responsible for a number, if not all, of the events . . . Who knows, that same person *may* have been responsible for Madeleine McCann's disappearance.'

When it first emerged that police were focusing on intrusions into homes, Chief Inspector Redwood had referred wistfully to what his team really yearned for. If forensic evidence could be found that might identify the man or men behind the intrusions, that above all could lead to a breakthrough. Maybe, just maybe, telltale fingerprint or DNA evidence was lying forgotten in an exhibit store in the Algarve.

Evidence. In eight years – across the whole case, not just in the matter of the intrusions – there has been *no* hard, usable evidence. That is perhaps the most bedevilling aspect of the Madeleine McCann mystery. From time to time it has seemed there might be some. As reported in earlier chapters, the initial Portuguese police team found – aside from prints and hair strands of those known to have had legitimate access to the McCanns' rented apartment – a number of prints that were at the time judged to be of no evidential value, as well as hairs of unknown origin.

Weeks later, of course, sniffer dogs used in the apartment – and around the car Madeleine's parents had rented almost a month after their daughter's disappearance – had seemed to pick up the smell of human blood. One of them, trained to search for dead bodies, had reacted positively. This had led to much excitement, lurid headlines and a nightmare of uninformed finger-pointing at Gerry and Kate McCann that lingers to this day.

In this book, we have laid out in detail the reasons for dismissing the dog 'discoveries' as having been of no consequence. Today, we can hammer the point home by reporting the views of two leading forensic scientists. One is Dr Maureen Smyth, who was Director of DNA with the Republic of Ireland's forensic science service until her retirement in 2014. The second, British, scientist we consulted is of similar prominence but asked for anonymity because he is engaged in another ongoing, high-profile investigation. Between them, the two scientists have more than sixty years' experience in their field.

Having perused the forensic files released by the Portuguese police, both experts agreed that this book's reporting of the forensic aspects of the case is accurate, and made several additional points. The first deals with the samples removed from the wall and floor near the sofa in Apartment 5A, at points where the sniffer dogs 'alerted'. Standard practice – the testing of such samples for blood at the scene, prior to DNA testing in the laboratory – was not followed in this case. It has therefore not been scientifically established that the samples sent to the laboratory *were* in fact blood.

The two scientists state, moreover, that – contrary to what some have suggested – the location of the samples taken from the wall and floor does not indicate that Madeleine, or anyone else, fell or was assaulted there. There is no typical 'smear pattern', no 'trail' of marks consistent with a scenario of someone bleeding as a result of being attacked, or bleeding as the result of a fall. Photographs of areas of the apartment's living-room wall that accompany the relevant reports, showing what appear to be smear marks, are consistent with what one might find in any average household. They do not support the notion that anyone cleaned the wall in an attempt to obliterate evidence.

The forensic reports as released, Dr Smyth said in summary, 'amount to a whole lot of nothing'.

That said, leaks from the ongoing investigation might suggest that police are now making progress on the forensic front. One report said British detectives had asked their Portuguese counterparts not only for strands of hair that were found in Apartment 5A, but for curtains that once hung there. Further laboratory analysis might yield fresh information. Has there been such progress? On this, it may be significant that, when repeatedly questioned, our Metropolitan Police sources proved tight-lipped.

A senior source remains optimistic. 'I am upbeat,' the source said. 'With effort and time and teamwork, this case is solvable. There are simply many angles and many people whom we should interview. We must just work through them one by one, until hopefully – in the end – we identify one or more perpetrators guilty in Madeleine's disappearance.

'Every case is solvable, and there's no reason to think this one can't be solved.'

Afterword

What lessons can be taken from the sad saga of Madeleine McCann? The man who for three decades headed America's National Center for Missing and Exploited Children – NCMEC – Ernie Allen, believes so. The overall issue of missing children, he told the authors in 2014, really gets the attention of policy makers 'when there is a human face attached to it. So much of our progress has come as a result of publicity about named children and their families. The story of Madeleine McCann has had that same kind of effect.'

NCMEC had been founded in 1984, following the abductions of two six-year-olds, Etan Patz from a New York City street, and Adam Walsh, from a Sears department store in Florida. Adam's murdered and mutilated remains were found quite soon after his disappearance, and the indications are that Etan was killed. In both cases, parents were initially suspected but later cleared. More than three decades on, as mentioned earlier, the McCanns learned of Allen's vast experience on the subject of missing children and hurried to consult him. Allen, who has moved on to run ICMEC, NCMEC's international arm, took an immediate and lasting interest.

The 'missing children problem,' Allen explained, 'is really at least five separate but related problems: runaways, lost children, family abductions, non-family abductions (committed by someone the child knows), and abductions by complete strangers. One of the greatest challenges is simply measuring how large the overall problem is. We simply don't have the kind of comprehensive, scientific data that we need on a global basis'.

According to the most recent, 2002, estimate, some 800,000 children – from all age groups from infancy to mid to late teens – were reported missing in the United States in a single year. More recent data will soon be made public. In the UK in 2012, according to British police data, 96,341 children under eighteen went missing. In the same year in Portugal, where Madeleine vanished, national police figures indicate that 2,973 children went missing. The vast majority of the children represented by these totals were sooner or later recovered safe.

A look at the broader picture reveals implausible disparities between countries. 'Exactly what are we counting?' asks Allen, 'Are there 2,973 missing children in Portugal each year? Are there some 43,000 in Germany yet just 5,513 in Italy or 383 in Greece? We doubt it . . . Every country is not counting the same things, and what you count, counts.'

A study conducted in the UK by PACT – Parents and Abducted Children Together – does appear to offer significant information. Forty-two per cent of all children under eighteen abducted in 2011, the study revealed, had been taken by a stranger.

Mercifully, according to American and British figures, kidnapping of children by a stranger is still a rare event. In the United States, as of the 2002 study, only some twenty children under the age of five – out of the total of 800,000 children who went missing in a year – were taken by strangers. In the UK in 2011, according to the PACT study, an estimated twenty-seven children under five – out of more than 96,000 children who went missing – were abducted by a stranger.

'Younger children are at higher risk of being the victims of the most serious, most long term abductions,' Ernie Allen told the authors. In the 'taken by a stranger' category, girls outnumber boys by 69 per cent to 31 per cent.

Child abduction is not new, and it is not only sex fiends who take children. Children were being taken – or traded – three centuries ago. Boys might be taken for their value as workers, girls as potential wives or for sale as prostitutes. In the first year of this century, a United Nations agency's best global estimate was that a 'stock' of more than a million youngsters, mostly from the developing world, were trafficked. They might be used as workers in farms, sent down mines, or as beggars to pull in money for their adult controllers. Females could be destined for prostitution.

Allen cautions, though, that, 'trafficking is a phenomenon that is happening in virtually every country, and it has been exacerbated by the Internet. Human trafficking has moved from the streets to the Internet . . . I do a lot of work in the battle against human trafficking, and particularly child sex trafficking . . . The first of the myths I cite is the "Somewhere Else" myth. Be in no doubt, it does not always happen somewhere else, on the other side of the world.'

Child pornography, ICMEC has reported, 'has become a global crisis . . . It has become a lucrative worldwide industry, fuelled by the Internet. Its victims are becoming younger . . . 19 per cent of identified offenders had images of children younger than three; 39 per cent had images of children younger than six . . . Children have become a commodity in this insidious crime . . .

According to the Internet Watch Foundation in the _
Kingdom, there has been a 1,500 per cent increase in the numbɛ
of child pornography images since 1997.'

There are no meaningful statistics for one category of child-
snatcher, that of the childless woman or couple who steal a child
to 'fill a void'. Childlessness and the desperation it can bring
know no economic boundaries. The traffic in children, it is said,
can touch the cosy world of the European and American middle
classes. There are well-to-do people who will not settle for the
child on offer from an adoption agency and, caring nothing for
the source, order to specification.

'There is a huge demand for blond blue-eyed children,' said
Allen, who as a lawyer for years handled international adoption
cases. 'Most of the focus of such demand in recent years has been
Eastern Europe.'

On the subject of the theft of children, there is ancient, Europe-
wide prejudice against one particular social group – and recent
events have shown that it is still prevalent. Most youngsters once
grew up knowing the rhyme:

> *My mother said, I never should*
> *Play with the Gypsies in the wood. . .*

The world's uncounted millions of Gypsies, or Romanis, remain
alien creatures to settled folk, little understood, not respected,
readily blamed for crimes ranging from petty theft to the drugs
trade, to murder and child abduction. Professor Emeritus Thomas
Acton, the pre-eminent British author on the subject, has said,
however, that he does not know of a single documented case of
Gypsies having stolen non-Gypsy children.

*

...ken, it is usual police practice first to look ... and for good reason. Parent taking a child ...e from spouse, is common – and the subject ...rangling, often across international borders. The same ... the murder of children. In England and Wales, 2014 figures from the National Society for the Prevention of Cruelty to Children show, a child is killed by a parent every ten days. In some 67 per cent of the killings of children, a parent is the principal suspect. The U.S. statistic is similar. In 60 per cent of cases where children under five had been murdered, a 2005 American study indicated, a parent was responsible.

To a father and mother agonising over the lasting disappearance of a child under five, with no evidence that the child has been killed, the American statistics offer optimism and pessimism in almost equal measure. The 2002 US figures, the only ones available, indicate that:

40 per cent are killed;
4 per cent are not returned and not located; and
56 per cent are recovered alive.

'The likelihood of safe recovery,' Ernie Allen told the authors in 2014, 'is highest in the initial minutes, hours and days, and that likelihood declines as time passes. However, the data illustrate that most of those who abduct children are not taking them to kill them. They take children for a host of reasons, most of which do result in harm to the child. However, in most of these cases, the child is not killed. That is why, in cases like Madeleine McCann's and many others, I continue to make the point that there is hope.'

On May 25th 2007, within weeks of Madeleine's disappearance, Kate McCann attended a gathering in the Algarve to mark

International Missing Children's Day. In their distress after the loss of their daughter, and as they looked desperately for information that might help find her, she and her husband came to understand the scale of the overall problem of missing children. Kate thought it 'terrifying'. 'I have asked myself many times,' she was to say, '"Why did I not know about this? Am I that naïve? Or is it the fact that the problem itself is not well publicised?"'

As the months and years passed, the McCanns became ever more involved not only in the hunt for Madeleine but in international efforts to improve the response of society when a child goes missing. They learned of Amber Alert, the emergency system that was long since developed in the United States. While the title is taken from the name of a little girl who was abducted and murdered in Texas, it is also a mnemonic that stands for America's Missing: Broadcast Emergency Response.

An Amber Alert brings together police forces, broadcasters and others to ensure an immediate response by the whole community when a child is abducted. With others, Kate has campaigned for implementation and coordination of child rescue alert systems across Europe. Only two European nations had such a system in place at the time Madeleine vanished. That figure had risen to eleven by mid-2013, and included Portugal.

Kate is today an ambassador for the organisation *Missing People*. Early on, she and Gerry received help from the charity, which works to return missing children to their families and to assist those who have lost offspring in the struggle to cope. The organisation runs the UK end of the free hotline 116 000, which enables citizens across twenty-seven EU countries to report that a child has gone missing. In summer 2007, it displayed Madeleine's picture, along with those of two other children, on London's Marble Arch. The two other children were recovered alive.

No one involved in the effort to ameliorate the missing children problem would say all these efforts are enough. Jim Gamble no longer runs the Child Exploitation and Online Protection Centre. He resigned in protest when the government decided to absorb CEOP into the National Crime Agency. The move, he said, was not in the best interests of children and young people.

Looking back, when he spoke with the authors in 2014, Gamble characterised the change as having been 'political vandalism'. 'Are we going to pretend,' he said, 'that CEOP is the centre we wanted it to be? Is there a 24-hour command hub there? No. Do they have their own communications team in there now? No. Do they have the ability to engage immediately with the social media networks? No. They've pulled out many of the staff we had that were young and vibrant, and some of the truly professional child protection officers with policing backgrounds.'

'In the Scoping Review on the McCann case,' he said, 'one general recommendation we made was to change things so that mistakes made in UK policing right after Madeleine vanished – the lack of coherent leadership, the confusion of too many agencies getting involved, the failure to use technology to bring all the information together in one place – are not repeated. I don't think this has been done. In fact I'm sure it hasn't.

'We need a UK national centre to coordinate child protection activity, a body that is at arm's length from government. The key is to place all the lessons of the past in the context of the present. Technology should enable better communication and empower every motivated citizen to play a part in making children safer. Collaboration is key, and in Europe our efforts should be consolidated through Europol. The national centre I mention would provide a platform above petty national imperatives, which in my opinion did not serve Madeleine well.

'If this were done, that would be something, a blueprint for ensuring that other parents would not have to experience the short-comings the McCanns endured. It would be a legacy of sorts for the McCanns and for other parents of missing or murdered children.'

Ernie Allen of ICMEC, for his part, believes 'you have to address these cases in a comprehensive way. We learned thirty years ago that these investigations are of necessity multi-jurisdictional. Most importantly, you reach out for help and overcome the natural tendencies to want to make this "your case". Be prepared. Have a plan and a system in place. Train your people. Cooperate with everybody. Share information. Ask for help and work together.

'Finally, I've said the same thing to so many officials. It doesn't matter how hard you've worked, how many resources you expended or how hard you tried. The goal is to find the child. If you did not find the child, well, you failed.'

ICMEC's Allen considers the McCanns' 'tenacity, and their commit-ment to their daughter, to be admirable, inspiring . . . A parent of another child, who had been abducted by a stranger and had been missing for months, once asked me, "Am I being foolish? I have other children. I need to be concerned about their well-being too. Should I come to grips with the reality that my child is probably dead and do the best I can to get on with my life?" My answer was, "No, continue to fight for your daughter. There are many scenarios under which your child could still be alive, still recoverable."

'That person's child is alive and well today. And there have been so many others. We keep finding abducted children who have been missing for years.'

As recently as February 2015, as this edition went to press, a

South African girl was found alive and well having been missing since her shortly after her birth in 1997 – seventeen long years ago. She had been snatched as she lay beside her sleeping mother in a hospital bed. Long after her baby's disappearance, her mother had said, 'I just hope one day someone will realise something and bring her back to us.' The father, for his part, said he would, 'never ever give up hope. I can feel it in my gut. My daughter is out there and she is going to come home.' So it turned out, after fellow pupils at the missing girl's school noticed a striking similarity between her and her biological sister, who was attending the same school. When DNA tests confirmed that she was indeed the lost child, a woman was arrested and charged with the abduction.

'It is essential, I believe, to keep hope alive and not stop the search until we know with certainty what happened to him or her, or find them. No one has the right to take away a parent's hope.'

The fact that only a minute number of very young children are abducted by strangers is of no comfort to a lost child's mother and father. For the parents, the present – and a future devoid of certainty – is a place of loss without end, black imaginings, and flickering hope.

Acknowledgements

A host of people helped during the writing of the book without knowing it, since so many people have views, sensible or otherwise, as to what happened to little Madeleine McCann. We thank especially Headline's publisher Simon Thorogood, our editor for the third time and a champion of non-fiction investigative writing at a difficult time in publishing. As always, too, our literary agent and loyal friend Jonathan Lloyd, chairman of Curtis Brown, and his assistant Lucia Rae.

Researcher Marta Simons rose to the challenge in Portugal, eventually juggling both our demands and those of Sky News. When it came to dealing with Portuguese texts, Oona Ni Dhuinnin and Luisa Maria Cardoso dealt patiently with our demands in Ireland. As in the past, Charles Cardiff handled Spanish-language requests. Press-ganged when she thought she was in Ireland on holiday, Hannah Cleaver took on interview tasks and carried out repairs to our rusty translations from German.

Martin Brunt, Sky News' excellent crime reporter, lent an ear and gave advice. David Mills, a colleague from days of yore at the BBC and producer of a landmark documentary on the JonBenét Ramsey murder in the United States, made available unique source material. Len Port, who lives near Praia da Luz and was the first journalist on the scene the morning after Madeleine vanished, offered local insights, valuable contacts and, with his wife, Joan, hospitality. Sky's weather forecaster Jo Wheeler, who has long had a home in the Algarve, provided background that turned out to be important.

At Headline, copy-editor Caroline Johnson, designer Lucy Bennett, and Holly Harris helped us navigate the last hectic weeks. In Ireland, interns Nick Winchester, Ailís Burke, Clara Roch-Perks and Alex Aldous brought enthusiasm and intelligence to dozens of requests – not always interesting ones. Sinéad Sweeney pitched in again to do transcriptions. As she has on so many books, Pauline Lombard made sense of our myriad office and clerical requests. Jenny Maher again gave loyal service.

Heartfelt thanks, too, to our stalwart friends and our family in the United States. And, once again – for tolerating our absences – to Ronan, Sara and Ava and our dear children, Colm, Fionn and Lara.

A.S. R.S.
July 2014

A Note on Sources

This book is the result of more than two years' work. Our contact with Madeleine McCann's parents, Gerry and Kate McCann, and with the leadership of Scotland Yard's Operation Grange, was limited. We met once with the McCanns early on, but conducted this project completely independently of them. In the light of related controversy, this has meant that we can be – and be seen to be – entirely impartial. Our aim in the book is in the main simply to tell the story, and any conclusions we draw are entirely our own – based on the available facts.

At Scotland Yard, Detective Chief Inspector Andy Redwood met with us at the outset, spoke frankly, but made it clear that he and his colleagues could not favour us – or any part of the media community – over any other parties. This was only correct.

The McCanns and the Yard urged us to be constantly careful that we do nothing during our research that might – however inadvertently – impact negatively on the search for Madeleine. This was in any case a paramount concern for us. It has meant that, contrary to the very extensive interviewing conducted for our previous eight books – we talked with more than a thousand people for one book – we limited the interviews conducted for this project.

Interviews with some individuals could have led to crossed wires with the ongoing police investigation. Interviews with police or officials in Portugal could have adversely affected the fragile relationship between UK and Portuguese forces. Nevertheless, we did speak with former senior officials in both Portuguese and British law enforcement, and list some of their names below.

The principal documentary source has been the voluminous Portuguese police dossier – to the extent that it is available to researchers – amounting to many thousands of pages. The dossier comprises a seventeen-volume main case file, thirty volumes of appendices and a fourteen-volume appendix of 'sightings'.

A chronological reading of the files tracks the way the Portuguese inquiry developed, through the removal of the chief investigator (more literally 'coordinator') Gonçalo Amaral and his replacement by Paulo Rebelo, to the Final Report and the letter on the status of the case by prosecutors João Melchior Gomes and José de Magalhães e Menezes at the time the case was 'archived' (shelved) in July 2008.

Not part of the available releases is some investigative material that was released to the McCanns but then withdrawn, and not included in the general release made shortly afterwards. The available Portuguese dossier includes a notification that, as agreed with British police, items have been withheld that relate to known paedophiles and sex offenders, related crimes and individuals' right to privacy. Some of the individuals involved were British.

There is also Kate McCann's personal memoir, *Madeleine: Our Daughter's Disappearance and the Continuing Search for Her*, published in 2011 and obviously essential reading. (The paperback edition, published the following year, contains added material.) There is also the blog initiated by Gerry McCann as early as May 2007 and still updated periodically in 2014. Entries from

Kate McCann's daily journal, begun on May 23rd, 2007 – but with some retrospective entries for that month – have appeared in her book *Madeleine*.

We have consulted former chief investigator Gonçalo Amaral's controversial 2008 book, *Maddie: A Verdade da Mentira* (*Maddie: The Truth of the Lie*). His book is useful as an insight into the way the Polícia Judiciária investigation developed during his tenure.

As always, chronology has been the key. The timeline for this book was created using not only official documents but also media reports from the UK and Portugal and on occasion other European nations. While we were open to all sources, principal resources in the UK have been transcripts of BBC and Sky News broadcasts, *Crimewatch*, *Panorama*'s 'The Mystery of Madeleine McCann' (2007) and 'Madeleine: The Last Hope' (2012), ITV1's *Madeleine: One Year On* in 2008, and Channel 4's *Madeleine Was Here* in 2009. For crosschecking where possible, or speaking with the reporters involved, the *Daily Telegraph*, the *Guardian*, and an excellent early piece by David James Smith in the *Sunday Times Magazine*, were especially useful. Not least because they were themselves on occasion 'part of the story', we read the voluminous coverage in the daily and Sunday tabloids: *The Sun*, the *Mirror* and the *Express*. We followed reporting in the Portuguese newspapers – *Correio da Manhã*, *Diário de Notícias*, *Jornal de Notícias*, *Expresso*, *Público*, *Sol*, the now defunct *24 Horas* and *Tal & Qual* – and viewed coverage by the Portuguese national broadcaster, RTP. There was useful reporting in English-language newspapers, the *Algarve Resident* and *Portugal News*. We also consulted *Vanished* by Danny Collins (London, John Blake, 2008).

The following declined to be interviewed because the case was ongoing: Chief Inspector Olegário de Sousa, former Yorkshire police dog handler Martin Grime, former National Policing Improvement Agency search adviser Mark Harrison, and John Lowe of what was at the time the Forensic Science Service. Forensic artist Melissa Little and then pro-consul for the Algarve, Angela Morado, did not agree to speak with us. Though we repeatedly asked Gonçalo Amaral for an interview, he courteously declined.

Of those who gave interviews or corresponded we thank especially Jim Gamble, former chief executive of the Child Exploitation and Online Protection Centre, who wrote the Scoping Report that paved the way for the current Scotland Yard probe. Also Ernie Allen, president and CEO of the International Center for Missing and Exploited Children. Dr Patrícia de Sousa Cipriano, president of Associaçao Portuguesa de Crianças Desaparecidas, the Portuguese Association for Missing Children, corresponded.

There is essential information on the issue of child abduction, exploitation and trafficking at www.ceop.police.uk and at www. icmec.org. We also consulted the websites of Missing Children Europe (www.missingchildreneurope.eu) and Parents and Abducted Children Together – PACT – at www.pact-online.org. The books Child Pornography by Tim Tate (London, Methuen, 1990) and Children's Sexual Encounters with Adults, by C. K. Li, D. J. West and T. P. Woodhouse (New York, Prometheus, 1993) were useful reading.

In Portugal, Fernando Pinto Monteiro, who was his nation's attorney general during the initial investigation, granted us a lengthy interview.

Brian Kennedy, the prominent businessman who gave fulsome support to the McCanns when they returned to the UK, then handled their private probe, talked freely with us.

The authors either interviewed or corresponded with Carlos Anjos, former president of the Polícia Judiciária's professional association;

Pat Brown, criminal profiler; Marcos Aragão Correia; the very helpful Praia da Luz resident John Ballinger who also provided photographs; Anthony Bennett; Lt. Col. Bruno Fehr, chief of the Kriminalpolizei in St Gallen, Switzerland; medium Christine Hamlett; journalist Peter Holenstein; Margit Holzer, Professor Wolfram Meier-Augenstein; Bren Ryan, Salisu Suleiman; George Thomson; former Método 3 Barcelona chief Elisenda Villena.

On the contentious issue of the abilities of cadaver and blood dogs, we were greatly helped by Marcia Koenig and by Andy Rebman of K9 Speciality Search Associates, and by Robert Noziska, K9 Coordinator of the US Border Patrol. We also referred to documents in State of Wisconsin v Eugene J. Zapata, Circuit Court, Dane County, Wisconsin.

In connection with the possibility that a possible abductor might have drugged Madeleine (and perhaps her siblings), we consulted Dr Shan Yin, Medical Director of Cincinnati Drug and Poison Information Center, Professor Robert Flanagan, Consultant Clinical Scientist of the Toxicology Unit at King's College Hospital, London, Dr Steven Karch, Assistant Medical Examiner in San Francisco, consultant anaesthetists Dr Alan Feerick and Dr Pachaimuthu Gnanamoorthy, and pharmacist Tom Feerick.

For information on the criminal use of chloroform, we corresponded with Linda Stratmann, author of *Chloroform: The Quest for Oblivion* (Stroud, Sutton, 2003). Stratmann's book, J. P. Payne's study 'The Criminal Use of Chloroform' (*Anaesthesia*, 1998), and María Martínez' and Salomé Ballesteros' 'An Unusual Case of Drug-Facilitated Sexual Assault Using Aromatic Solvents', were invaluable.

For this edition, we are grateful to Dr. Maureen Smyth, former Director of DNA for Ireland's forensic science service, for patiently answering our questions.

Photo Credits

1. Courtesy of REX / 2. © solarpix.com / 3. © Getty Images / 4. © Chris Radburn/PA Archive/Press Association Images (top) solarpix.com (bottom) / 5. Courtesy John Ballinger / 6. © Steve Parsons/PA Archive/Press Association Images / 7. © AFP/Getty Images (top and bottom) / 9. © Reuters/Nacho Doce / 10. © EPA / 11. © AFP/Getty Images / 12. © Steve Parsons/PA Archive/Press Association Images / 13. © The Sun / NewsSyndication.com (top) © solarpix.com (bottom) / 14. © The Sun / NewsSyndication.com / 15. © Denis Doyle/Getty Images (top and bottom) / 16. © solarpix.com (top) © REX (middle) © REX (bottom left) © mirrorpix (bottom right) / 17. © SNS Group / 18. © EPA / 19. © AFP/Getty Images / 20. © Rebecca Naden/PA Archive/Press Association Images (top) © Rafael Marchante/Reuters/Corbis (middle) © Geoff Pugh/REX (bottom) / 21. © The Sun / NewsSyndication.com / 22. © Alex Lentati/Evening Standard/eyevine / 24. Courtesy of REX / 25. Courtesy of REX (left) PA/PA Archive/Press Association Images (centre) REX (right) / 26. © PA/PA Archive/Press Association Images (left) courtesy of REX (centre and right) / 27. © Reuters/Rafael Marchante (top and bottom) / 28. © Teri Blythe/Metropolitan Police/PA Archive/Press Association Images

Index